ANGOLAN
rendezvous

Tamar Ron & Tamar Golan

ANGOLAN
rendezvous

Man and Nature in the
Shadow of War

30° South Publishers

Published by 30° South Publishers (Pty) Ltd.
3 Ajax Place, 120 Caroline Street, Brixton
Johannesburg 2092, South Africa
www.30degreessouth.co.za
info@30degreessouth.co.za

Original edition in Hebrew: *Gorilot ve-Diplomatia*, Am Oved Publishers, Tel-Aviv, 2006
Portuguese edition: *Encontros em Angola: O Homem e a Natureza na Sombra da Guerra*
Cha de Caxinde, Luanda, and Prefacio, Lisbon, 2007
French edition: *Rendez-vous en Angola avec l'Homme et la Nature dans l'ombre de la guerre,*
L'Harmattan, Paris, 2009

Editors: Neels Blom & Lisa Witepski
Tamar Ron's chapters were first edited by Sandie Sowler
Tamar Golan's chapters were translated from Hebrew by Ora Cummings
Illustrations: Tamar Ron
Cover design: Kerrin Cocks, Cover Photo: Tamar Ron
Design and layout: Melissa Schäfers

Printed and bound by Pinetown Printers, Durban

ISBN 978-1-920143-42-8

In the memory of Antonio

and for the street children of Luanda.

Tamar and Tamar

ای ای ای

In the memory of my mother, Jehudith Ron

𝒯 ℛ

For Avi'hu, who accompanies me all my life

𝒯 𝒢

Contents

ANGOLA

ANGOLA

CONGO

Brazzaville
Kinshasa

DEMOCRATIC
REPUBLIC
OF THE
CONGO

Kikwit

Kasai

Kwango

Kwilu

Loange

Kwenge

Wamba

Zaire

CABINDA

Cabinda

Nóqui
Soyo
M'banza Congo
ZAIRE
Damba
Quimbele
Bembe
UÍGE
N'zeto
Bungo
Ambriz
Uige
Negage
Caxito
Camabatela
Marimba
Luremo
Cuango
CUANZA
NORTE
N'dalatando
Luanda
Quela
LUANDA
Lucala Malanje
Cabo Ledo
Dondo
Cangandala
Cabo de São Bráz
Cuanza
Xá-Muteba
MALANJE
Mussende
Luando
Quirima
Porto Amboim
Quibala
CUANZA
Quimbango
ATLANTIC
Gabela
SUL
Andulo
Sumbe
Uaco
Cungo
Nharea
OCEAN
Cassongue
Bimbe
Camacupa
Balombo
HUAMBO
Cuemba
Chicala
Lobito
Benguela
Cubal
BENGUELA
Huambo
Kuito
Ponta das Salinas
Ganda
Cuima
Sambo
BIÉ
Cabo de
Santa Maria
Caconda
Chitembo
Cabo de
Santa Marta
Quilengues
NAMIBE
Cubango
Cuchi
Menongue
Bibala
HUÍLA
Matala
Lubango
Techamutete
Namibe
Chibia
Cuito
Cuanavale
Virei
Chiange
Cuvelai
CUANDO
Mavinga
Tombua
CUNENE
CUBANGO
Curoca
Cahama
Savate
Xangongo
Ondjiva
Chitado
Santa Clara
Cuangar
Cubango
Mucusso

Dundo
Cuilo
Andrada
Lucapa
LUNDA
NORTE
Lubalo
Saurimo
Cacolo
LUNDA
SUL
Muconda
Luau
DEMOCRATIC
REPUBLIC
OF THE
CONGO
Lulua
Cassai
Lumeje
Cazombo
Luena
Luatamba
Lumbala
Lucusse
MOXICO
Lungué-Bungo
Lumbala
N'guimbo
Zambeze
Chiume
ZAMBIA
Luiana
Zambezi
Lungwebungu
Cuando
Cuito
Cubango
Utembo
Zambezi

NAMIBIA

BOTSWANA

Kasai

Lóvua
Chicapa
Cuilo
Cassai

Luembe

Cambo

Longa
Cutato
Cuvo ou Queve
Cuando
Coporolo
Cunene
Cunene
Cunene

- - - International boundary
- · - Province boundary
⊚ National capital
◉ Province capital
○ Town, village
Road
Track
Railroad
+ Airport

| 0 | 50 | 100 | 150 | 200 km |
| 0 | 50 | 100 | 150 mi |

The boundaries and names shown on this map do not imply
official endorsement or acceptance by the United Nations.

4°   14°   18°   22°   4°
8°
12°
16°
20°   14°   18°   22°   20°

Map No. 3727 Rev. 2   UNITED NATIONS
October 1997 (Colour)

Department of Public Information
Cartographic Section

About the authors

Dr Tamar Ron was born and raised in Jerusalem. She obtained a BSc in Biology and an MSc in Environmental Biology at the Hebrew University of Jerusalem. Her PhD in Zoology was completed at the University of KwaZulu-Natal, Pietermaritzburg, South Africa.

Her life is dedicated to nature conservation, as well as to the welfare of wildlife in captivity, and to education about these issues. She was trained in endangered wildlife management at the Jersey Wildlife Preservation Trust, in Jersey Zoo. Over a six-month period, she conducted an ecological and behavioural study for Chimfunshi Wildlife Sanctuary, a chimpanzee rehabilitation centre in northern Zambia.

During 1989–1991, she lived in Mkuzi Game Reserve in Zululand, South Africa, and followed the social behaviour of Chacma baboons for her PhD thesis. During 1992–2000, she served as the wildlife ecologist of the scientific division of the Nature Reserves Authority of Israel.

In 1998, the Angolan Vice-Minister of Environment invited Tamar to his country, where she served two short consultancy missions as a representative of the Department of International Cooperation for Israel's Ministry of Foreign

Affairs. In 2000, she returned as a long-term consultant on biodiversity conservation to the Angolan government, with the support of the Norwegian government, through NORAD. In 2001, she was recruited as UNDP-Angola chief technical adviser (CTA) on biodiversity conservation, with continued NORAD support. She ended her mission and returned to Israel in 2005.

She now works as an independent biodiversity conservation consultant and, among other projects, has developed a Southern African Development Community (SADC) framework for transfrontier conservation areas (TFCAs).

Haifa-born **Dr Tamar Golan** is a former member of Kibbutz Lahav in Israel's southern region; where she returned to live after completing her mission in Africa.

She first went to Africa in 1961 with her husband Avi'hu, to lecture at the Agricultural College of Ethiopia in Harar City on behalf of the Department for International Cooperation of the Israeli Ministry of Foreign Affairs. Avi'hu died there.

In 1964, she was sent to New York, where she completed a doctorate in law and government at Columbia University, specializing in Africa. From 1967, Tamar Golan worked as a journalist for the BBC's African Service; the Israeli daily, *Ma'ariv*; and the Israeli Army Radio Station, reporting from Africa, the Arab states and Paris.

In 1994, Tamar Golan was appointed Israeli ambassador to Angola. With presentation of her letters of credentials to President José Eduardo dos Santos on July 7, 1995, she launched the official Israeli presence in Luanda. After completing her term as ambassador, Tamar Golan returned to Angola at the request of the President of the Republic, as a United Nations expert to assist in establishing a National Commission for Landmine Action, annexed to the Angolan Presidency. She returned to Israel in 2002.

Today, Tamar Golan lectures on African Affairs at Ben-Gurion University of the Negev. Tamar Golan has written two books: *Black White; White Black* (MOD Publishers) in 1986 and *Africa, Africa* (with Amnon Dankner, Ma'ariv Publishers), 1988.

Foreword

"Calma, calma" —Relax, relax—no expression can be more annoying than that.

There's a fire in town and the fire brigade doesn't have water. Calma, calma.

Unita rebels have blown up Luanda's power station. Calma, calma.

A United Nations aircraft has disappeared from the airport control radar. Calma, calma.

These two words intended to calm you down, always said in a quiet voice and with a big smile, usually indicate that there must be something serious to be worried about.

Calma, calma. It is difficult to translate the term precisely. Calm down, relax, don't worry. Maybe, don't worry, everything will be all right. Or maybe, calm down, nothing will be right, but worring won't help, anyway. And also, wait, wait, eventually things will somehow get sorted. It always does, one way or another.

"Calma, calma!" is the answer we got for every problem we encountered in Angola. Your visa has expired and your passport has been with the immigration authorities for the past two months? "Calma, calma!" Your body and brain are wracked with malaria? "Calma, calma!" There's a power cut in your building leaving you stuck in the elevator between the 15th and 16th floors? "Calma, calma!" That's what you hear in the worst situations and it only adds fuel to the fire. "Calma, calma!"

Surprisingly though, in Angola problems quite often manage to sort themselves out, even if it is at the very last minute, when everything seems lost and you have given up all hope. Somehow, eventually, the passport comes back, with the visa, just two days before you are due to take off; your malaria passes; you even make it to the 16th floor—if not in the lift then at least by way of the stairs. Eventually the fires are extinguished and the power is restored. Even peace arrived when it seemed it never would.

But we never stopped worrying, and the more we heard "Calma, calma!" the more worried we became. Maybe that is the real reason why we will never fit in, be anything but foreigners in Angola, in Africa. Maybe what we are missing is the Angolan capacity to let things sort themselves out, to accept life as it comes. Yet, for all the pain and suffering that is part of Africa and Angola, there is a pleasant air, something warm and soothing, something that cannot be expressed in any way other than with those two words: calma, calma!

T R and T G

We share a great love of Africa, the continent that brought us together. Angola has especially touched our hearts. We each have our own Angola. We wanted to tell people about it, but we found it difficult to agree on the way. We sat next to each other, each with a computer, reading each other's screen, commenting, correcting, and debating. It was not an easy process. Doing things together, in a tribal way, is one of the characteristics of life on the African continent, yet we are two Israelis, Western women. We grew up in a place which emhasizes the individual in the centre, rather than cooperation, but, eventually, the African way won and dictated to us how to write one book together.

Over the years of our stay and work in Angola, we shared and discussed our experiences, and they form the basis for the chapters of this book. Each chapter is a story on its own and together they reflect our experience in Angola and the mark that this very special country has left on each of us.

T G and T R

We have resolved to writing together, in two voices.

Tamar Ron's voice is symbolized by a sketch of the Palanca negra, the giant sable, an antelope sub-species endemic to Angola and a national symbol:

Tamar Golan's voice is symbolized by a sketch of the Pensador, the Angolan symbol for the Thinking Man:

When I told my friends at home that I was going to work in Angola, their reactions were similar. "Where? Are you out of your mind?"

In the minds of people who are unfamiliar with Africa and Angola, and indeed, even in the minds of many foreigners who live here, the country is associated with war, disease, oil, diamonds, weapons, corruption, destruction, death—a lost and forlorn world. Most people accept snippets of news from here and there, nod their heads and turn to more optimistic stories. In Angola, we saw all these, but much, much more. We fell in love with the country, with the wonderful people we met, the children and the women, whose daily struggle for survival arouses sympathy and admiration. And we fell in love with the vast open spaces, the enchanting natural beauty and the fiery sunsets over the endless ocean.

T R

As in Angola itself, everything in our book is jumbled: life and death, war and peace, children who have no childhood and adults who dream of their lost innocence; women and men, tough fighters, suddenly finding tenderness and warmth and joy; betrayal of tradition and a return to it; man and nature and their fate intertwined.

In our long conversations, we discussed the children who are more mature than the adults, and the adults who are children in a world in which there is no room for childhood. We talked about the way women play a pivatol role in society; women who are at once fighters and mothers. We talked about our involvement, as women, in this world. We talked about the war and about death that followed the writing of this book, like a shadow.

More than once we were dragged into a debate over who suffers more from the war—man or nature? You, Tamar, reminded me then that the war itself is man-made.

T G

When I arrived in Angola, I encountered many raised eyebrows, and was asked in a sceptical tone: "How come you are dealing with nature conservation when the country has been subjected to the horrors of an armed conflict for so long? Don't you see that there are much more important problems here? People are dying and you care about animals?" I was certain, but found it difficult to convince others, that the destinies of man and nature are irrevocably intertwined. Both fell victim to the war, but the chances of Angola and the Angolans being rehabilitated and flourishing depend on their ability to save whatever is left of the glorious natural richness with which the country was blessed. The war has accelerated a process of extinction of wild species populations. The continued loss of the wild fauna and flora of Angola will take with it any hope of a better future for the country and its citizens.

T R

One day as we were writing, you said to me, "Have you noticed, Tamar, that each one of your chapters contains at least one dead body?" You were right.

T G

Already, during my first visit to Africa years ago, I was surprised to find out just how much life and death are intertwined in a way that people of Western upbringing find difficult to comprehend. Death and the dead have an integral and important role in life, and life itself is always to be found on the edge of the dying. Even more so in Angola, where for so many years, war was an inseparable part of daily life.

It is difficult for us to digest the unbearable lightness of death in Africa, but the Africans are no less surprised by our inability to accept the presence of 'the other world' in our lives; the world of the dead, the spirits, the magic and the witchcraft; the world that is beyond our narrow human conception and understanding. It is a world that many Westerners fiercely reject, as though the acknowledgement of its presence is tantamount to admitting insanity. Without accepting that there are things that we are not capable of comprehending logically, we will never be able to understand Africa and the Africans. We will never really be part of this beloved continent.

T R

For us, who grew up in a Western culture, death is a devastating and heartbreaking end. Even the believers among us make a distinction between life on earth and in heaven. In Africa, there is no such clear distinction. It took me years to internalize or even understand the profound difference between these two concepts. The hardest lesson came many years ago when Avi'hu, my beloved man, was killed in Ethiopia. In 1961, Avi'hu and I were engaged as lecturers at the College for Agricultural Studies in the historic town of Harar in the west of the country. After the fatal accident in which he died, I received 150 letters of condolence from our students. With the exception of one from a young man called Taifu, all the letters included the same phrase, 'to accept'. Africa taught me to accept—and to go on loving. Because the dead continue live on with us.

Looking back, I understand that, more than anyone else, those who taught me that painful acceptance were the women, my African sisters. In Angola and in other countries on the continent, I met some amazing women; strong, courageous women. They gave me a feeling of family and of belonging. There was something unique, at once liberating and painful in those friendships; liberating, because it was with them that I felt truly free; painful, because of my deep solidarity with the hardships of their lives.

τ 9

In almost every discussion we have mentioned our admiration of the women of Angola. The women are those who weave the fabric of life and make existence in the chaos of war and poverty possible. With their backs straight they carry the heavy loads on their heads, and the heavy burdens in their hearts. Despite the allegedly inferior status of the woman in most African societies, no words here are whispered with greater reverence than 'my mother'.

A friend—a senior government official—told me that there is only one thing in the whole world that can make him jealous, and that is the sisterhood of women. The women of his family gather in the large kitchen and together they stir the pots, add spices to each other's dishes and get carried away with the telling of stories. They talk together in the old tribal language, which is passed only from mother to daughter and on to granddaughter, but not to the boys and the men. Maybe it is because the girls are those who accompany their mother throughout their childhood and adolescence, and even into adulthood, and maybe they do so intentionally, to create their own world in which the men have no part.

"If only I could be a fly on the wall in this kitchen," he sighed. "Even if just once."

"The woman determines the family relatedness," he explained on another occasion. "My cousins, the children of my mother's sister, are closer to me than my own brothers and sisters, and my obligation to my sister's children is even stronger than to my own children."

I learned that the title 'mother', 'sister', 'brother', 'daughter' and 'son' do not necessarily refer only to biological ties. They can also indicate a strong feeling of emotional closeness between people who are not relatives, even between black and white, African and foreigner. Yet, these titles should not be taken lightly. Especially not 'mother'.

I felt that my belonging to such an 'extended African family' was a great privilege and honour, and also an obligation.

T R

This book is a personal attempt to touch some of the many faces of one country in Africa, in the hope that it will also touch you, the reader.

Shimon Peres and the late Yitzhak Rabin were responsible for my appointment to the position of Israel's ambassador in Africa. They had both known me for many years and it was virtually impossible, whenever we met, to avoid talking about what Yitzhak Rabin referred to as my 'obsession with Africa'. Sometimes he'd say it with a wry smile, at other times he would flick it away, as one would a pesky fly. Shimon Peres, a sophisticated man of the world, tended to treat me and my 'obsession' with polite tolerance.

Over the years, whenever the African issue forced itself on the over-burdened agenda of the two leaders, they would turn to me with questions. "What's your take on this president?" "What exactly is going on in that country?" they would ask. Rabin and Peres even granted me the privilege of organizing several more or less clandestine meetings with African leaders and made it possible to make my own contribution to renewing diplomatic relations between Israel and some African states.

For several hope-filled years following September 13, 1993, when Israel signed the Oslo Accords with the Palestinians and Yitzhak Rabin and Shimon Peres shook hands with Palestinian Liberation Organization leader, Yassir Arafat, on the White House lawn, Israel was the international flavour of the month. In Africa, too, a fresh wind was blowing; in 1994 South Africa's infamous Apartheid regime came to an end and Nelson Mandela was elected as that country's first black president.

Knesset member, Colette Avital, who had served as Israel's ambassador to Portugal, paid a secret visit to Angola, a former Portuguese colony. On her return, she suggested to then Foreign Minister, Shimon Peres, that he appoint me Israel's first ambassador to Angola.

It would take a while to pass a government decision to appoint a woman who was not a member of the Foreign Office's diplomatic tribe to an ambassadorial position, but on July 5, 1995, I landed at Luanda Airport to head the small Israeli delegation in Angola. It was not my first visit. As a journalist, I had already spent several weeks there on special assignment for the BBC African Service and an Israeli journal, and this made it somewhat easier to handle the shocking encounter with the battle-weary city—its bullet-ridden houses, unpaved streets, foul-smelling sewage flowing into every corner, thousands of street urchins and limbless landmine victims begging for alms everywhere I looked and, at night, rounds of rifle fire that shook the city to its foundations.

The crowd at the airport couldn't believe its eyes as the lady ambassador, a grim-faced armed security guard at her side, disembarked with a small cage in each hand, each containing a wailing cat.

We set up the Israeli Embassy in the town's veteran Presidente Meridien

Hotel, a temporary arrangement which lasted for two years. Eventually we found permanent premises and, later, an apartment capable of conforming with the strict security demands of the State of Israel. It wasn't long before our small hotel suite had become a hub of social and diplomatic activity.

Two days after my arrival in Angola, I presented my Letters of Credentials to President José Eduardo dos Santos.

One of the embassy's objectives was to bring Israelis to Angola to learn as much about the country as possible and to allow the local population to learn as much as possible about Israel. Some Israelis were wary of coming, because of the war, the constant skirmishes, the frequent electricity cuts, the risk of malaria, the foul water. But there were others, those who saw in Angola a challenge and came in order to take part in its rehabilitation. One of these was Tamar Ron.

T G

The telephone was ringing in my apartment in Jerusalem. It sounded as it always did. I had no idea that this call would change the course of my life. "Would you like to go on a mission to Angola, to help look for a large and rare fish?" I was asked by the Department of International Cooperation at the Ministry of Foreign Affairs in Israel. "Of course!" I said, without a moment's hesitation. The ambassador of Israel in Angola, Tamar Golan, had telegraphed the invitation by Professor João Serodio de Almeida, the Angolan Vice-Minister of Environment, to the ministry of foreign affairs in Jerusalem. He had suggested that I serve as a biodiversity conservation consultant to his ministry. The vice-minister was specifically interested in a 'big fish' that lived in the rivers and lakes of Angola, and that its conservation was of special importance. The Latin and the Portuguese names of the fish were indicated. Unfortunately, I am not one of those zoologists who memorize the Latin names of all of the creatures on earth. My acquaintance with fish is particularly poor, and I was then completely unfamiliar with Portuguese. Still, I had no intention whatsoever to forego this opportunity to get back to Africa.

I was working as the wildlife ecologist at the Nature Reserves Authority of Israel at the time. I had achingly missed Africa ever since I had left the continent. In fact, the longing for Africa started to simmer in my blood long before I first arrived there. It was ignited by reading children's books such as *Tarzan* (Edgar Rice-Burroughs' original trilogy, which my mother kept from her own childhood), and was later fed by Jane Goodall's famous *In the Shadow of Man*, and other books written by field biologists who worked on the continent. Throughout my youth in Jerusalem, I had secretly nurtured a strange yearning to go to Africa one day and study the behaviour of the wildlife that roamed in those vast spaces. I was certain then that it was merely a crazy dream and not something that I would ever realize, but ever since it started to nest in my bones, this dream had occupied a permanent place in my life and my thoughts.

Years later, I found myself living in a tiny caravan situated in the heart of an enchanting nature reserve in Zululand, South Africa. Every day, for more than two years, I followed a troop of chacma baboons on foot. I got to know each of the troop members personally, and recorded the development of their fascinating interrelationships. I still remember vividly the pain of my departure from the beloved reserve and from 'my' baboons. I could never bring myself to visit there again. I was afraid of losing the reserve that was engraved on my heart.

The phone call from the Ministry of Foreign Affairs, eight years later, could not have fallen on more attentive ears. It was the opportunity that I was waiting for. I immediately promised to find out what species of fish this was and why its protection in Angola was so important. I feverishly searched any possible references and the Internet. I consulted with experts specializing in freshwater fish, but all to no avail. The name of the fish that the ministry had sent me was not mentioned anywhere, and did not ring any bells with anyone. I had no option but to get back to the ministry with these embarrassing findings: "There is probably a mistake in the name provided, and maybe it is not a fish." Several days later the ambassador's response arrived. She had checked the name with the vice-minister, and he verified that the name he had given her had indeed been distorted by the time it reached Jerusalem. "Besides," wrote the ambassador, "it is not a fish, but a large creature which lives in rivers and lakes and can weigh as much as some

400 kilograms. The first discoverers of the creature thought it to be the legendary mermaid. A rather chubby mermaid, in my view," she added. "During courtship," so it was written in the official telegram to the foreign ministry that was solemnly read to me on the phone, "the creature utters grr ... grr ... sounds."

Of course. Why did I not realize it before? It was the manatee, the 'sea-cow', a mammal that lives along the coastal zone in the rivers and lakes of western Africa, from Senegal to Angola. Other sub-species are found in Florida in the United States, in Central America and in South America. The seamen that first discovered the manatees and their relatives, the dugongs, and saw the females holding their suckling calves in their arms, with the upper part of their body raised above the water surface, wove the famous legend of the mermaids around them. It must have been a very long time since they had last seen a real woman.

Apparently, this information was enough for the Israeli Ministry of Foreign Affairs to enter into a programme of cooperation in biodiversity conservation with an African country for the first time. And so I arrived on my first visit to Angola. As I descended from the aircraft, a representative of the embassy waited for me with the special protocol vehicle that took me straight to the luxurious waiting room of VIPs. The Israeli ambassador and the Vice-Minister for the environment received me there, together with several journalists.

"Are you sure that such an animal really exists?" asked one of the journalists. The manatee, known in Angola more as the peixe-mulher (fish-woman), is thought to be a mythological creature, and all sorts of legends are associated with it. Many people do not even believe that this mammal exists and very few have been lucky enough to see it.

Next day, the manatee was the top news item on the national television channel. Even the BBC correspondent interviewed me at length. The journalists in Angola, local and foreigners alike, were tired of covering nothing but war and the horror and the suffering. They jumped at the chance to report on something completely different. From a mysterious entity, with a mythological touch, the manatee had turned into a momentary celebrity.

I stayed in Angola for two months. With the vice-minister and his team, we visited several lakes and rivers, where the manatee had been reported in the past.

We asked the fishermen if they had seen it recently. At de Almeida's request, I prepared a comprehensive proposal for the study and conservation of this aquatic mammal. Several months later I was invited for a second visit.

I had expected a similar reception to that of my first visit. This time, however, I was rather surprised to find myself waiting, without an entry visa, at the end of a long and sweaty queue in the crowded reception hall of the airport. My hosts, the ambassador and the vice-minister, were both out of the country on that day. Representatives of the embassy and the Ministry of Environment arrived at the airport with my visa, but they were not allowed to enter the arrivals hall. And so, my visa and I were waiting on different sides of the immigration desk, but could not meet each other.

The immigration officer looked at me with a hollow stare. I have always believed that everywhere in the world, it is the cruellest of characters that are recruited as immigration officers, and they take their revenge on those who enter their country for all their frustrations since the day they were born. When he realized that I did not speak the language he said simply: "No visa—out!" "Ministro ... ambiente ... [minister ... environment]," I tried my poor Portuguese vocabulary. "Manatim ... peixe-mulher." (Manatee ... fish-woman). The officer's gaze became completely misty. He instructed me to wait and called the chief of the immigration police at the airport. At the sight of the commander I nearly fainted. He was a huge, bald, muscular giant, and his thick eyebrows were slanted in an angry expression.

"What's the problem?" he asked in English with a deep voice from the heights of his tall figure, his eyebrows getting threateningly close to each other. "Don't you understand? No visa—no entry. You cannot get into the country. You must return on the flight that you came on."

"But ..." I mumbled weakly, "visa ... outside ... minister ... environment ... Serodio ... there is a visa ... Israel ... manatee ... search ... peixe-mulher ... peixe-mulher ..." I fell silent. I could not utter a single sensible sentence. I expected the worst.

To my great surprise, the chief's face lit up with a huge smile. His eyebrows separated from each other, and his voice softened. "Peixe-mulher. I know you! I saw you on the television. You are peixe-mulher, the expert that came here to look for the fish-woman. Why didn't you say so immediately?" He accompanied me out, carrying my suitcase. There we met the worried representatives of the ministry and the embassy who were waiting with my visa. He stamped my passport and departed with a big smile, a warm hug and wishes for success in my search for the manatee. "My name is Rui Neto," he said. "Remember this name if you ever need any help."

A year later I returned to Angola, this time as a long-term consultant on biodiversity conservation to the Ministry of Fisheries and Environment, with the support of the Norwegian government. The ambassador of Norway in Angola had decided that it was the right time to invest in environmental issues and sustainable development in the country. Later on, the United Nations Development Programme (UNDP) also joined the initiative.

When I needed to renew my work visa for the second year of my work there, I encountered an especially nasty immigration officer. By then, Rui Neto had been promoted to the deputy chief of the immigration police of Angola. After two weeks of failed attempts to have my visa renewed, I asked for a meeting with him.

"The chief is a very busy man," said the officer. "He cannot help you."

"In that case," I insisted, handing him the file with the necessary documents and my passport, "tell him only this: tell him that this visa is necessary for the peixe-mulher. That's all."

After several minutes the officer returned with his knees shaking. With an astonished stare and a trembling hand he handed the passport back to me, with the new visa stamped in it. "The chief didn't say anything," he mumbled. "He only smiled and immediately stamped the passport. I don't understand. He never does this. What is peixe-mulher?"

"I am sorry," I whispered, "this, I cannot tell you."

Rui Neto followed my work in Angola, and he got me out of trouble on other occasions too.

I did not find the manatee, the peixe-mulher, but the search for her brought me to the most surprising and exciting places.

TR

CHAPTER ONE

Thus it happened ... or did it?

Africa's history may not be well documented, but it is a continent steeped in rich tradition. Whereas the Arabs and the Europeans were the first to bring writing to Africa, the African people had already raised the oral tradition in history, literature and law to the highest level.

One of the secrets of Africa's charm is the absence of boundaries between the spirits of the dead and the living, between daily life and life on the other side, between description of reality and its interpretation.

To people who grew up in a Western culture and seek definitions for our lives and the world around us within clear-cut frameworks, it is hard to accept this lack of division. Yet it may be exactly this that so draws us to Africa.

Our journey in Angola begins among creatures whose entity is profoundly mysterious; disappearing kingdoms, enchanted carvings, between things that happened and things that might not have happened.

Palanca negra

We stood quietly around Kataba's grave: a single mound of earth at the edge of the woodland on the way to the village. Old Kataba, 'Velho Kataba,' was the legendary first shepherd; the pastor of the palanca negra gigante, the black giant sable, the most beautiful antelope of them all which lives only in Angola, and had become the country's national symbol.

The guide, Figueira, and I had been walking for several hours that morning through the wood. We had left at dawn and were looking for the giant sable's spoor. It was one more attempt, after many concentrated efforts over several days of searching, to find the ellusive antelope in the Miombo Woodland in Cangandala National Park. We had travelled through the open woodland, heading toward Cazela River. The soil was very dry. It was the beginning of the rainy season, but the rains here were late.

We crossed the river and walked through a meadow of tall grass, up to our waists in dainty yellow flowers. A swift movement suddenly disturbed the grass. It stopped and a tiny head emerged. A banded mongoose stood upright for a moment, perched on its hind legs and tail, surveying the area. It fled as soon as it noticed our presence. We could see only a flicker of grasses as the mongoose vanished.

We reached the Sable Forest, Mata da Palanca. It was an open woodland dotted with yellowish-red autumn leaves, though a few green buds had started to take their place, here and there. At a distance of about twenty metres from us we saw a duiker. The small, dainty antelope stood for a moment, its body shivering and nostrils flaring, and then disappeared into the wood, leaping as it went. The wildlife that remained here were few and they had learned to fear humans.

It was then that we saw the tracks of a large male sable. The spoor was about a week old. From the first day of the survey in the park we had encountered many sable antelope tracks, some that were fresh. Was this the giant sable, the palanca negra that we were after, or just a roan, which is a more common species? It is difficult to distinguish between the spoor of these two species with certainty.

Does it really still exist, that legendary, mysterious animal, with a noble and powerful gait, large back-curving horns and spectacular colouring? The antelope around which so many myths, dreams, passionate feelings, plans, conspiracies, and adventures are woven? The animal that is found only here, in the Miombo woodland around Cangandala and Luando, in the province of Malange, in the northern centre of Angola, in the very heart of the country? Many people had been preoccupied with this question. During the long years of the war it had concerned Angolan leaders and citizens from both warring sides.

Does it still exist? Or, does it remain only in stories and in the imagination? Maybe all that lingers is its name and its iconic image on many national symbols: the Angolan football team, the national airline, the electronic rendering which appears at the end of the daily television programmes to the strains of the national anthem.

The giant sable became known to science only in 1909, almost accidentally. It was first described by Frank Varian, a young Belgian engineer, an adventurer and amateur naturalist who worked on the construction of the Benguela railway line. The railway was laid during the Portuguese colonial era to transport the country's natural wealth out of the continent.

This remarkable sub-species, the black giant sable—*Hippotragus niger variani*—or palanca negra gigante, is identified by its typical white facial pattern and the radiant black fur of the male, but above all its glorious long horns which arc perfectly almost all the way to its back. The trophy of these magnificent horns cost the lives of many animals of this subspecies. However, it became the target of considerable conservation efforts. Two protected areas were established for the species; the first as early as the late 1930s.

It is the spectacular male giant sable that has conquered hearts. The female is closer in appearance to other sables and to the roan antelope, with its reddish-brown colour. Those lucky enough to encounter the large adult males wrote the most thrilling descriptions of the palanca negra. Each observer has described the exciting combination of power, grace and refinement. The descriptions have always focused on the horns. Every prosaic researcher privileged to see them turned into a poet in the presence of these animals, and dry scientific writing became suffused with awe and praise.

The scientific world was overwhelmed by the discovery of the giant sable. Researchers, adventurers, and eccentrics were impassioned and enthused, driven to view it with their own eyes. Hunters from around the world developed an irresistible desire to hold its horns and undertook long and dangerous journeys into the heart of the Dark Continent, squandering fortunes and lives for a glimpse of the enchanted beast.

Only a lucky few have succeeded in seeing or photographing the giant sable, and fewer yet have hunted the animal and returned with a trophy. Some were content with the memory or pictures, but others returned with the antelope's head, horns or skin, for display on their walls or in natural history museums. Most search parties returned empty-handed, but the yearning for the giant sable kept haunting them all. Some were longing for a memory, others merely for an image they had in their minds.

ooo

On our way back to the camp, Figueira told me how he used to go to the forest as a child, with his uncle Kataba, the first ever giant sable shepherd. It was before independence and before the war. They had followed the giant sable herds in the park, and protected them. Kataba taught him all about their behaviour and life history. He also instructed him how to identify the heart-shaped footprints of the giant sable, and how to recognize the spoor, the scents and the sounds of the woodland dwellers. But now very little wildlife remained, and they had learned to avoid human beings.

"You know," he said with a mysterious smile, "not many people have ever seen the palanca negra. It does not show itself to just anyone."

We continued walking in silence. Several minutes later he said: "Only if you do not look for it, will you see it. This is why no one succeeds in taking photos of it. It appears only in the most unpredictable moments." His gaze was fixed on the ground. "Maybe ..." he suggested quietly, almost in a whisper, "maybe Kataba can help us? Sometimes he helps those who ask him. It may be worth a try."

At camp we met with two more of the guides, João and Manuel. They were also descendents of Kataba's family, shepherd of the giant sable. We had resolved to go together to Kataba's grave and ask for his help. Several of the villagers joined us. Manuel cleaned the grave of the grass that had grown over it. Figueira hoed around the grave. Others helped until the grave and its surrounds were tidied. João poured wine from a cardboard box into a large tin container. He blessed Kataba, asked for his help with our mission and poured some wine on the grave. Then the tin was passed between us all. Each of us drank a sip, added some blessings, poured some wine on the grave, and passed the tin on. João emptied the remaining wine onto the grave. Then he buried the wine box and the tin in the ground next to the grave.

When we returned to camp after the ceremony, João, Manuel and Figueira told me the story of the legendary Kataba.

One day, in the mid-1950s, about ten years before the designation of Cangandala as a national park, a senior official of the colonial regime arrived to visit the region. He asked the local residents to lead him to the giant sable.

The local communities are members of the Songo tribe. Protecting the palanca negra, or 'kolo' in their language, is an old tradition of this tribe. Some even think that the giant sable was discovered to science so late because of the tribe's considerable effort to conceal it from foreigners and so to protect it. Some claim that until today, the Songos had sabotaged attempts of strangers to locate the giant sable, especially if they were suspicious of the searchers' intentions.

After the official's attempts to find the giant sable had failed, even with the help of all of the other surrounding villages, he traveled to the village of Bola Cachasse, situated today on the border of Cangandala National Park. Two communities occupied the village, the Bolas and the Canzambas. The traditional authority of the Bola community, the Soba, did not want to help the official of the colonial regime, and suggested that he should ask Kataba, the deputy Soba of the Canzamba community. A bitter rivalry still prevails between the two communities in the village, even today. Some say that Kataba agreed to help only because the official had threatened to kill his entire family if he refused. Others say that less drastic means of persuasion were required. One way or the other, Kataba was the only one to successfully find the giant sable and show it to the official. He was then nominated as the first 'pastor', shepherd, of the palanca negra, the first guard of the giant sables. Since then, and until his death shortly before independence, he dedicated all his time and effort to the protection of his charges.

The sable shepherds' knowledge and their position passed from Kataba to his relatives. The last shepherd was killed during the war in the mid-1980s. Since then, no other guard has been nominated to protect the sables, and they were left to their destiny. The shepherds' faith was the faith of the villagers too, who had no alternative but to leave their village and move to crowded refugee camps many kilometres away. Some moved to the province's capital.

Manuel and his family chose to stay in the park, together with a few other families. They escaped from the village into the bush, and managed to survive for several months until the fighting had ceased and they could get out again. "We decided to stay with the palanca negra," Manuel said. "To live with them in the bush, or to die with them. And so we have survived, us and them."

When the war ended, the two communities returned to their derelict village. They had nothing left and received no support, but through sheer determination and hard work they managed to recultivate their fields and rebuild their village. The difficulties they had to overcome were enormous. There was a teacher in the village who wanted to establish a school for the children, but there were no books or notebooks or pencils, let alone schoolrooms or equipment. The only means of transport were a number of bicycles. Those who needed medical treatment had to make their own way to the regional clinic, about thirty kilometres away from the village along a potholed road. The clinic itself was poorly equipped. Medicines were scarce.

Kataba's relatives, the giant sable experts, were treated with special respect in the village and they continued with their efforts to protect the sable even when nobody asked them to do so, let alone pay them for their services.

Much of the Angolan wildlife had perished during the war and damage to populations continued when the war eventually ended. In the heat of the armed conflict some of the wildlife populations had enjoyed refuge in places that were inaccessible to people. With peace, many of these areas have become open to all. Large quantities of arms are still available everywhere and poverty prevails. Former soldiers, whose only professional skills are the use of weapons, are desperately looking for ways to support themselves and their families. Nature conservation is not a priority in a country recovering from a long armed conflict. The wildlife of Angola became victims of the war, and of the peace.

Will this also be the destiny of the national symbol? Will the enchanted antelope that has fired the imagination, and that exists only here, in the heart of Angola, perish forever? Will old Kataba manage, from his grave, to save it, or will it be his living descendents who will succeed? The giant sable has survived the war. Will it survive the peace?

ООО

From the early 1970s and until the civil war erupted several years later with the declaration of independence in Angola, the giant sable had became an attractive research subject. In those days, the research was led by three young scientists: predominantly Richard Estes, an American, as well as João Crawford-Cabral, from Portugal and Brian Huntley, a South-African. Years later they all became leading ecologists with international reputations in their fields of expertise. The giant sable has always occupied a very special place in their hearts, not necessarily a very scientific place, but rather one of love, passion; a feeling of ownership and a great desire to protect. These intense feelings have not diminished over the years.

At that time, the giant sable enjoyed full protection in the two designated protected areas in Malange province—Cangandala National Park and Luando Reserve. Most of the giant sable population, then estimated at about 2,600, occurred in Luando Reserve with a further one or two hundred in Cangandala National Park. Several herds were habituated to human presence and the mystery surrounding the antelope had somewhat faded. It was easy to observe them, to follow their movements, and to photograph them in numerous poses, always beautiful, photogenic, and noble.

Richard Estes last photographed the giant sable in 1982. It was to be the last photograph to be taken for many years. The glamorous days were over. When the civil war erupted the giant sable found itself in the midst of the battle. The shepherds, the rangers, the researchers, the tourists, were all gone. They carried the sable in their hearts, but had no choice but to abandon it to its destiny. Their place was taken by warriors and dislocated people who lived in temporary camps at the margins of the area. Famine haunted them all; a multitude of people with no access to food, housing, or clothing, but with large caches of arms and ammunition. The reserves turned into the hunting grounds of the starving soldiers and citizens alike.

This was the fate of most of the wildlife in the various protected areas of Angola. Soldiers from both warring sides hunted wildlife indiscriminately, on foot patrols, from vehicles and from the air, day and night. They hunted them for food and for commercial purposes, and often simply for target practice or out of sheer boredom. And yet, rumours circulated that even the hungriest and cruelest of the soldiers kept one rule: do not touch even one hair of the giant sable, the national symbol that is sacred to all.

Was that really so?

Can every soldier that sees a reddish-brown creature passing briefly before him distinguish between the giant sable female and other similar species? Does every battle-hardened soldier, whose eyes have been drowning in blood for years, really care? Can every refugee, whose belly has been empty for days, allow himself to let a big antelope escape his rifle's sights, taking with it a chance for survival for a few more days? It is difficult to imagine that during those dark years, when the whole country was mired in destruction and death and loss and desperation, when most of the wildlife were exterminated, that the giant sable population had remained intact.

Is it possible that tradition and their sacred status had saved at least a core population? Some people claimed to have seen them during the war and later, especially residents of the adjacent villages, in Malange. There was much speculation, but no one really knew. There was no definite proof.

The devoted admirers of the giant sable, from Angola and elsewhere, never stopped worrying about the antelope during all the years of the war. Some were even more concerned about the threat to its survival than about the horrors of the war and the great human suffering that it caused.

Various actions were proposed at that time in an attempt to secure a future for the antelope. Some suggested capturing several giant sables in the wild and removing them from Angola. The declared goal was to establish a captive breeding herd outside the country to conserve the species for future reintroduction if the wild population in Angola became nonviable or extinct. These plans seemed rather vague and unrealistic. How did the foreign researchers intend to capture these ellusive antelopes in the thicket and in the midst of the battle fields? It seemed that, again, some of the experts had allowed their hearts to rule their heads and were overcome by the longing for the giant sable.

There were also the avaricious ones, whose main motive was financial—a giant sable, offered for sale to zoos or game ranches, would fetch hundreds of thousands of dollars, maybe even a million or more ... and if they could only get a pair ... even semen from one male could probably be sold for a fortune. Sable sub-species can be crossed, and it was said that attempts made to create a pseudo black giant sable by interbreeding in captivity were revealed in genetic examinations, conducted by zoos that had been offered the animals.

Among the unscrupulous were those who wanted to become rich by offering the hunting of giant sables—real ones or fakes—in the wild or on game farms. Stories about such attempts appeared from time to time in the national and international media. In fact, almost any story about the giant sable—real or otherwise—immediately received wide media coverage. The thirst for any information about the antelope was intense.

"No one will remove the palanca negra from Angola. It belongs here," every self-respecting Angolan would say. There was talk of a foreign crook who had arrived in the country to hunt some giant sable. He said his intention was to establish a breeding colony for the conservation of the species so that it could be reintroduced into the wild when the war had ended. But the Angolans had no doubt that it was yet another attempt—one of many—to steal their national treasure.

The responsible minister rejected the foreigner's request for a permit. Even if there are some Angolan politicians who are willing to allow the country's natural resources to be plundered for their own interests and greed, this national treasure is sacred to all. Probably no minister could approve the removal of giant sable antelopes from Angola and still remain in power. The scoundrel was deported that same day.

The rumours spread quickly. By the time the foreigner had packed his bags, a large and angry crowd had already gathered at the entrance of the hotel where he was staying. They were ready to tear him apart. Eventually he had to sneak through the back door to a waiting vehicle that took him to the airport and out of country.

The citizens of Angola felt proud. They had successfully protected their palanca negra from another kidnap attempt. But still, no one really knew what had happened to the antelope during the long years of war.

One group of American and South African giant sable admirers—some with good intentions and others whose intentions were questionable —made every effort to reach the giant sable's reserves in Malange during the war. They asked for the help of the senior generals. The generals did not want to refuse outright, but they had no intention of taking this group of foreign madmen into the middle of the battlefields. The foreigners persisted and the generals dismissed them with promises, which they believed, so they put on more pressure. The generals gave more promises, and so it went on, for years.

Only when the war had ended did the group realize their long-awaited ambition with the help of the generals. To their surprise, many of the local devotees of the giant sable joined their flight over the reserves in Malange. It was the first opportunity in more than two decades to look for the antelope and everybody wanted to take part. They landed briefly in Cangandala National

Park from where they travelled on foot, accompanied by local guides. It became obvious that travelling in a large group was not going to yield the desired results, especially not at a time when animals avoided humans, which they learned to recognize as the source of death. The group split into small parties. On their return, one of these groups claimed that they had seen the giant sable, but none of the experts had been in that group.

The story soon hit the headlines: "The black giant sable has been rediscovered in Angola!" they stated. Maybe, but no one had any proof.

In the same week that this group were looking for the giant sable in Malange, Santos Virgilio, the director of the Department of Communication and Information of the Ministry of Fisheries and Environment, arrived at the same place and with the same objective. He had been sent on a one-man mission, by the minister, Fatima Jardim. Santos went to Cangandala National Park, met with the community of Bola Cachasse near the park, spent several days with them and asked for their help. Unlike the large group that concentrated their efforts on aerial surveys, he walked through the park with guides from the community, on foot and on push-bikes. When he returned he said that he had briefly seen one giant sable male moving quickly through the bush. But he, too, had no proof.

Since then an increasing number of people claimed to have observed the animals, but none of them could provide any proof of their sightings. Everybody now focused on a single objective—to photograph the giant sable, to produce unequivocal evidence that it still really existed here, in the wild, in Angola, in the sable reserves of Malange province.

The national pride was at stake. After so many years it had to be an Angolan that would bring the first sign of survival, the first photo. It was unacceptable that the giant sable would be rediscovered by foreigners. A delegation of the national television channel, TPA, went into the park weighed down with sophisticated filming equipment. They returned empty-handed. They had a lot of footage of the crew, the area, the trees, and antelope spoor. But not a single giant sable, not even its shadow.

In September 2003, about a year and a half after the war had ended, I arrived at Bola Cachasse with an Angolan delegation to look for the giant sable. The expedition was led by Pedro Vaz Pinto, a young researcher from the Catholic University in Luanda. He was joined by another young Angolan researcher, Miguel Morais, two government representatives, Santos Virgilio and Joaquim Lourenço, and me, the UNDP consultant. Our objective was to return with a photo, proof beyond any doubt that would convince the Angolans and the world that the giant sable is still extant. For two and a half weeks we split up and scoured the Cangandala National Park, walking many kilometres each day.

We asked the Soba to nominate two or three guides to work with us and to direct us in our searches of the park. "No," he said adamantly. "There are six palanca negra experts in the village. I will not choose between them. You will work with them all." The six were João, Figueira, Manuel, Esteves, Valente and Domingos, all of them descendents and relatives of old Kataba.

After consulting the Soba, we set up a small camp next to the village. The children gathered to watch us while we erected our tents. We bought mattresses from the villagers and spread our sleeping bags on them. We even had a small bathroom: a small pail filled with clean water from a spring set on a bed of fresh, soft banana leaves in a small hide made of branches. It was so good to find it waiting after the long tiring walks in the park.

The women of the village, beautiful and impressive, wrapped in colourful pano skirts, passed every day near our camp, on their way to the spring. They carried pails of washing and returned with the clean laundry and large water containers carefully balanced on their high-held heads. They watched us with interest as they passed, smiling shyly. Our improvised cooking caused them to burst into laughter, but they did not say anything.

On one of the first days of the survey we went to a small spring near the Maubi River. Figueira said that in the dry season, when the water sources dwindle, sable herds sometimes come to drink at this spring. We had walked for several hours, when we suddenly heard a gunshot coming from the direction of the spring. We stopped dead in our tracks. Then we saw them: three armed poachers at a distance of several hundred metres from us. "We must escape, and fast," said Figueira. "These men are dangerous!"

We ran away.

The army officer who had accompanied our delegation sent an urgent message to the municipal administrator and asked for help from the police. The next day, six armed police officers arrived at the village. Close to the spring, near the Maubi River, they found what was left of the poachers' temporary camp and the remnants of at least fifteen antelopes, mainly duikers. There was, however, no evidence that they had been hunting giant sables, but there was also no doubt that the presence of poachers in the park would jeopardize the sables' survival.

"Since the battles ceased, there are many poachers in the park. Whenever we see them we inform the authorities," the guides told us, "but this is the first time that our information has been taken seriously, and assistance has been sent. We have no weapons and we cannot confront the well-armed poachers alone. After all, many of the poachers are former soldiers or policemen. Who else has so many weapons and ammunition? And they hunt antelopes to sell as bush meat in the market."

The Soba of the Bola community convened an urgent meeting of the other Soba and traditional authorities of the villages around the park. Messengers walked for ten, twenty and thirty kilometres, and returned with the old Soba and their accompanying parties of several young men.

The meeting began at noon. The Soba sat on logs in the shadow of a large wild fig tree. They were bent over, immersed in the heat of their discussion until the sun disappeared below the horizon in a burning sunset that gave way to a busy African night. Then they lit the fire and continued debating around it, far into the night. The younger men stood around the elders, or sat on the ground, with the six guides, Kataba's relatives, among them. No one else dared approach. In the morning the distinguished visitors returned to their villages.

João gave us a brief report. The debate had been difficult and tiring. The Soba discussed the severe poverty and its devastating effect on the communities and their traditions. They also talked about strangers from outside the communities who had come to hunt in the park. Above all, they agreed to work together to protect the giant sable in the park and to prevent the extinction of the antelope that had always held such an important place in their local tradition.

The guides suggested that we should look for the giant sable in the southern part of the park, near the Kuki River. The animals were known to go there sometimes during the dry season, in search of water. We assumed that the poachers had scared them away from the Maubi River and surrounds. We left at dawn in a convoy, heading towards the Kuki River about twenty kilometres from our camp. When we arrived there, we split into small parties. Again, we found a lot of spoor, but no sable. In the mud of a riverside pasture we found fresh spoor left by a herd of sable females and calves. At the edges of the pasture were tall termite mounds. The next morning at dawn I hid behind a termite mounds for several hours. From there I could survey a large area of pasture and woodland with the binoculars. I saw one vervet monkey hurrying away, jumping rapidly from branch to branch, but there was no sign of the sables.

Pedro and João returned from a long walk. They told us, furiously, that on their way they had collected a large number of wire snares that had been hidden by poachers. An antelope that gets caught in such a trap dies in terrific agony. Snares do not distinguish between a giant sable and any other, less rare, antelope. They kill them all. The poachers had arrived here too.

In the evening we spread our sleeping bags under mosquito nets on a bed of leaves near the river. We fell asleep to the soothing sounds of croaking frogs, buzzing cicadas, chirruping fruit bats and the hoots of owls. The night was lit softly by a full moon and phosphorescent flickering fireflies moved around frantically.

On one of our walks we encountered very fresh sable tracks. We followed them quietly and carefully for about an hour and a half. We found more and more fresh spoor belonging to a female and a calf. We became very excited. We may soon find them, we thought. We sidestepped the tracks and hid in the thicket, our cameras poised for action and our eyes searching for the slightest movement. We dared not breathe.

There! A reddish-brown creature, about a metre high, passed by us, and then another, smaller one. They moved very quickly. We saw only a blurred brown shadow moving swiftly and disappearing. No one could get a picture. Had we just seen the giant sable? Maybe. Maybe not.

We turned around and started heading back. Once the animals had noticed us there was no point in going on. In one of the fresh tracks we found hairs, which we collected.

On the last night of our stay in the park all of the villagers from Bola Cachasse, the Kanzambas and the Bolas, came to see us off. We gave them some equipment and supplies—a contribution from UNDP to the village and to the project. The guides received their fees and some special gifts. One of the village youngsters brought a tambourine and the party began with singing and dancing. The village women prepared a special meal of chicken cooked in tomato and onion sauce, with cooked cassava leaves (kizaka) and cassava root porridge (funge). It was delicious.

"Next time you come here," they told us, "let us do the cooking. You should only bring the ingredients. You would be better to trust us with the cooking."

We returned to Luanda with swollen feet and in low spirits. The only photo we had of the giant sable was a picture of a large painting of a whole herd that we found on our way to the park, painted on a wall in one of the restaurants in the capital of the province. We had hoped then that it was a good sign of what we would find in the park. Now we knew that it was all we had.

We sent the collected sable hairs for genetic analysis in South Africa. Maybe, after all? Two weeks later we received the first response. "The results are still uncertain. We are still working." Every additional day further strained our stretched nerves. Only on Christmas Eve did the final result arrive.

"We are very sorry," said the correspondence. "The hairs do not belong to a giant sable." The reddish-brown animal that passed us in a blur was a roan antelope.

We published the results of our survey in all the media channels in Angola. We alerted everyone, in every possible way to the danger that the palanca negra was facing. If measures for its protection were not taken immediately, it may soon become extinct. In conjunction with the provincial government we mobilized support from UNDP for the temporary employment of the six guides, Kataba's relatives, as the giant sable's guardians, shepherds, in Cangandala National Park. That was a temporary measure to support their work until Pedro Vaz Pinto could find a permanent source of funding for the protection of the giant sable. He also recruited several more shepherds from other villages around the park.

With further donations he bought uniforms, bicycles and some equipment. The provincial governor also requested the assistance of the police with law enforcement. Poachers, however, continue to penetrate the sable reserves and threaten the giant sable's survival.

○○○

Pedro did not give up. On the contrary, the more difficult the task, the more persistent he became. He simply had to get a picture of the giant sable to prove its existence. There was no doubt left. His yearning for the palanca negra already had hold of his soul. It governed his actions. It was that famous disease. He returned to visit Cangandala several times, but each time in vain. He organized an aerial survey with a microlight, above Luando Reserve. He and his companions on this survey saw lots of sable spoor, but not the animals themselves.

With the help of the local community and the sable shepherds he installed hidden infrared-activated cameras next to salt licks on the sable tracks in the park. He caught lots of grasses that had activated the cameras on film and a few animals that came to the salt licks, but not a single giant sable. They also collected sable faeces in Cangandala and Luando and sent it to geneticists, but again and again the results were disappointing.

Many people despaired. Some said publicly that the giant sable was already extinct. But Pedro persevered. Then, one day towards the end of 2004, he informed me with great excitement and happiness: "We have proof at last. Some of the faeces collected in Luando Reserve has now been proved genetically to come from the giant sable. Our national symbol still exists."

Several months later, on March 2005, I received another message from Pedro: "We have photos!" Twenty-three years after the last photo of the giant sable was taken, a herd of twelve was captured by the lens of an infrared-activated camera that has been installed by Pedro near a salt lick in Cangandala National Park. Most of them were females, but there were also calves and juvenile males. The species' typical facial patterns were clearly distinguishable. This was indisputable. The palanca negra gigante is still here.

TR

The Boneco

"The Boneco, the statue, it is all his fault!"

Stella, Julia, Isabel, they all believed in it.

We had our doubts.

Tamar Golan's famous passion for African art attracted the art traders of Angola to the Israeli ambassador's residence. Filipe was the first to discover that here was a good opportunity to make a living, and with the private lessons he received on the artworks, he could also impress his other customers.

He knew very well, as we all did, that if Tamar fell in love with an antique statue, she would not rest until she had rescued it from the trader's dirty jute sack and provided it with a place of prominence in her home. Once installed, she would endow upon it all the polishing and shining that it deserved, and proudly position it where it would receive the appropriate attention.

Diplomats and other visitors who saw the ambassador's meticulously nurtured 'museum' were envious, and several began to collect antiques themselves. The ambassador could assess the age, origins and value of each and every piece. She could select the truly valuable antiquities from the many cheap imitations and she enjoyed telling the provenance and personal tale of each of her works of art.

And so a habit developed—Filipe used to go on his journeys around the country and return with his sack full of treasures. He would arrive at the ambassador's residence, open his sack, and set out the statues on the living room floor. When Isabel, the embassy secretary, got wind of Filipe's imminent arrival, she would often invite all those interested to come along to the viewing. Tamar lovingly caressed the pieces and started the art lessons.

"This statue, of a woman holding her rounded belly, helps women fall pregnant. Look how smooth it is—so many longing and loving hands have caressed it already. This is why it transfers to us such positive energy and a strong will to touch it."

"And this one—is this a statue that helps women fall pregnant too?"

"No, this statue has a different function: after the birth it helps with the milk production, so that the baby can grow well and strong."

"This large statue has an interesting story. You can see that it originates from the Tchokwe tribe. It is a special masculine figure that serves to strengthen the power of the chief, the leader of the tribe."

And so on.

Some of the pieces were lucky enough to join the well nurtured collection. Others were purchased by the visitors—but not before they had sought advice from the ambassador.

Tamar had one rule: she never bought what she would call 'bad' statues, those images used in witchcraft ceremonies and for cursing victims with the 'evil eye'. These figures are easy to identify. They have formidable, sharp teeth and are ornamented with a multitude of symbols associated with witchcraft. Some have what may be termed 'satanic' features, like a goat beard or a large horn. They all look evil, threatening and frightening. She resolved not to keep in the residence statues that could cause discomfort to their observers, to the relief of the household employees and visitors.

One of the many visitors who arrived at the ambassador's residence was a correspondent from a well-known American journal. As most of the foreign journalists in Angola, he wanted to write an original article about the 'real situation' in the war-ravaged country. He had a strong desire to interview José Eduardo dos Santos, the 'silent' president. Unlike media-oriented presidents, dos Santos made few public appearances, and especially avoided media interviews, in particular with foreign agencies.

The American journalist did not stand a chance, but he persisted. From time to time he would announce happily that he had made tentative appointments through people related to the presidency. He ignored all our sceptical comments. Each time he returned disappointed; the meeting with the president had not happened. He repeatedly postponed his return to the United States, until eventually he returned home empty handed, his nerves shot and without the interview.

He brought the ambassador a huge book, as heavy as a brick, a biography he had written. While he was waiting for the presidential interview, Tamar tried to cheer him up. And so he was introduced to Filipe and to his mobile statue exhibition. Unfortunately, it was exactly when he returned from one of his unsuccessful attempts to meet and interview the president. He was in despair and ill at ease. He observed the statues with intense concentration and examined them one by one. Then he stood in front of the statue line-up, with his legs apart, his eyes narrowed, and scrutinized them as though they were subjects in an identity parade. We all followed his gaze worriedly. Eventually he held out his hand and stated firmly: "This one! I want this one!"

He chose the most frightening statue I have ever seen. It was made of wood, gigantic and dark, with eyes that bulged with an evil expression. Two lines of sharp teeth crossed the face in a wicked smile. A large, sharp, curving horn grew from the centre of the head. The loins were covered with a belt, decorated with many witchcraft symbols known to be used by witchdoctors for getting rid of their clients' enemies. The statue was as tall as a person, and stared threateningly at anyone unfortunate enough to pass by his monstrous face. The ambassador tried to dissuade the journalist from making this dubious acquisition. But he was adamant: "I want this one!"

As though this was not enough, the American journalist asked Tamar to keep the horrid creature in her residence, until he went home. He would then send it by sea with more of his belongings. He was afraid that if he took it to the hotel it would be stolen.

Who, we wondered, would dare steal such a terrifying statue?

Despite the horrified expressions of the embassy's staff members, and their quiet protestations, Tamar was too embarrassed to refuse, and so 'the Boneco' (flatteringly, something between a toy and a statue, a Portuguese term), remained at her home.

Trouble soon followed.

The next day, Stella, the housekeeper, and Isabel, the embassy secretary, quarrelled bitterly. They were friends at heart and used to do everything together, wandering around Luanda, shopping, and gossiping cheerfully about the embassy's staff, including the ambassador. Their friendship was known to all and when they were not together, they spoke on the phone. Even when they argued from time to time, their disputes ended quickly and gave way to wide smiles and warm hugs. But this was the most serious quarrel they'd had since they met. They burst into tears, ran out of the house and refused to be reconciled.

In the evening I saw Julia approaching the Boneco fearfully. She carried a broomstick, with a large towel hanging from the end. In a single, brave move she threw the towel over the Boneco's face from a distance. The towel covered the hideous thing and Julia smiled to herself with satisfaction.

Isabel and Stella, still shaken from their fight, did not return to work the next day. They stayed at home, each of them separately mourning their lost friendship, and Julia was left to run the household on her own. That afternoon, several guests arrived for a formal meeting. Julia had prepared refreshments and had piled the teacups and saucers on a tray. Everything was ready.

Suddenly, in the middle of the diplomats' meeting, a loud noise came from the kitchen. The security officer hurried over and found Julia sitting on the floor, with her hands held out and despair in her eyes. The precious china was in pieces, chocolate cake swimming in thick brown tea around her.

That evening I found Julia meticulously sewing a large jute sack. The Boneco was imprisoned within the sack.

"That's it. Now he will not be able to get out," Julia clapped her hands together with satisfaction. Just to be on the safe side, she again threw the large towel over his head.

Several days passed quietly. It seemed that the Boneco, wrapped inside the sack, was defeated and had stopped making mischief. But apparently he was only gathering strength for a real strike.

"Come quickly to the military hospital," I was told on the phone from the embassy. "The ambassador has fallen and broken a joint in her hand. She needs treatment urgently. We may need to fly her out today to a hospital in South Africa."

The fracture was bad and Tamar had an operation in the excellent hospital in

Luanda belonging to the French oil company, Elf, following the intervention of the French ambassador, one of the most loyal and enthusiastic members of her African art club.

I accompanied her on her return home. The big jute sack, hiding the Boneco inside it, was standing quietly in the kitchen, a silent witness to its misdeeds. "Enough," I insisted, "No more! The Boneco must go!"

"Yes" she murmured, "I agree ... but I have promised the journalist to keep it for him and he keeps delaying his return home. He still believes that he will get an interview with the president. How can I tell him that I do not want to keep the Boneco any more because I have broken my hand? He will think for sure that I have lost my mind."

"There may be a solution," I said.

The apartment adjacent to the ambassador's residence housed a couple of annoying diplomats. Tamar and the American journalist were among their few friends. "We will transfer the Boneco to their apartment," I suggested. "Since you are injured and need to recuperate, it will be more convenient for the journalist to pack up his belongings at their place."

The security men carried the jute sack with its troublesome burden to the neighbours' apartment, mumbled some brief explanation, left the Boneco there and escaped before the couple could refuse. The residence staff felt relieved and the frightened expression left Julia's face, giving place again to her warm, wide smiles.

Finally, the journalist gave up on the presidential interview. He packed his belongings, with the Boneco among them, and sent them home by sea. We were all relieved when he and the Boneco left, but he promised to return. He would get his interview, no matter what.

Shortly afterwards, in a moment of frankness, Tamar told the neighbours the real reason for leaving the Boneco on their doorstep. "Aha!" said the neighbour, "now I understand. From the minute this thing entered our house, we never stopped quarrelling." They did not stop quarrelling many days after that.

Several months passed. The Boneco was almost forgotten. Even the journalist and his original article gave way to new events. One day, a long letter arrived from the journalist. The ship that carried his cargo, he wrote, had been lost at sea. The crew was saved, but all the cargo had gone to the bottom of the ocean. The journalist has reconsidered and resolved never to return to Angola again. Not ever.

TR

The plant

Life in our little embassy resembled that in a submarine, or perhaps a tightly knit family. And as in all good families, we, too, sometimes experienced difficulties. One of our problems was dealt with in a rather African manner.

Isabel was the most important person in the embassy. Anyone unfamiliar with the true situation could have been forgiven for believing that, as ambassador, I held the strongest position. But I knew the truth—the real power lay in the hands of our secretary, Isabel.

In the days following the official opening of the embassy at its temporary location on the 18th floor of the Presidente Meridien Hotel, we had no typewriter, not to mention a computer, a telephone line or even official note paper. We didn't know a soul in the place and the Portuguese spoken by the Israeli security officer Roni and I was strictly limited. We decided to seek someone to serve as our liaison with Angola.

A few hours after the first report in the local media on the opening of the new embassy, we were flooded with applicants. Did we need a secretary, a chauffeur, a gardener, cook, housekeeper, cleaner, servant, or, generally, anyone else to help us out? Jobs are scarce in Luanda and people would jump at any job with newly arrived foreigners and a salary in a foreign currency.

Roni was responsible for sifting through the applicants and for asking security-related questions. But, in a foreign place, a country where we had never had any kind of diplomatic representation, it was virtually impossible to pinpoint exactly who had a terrorist background, or was an enemy agent, or even to discover whether any of the applicants had a criminal history. Besides, almost everyone here owns some kind of a firearm, so who's to say what should be regarded as suspicious. On the third day I noticed that the young girls Roni was sending to me were especially attractive. Although Angolan women are generally regarded as beautiful, with their hair plaited into dozens of intricate braids, their bright, shining eyes and their firm, upright breasts and buttocks, he was making a point of choosing the most attractive of the lot. Unfortunately, however, none of the candidates Roni picked could use a typewriter, and most of them had never seen a computer in their lives. Even I could see that their command of Portuguese was feeble, and other foreign languages, especially English, were not worth mentioning. During the Marxist regime, English—the language of international imperialism—was no longer taught in Angolan schools; the second foreign language in use at that time was, of course, Russian.

Job applicants kept streaming in. One day there was a phone call from someone who found my own linguistic handicap so difficult to overcome that she was forced to address me in fluent French. What a relief. I invited her immediately to the 18th floor of the hotel.

She was so sorry, she said, but she would only be able to come later in the afternoon, because she was working at the Yugoslav Embassy, where office hours ended at two o'clock. I sensed that here was a real find: a French speaker, experienced in work with a diplomatic delegation.

Roni wasn't overjoyed when Isabel arrived at the embassy. She was quite short, slightly dumpy and modestly dressed, but she captured my heart immediately and my affection for her grew when I learned that she was a member of the Bakongo tribe, of which I have always been very fond.

An hour after turning up at our hotel suite, Isabel had managed to obtain from the hotel management an old-fashioned typewriter, a pile of white writing paper and, no less important, a telephone directory that was only four years old.

The Yugoslav Embassy in Luanda was in a bad way. Internal wars had torn Yugoslavia apart and the ambassador no longer knew where his orders, or his next budget, were coming from. Isabel and I agreed that it was not good form for her to leave her job immediately or for me to most undiplomatically appropriate a member of a fellow ambassador's staff.

For the first month, Isabel would come to us after completing her work at the Yugoslav Embassy. Later she became the first regular staff member of the Israeli Embassy in Angola. To this day she continues to be the kingpin of the delegation in Luanda; after all, ambassadors and diplomatic attachés come and go, but a good secretary stays forever.

As our workload increased and the Foreign Office in Jerusalem agreed to employ a second secretary, Alves was taken on as deputy chauffeur. Alves had been recommended by the wife of the German ambassador, who was happy to report that he was an excellent timekeeper. A tall, handsome young man, always impeccably dressed, he was also able to converse in English, something that was both rare and of supreme importance, since the Portuguese-speaking Israelis that came to us were few and far between. Alves told us that, as part of his national military service, he had been accepted for a helicopter training course, but, for some reason, he never completed it and instead returned to civilian life. When he was alone in the embassy car, it was easy to mistake him for an ambassador in his own right.

Some months later, it was obvious to us all that Alves' talents far exceeded those required by a deputy chauffeur. Any guests from Israel found in Alves a devoted and knowledgeable tour guide. By day, every second secretary arriving from Jerusalem to join the embassy's diplomatic staff was helped by Alves as interpreter vis-à-vis the authorities and, by night, as a guide to Luanda's night life.

A second desk was therefore found, slightly smaller than Isabel's, and placed in the tiny office allocated to the secretariat. It was overcrowded, but we had no doubt that Alves' promotion was good for us all, even for Isabel, who was overworked to exhaustion.

One morning Isabel failed to come to work. We sent someone to her home to see what had happened, since she didn't have a telephone or a car of her own. The emissary returned with the news that Isabel had a terrible headache and was lying in a dark room with a towel over her eyes. The emissary went back to Isabel's home to ask whether she would like to see the embassy's Spanish doctor.

Isabel declined and, on the third day, she returned to work, pale and introspective. She still refused to go to the doctor or take any kind of medication and life in the embassy resumed its busy schedule. When we had almost forgotten about Isabel's problem, she fell ill again. Again, she had a terrible headache. The third time it happened, I was really concerned. Isabel had been the kingpin at the embassy. On the days that she was not there, Alves would move over to her desk where he managed the day–to-day affairs of the embassy. One day, after work, Isabel announced that she would like to take a long leave of absence on health grounds. In fact, she wasn't sure she could ever return to work with us.

I invited her to my home. We drank tea and talked. Something in Isabel had changed. It was very late when she finally opened up and confessed, "I can talk to you. You know that the people of the Bakongo can feel everything. We live in the world of secrets. Something terrible is happening to me. Someone is trying to kill me and no white doctor can help me. I'm going to die".

She asked me to take care of her two young daughters. Her ex-husband was a good-for-nothing and already had children by another woman.

We call these things witchcraft, or the evil eye, and I had learned long ago to take them seriously. Whether real or imagined, their practical effect on the lives of people in Africa is a proven fact.

It was very difficult to get Isabel to tell me who it was who was trying to kill her and how. In a whisper she admitted that it was Alves. He'd been placing 'things' in her desk drawer. As soon as she'd come to work and take her place at her desk, she would feel the 'thing'. Her headaches would come on. She had no choice, therefore, but to leave her job at the embassy. Maybe this way she would be able to save herself from death.

I was horrified. Alves was a modern, urban young man, who had no respect for tradition. I invited him to my home for tea and cake. With great hesitancy, I related Isabel's suspicions. He was shocked and firmly denied them all. His family, he explained, was no ordinary village family. His father and grandfather had worked for the Portuguese in Luanda and not in some remote province. And, besides, why would he want to do anything to harm Isabel? He was happy with his lot and glad that he was no longer required to sit behind a driving wheel and that he had a respectable desk of his own.

I told this to Isabel. I told her that I was convinced that if anyone was doing 'things' to her, it surely was not Alves. Isabel was not placated. I offered to replace her desk with a smart new one. And we did. Isabel's smile returned and the new desk was really beautiful and quite compatible with her senior position in the embassy.

But after a while, the headaches returned. Again she failed to come to work and lay in her dark bedroom at home, a towel covering her face. We took our Spanish doctor to see her. Isabel was reluctant to talk to him and refused to reveal the source of the 'evil' that was causing her problems. I decided to take action; I had no choice. I invited Isabel and Alves to my home a few minutes before midnight. I prepared a new, unopened bottle of gin. Many years ago, I had learned what I was about to do in a small village in Ghana.

We stepped out to the broad balcony that overlooked Luanda Bay and the ocean. A full moon hung in the sky; significantly, because the ceremony had to be conducted by the light of a full moon. A spectacular green-foliaged tropical plant stood in an enormous pot in the corner of the balcony. The two joined hands and bowed down before me and I poured a little of the gin on their hands and on the plant in the planter. I said a few words in Hebrew, exorcising them of the evil spirit and calling on them to return to being friends. I then said a blessing for our embassy. Finally, I laid a hand on each of their heads and asked them to remove all bad thoughts from their heart's and to fill their heart with love. We embraced and kissed each other. Above us the moon shone.

"You see," Isabel exclaimed, "this ceremony has removed that thing from Alves. Now we have all been purified."

A month later, we threw out the plant. It had died.

TG

The chieftain's throne

This is the story of a pair of majestic thrones of the Tchokwe tribe; two intricately carved wooden chairs both with an upright back, adorned and decorated with crude copper inlays. The king's throne is only slightly taller than that of the queens. No one knows their exact age, but they have come a long way since they seated a royal couple somewhere in northeast Angola toward the end of the 19th century. Today they are proudly displayed in an office building belonging to the Kennedy family in Boston, USA.

It all began with a woman. In the 15th century, Queen Lueji headed a small kingdom, part of the large Lunda empire in southeast Congo. The queen had decided to marry a prince of the Luba tribe. The tribe's elders disagreed with her decision and refused to accept the authority of a foreigner. They decided to take action and, together with their families, they crossed the Kalani River and made their way south, to the region which is now northeast Angola. Using peaceful means though occasionally, war, they settled and multiplied in the area and established the kingdom of the Tchokwe.

Hunters and farmers, the Tchokwe were also gifted and talented artists and mathematicians. They believed in the supernatural powers of a single great force that controls the lives of mankind. The realms of the Tchokwe, deep in the heart of Africa, were first discovered by the white man only in the late 17th century.

The Tchokwe were brave warriors who withstood the slave traders and prevented them from capturing their sons to be sent to work in the Americas. Moreover, they had great confidence in themselves and in their culture, which allowed them to adopt the customs, accessories and techniques of the white man and to adapt them to their own needs. Thus they learned how to weave fabric from raffia, exchanged the bow and arrow for rifles that shot stones and replaced the traditional low round stool with tall, high-backed chairs.

A sketch dated 1878 depicts their famous king, N'dumba Tembo (tembo means lion), sitting, ramrod straight on his elegant, carved wood chair.

Several months after my arrival in Angola, I had the honour of meeting Filipe, a young 'antiques dealer' from the northeastern part of the country. He tried to sell me some of his wares and swore that the masks he was offering were genuine antiques and absolutely authentic. It was easy enough to show him that the masks were fakes, which had been buried for a few months in damp soil in order to obtain that 'antique' look. Dealers such as Filipe were not familiar with the traditions of the various tribes and often fell victim to highly sophisticated manufacturers of so-called antiques. Filipe's great advantage was the fact that he originated from the Angola-Congo border, a region with an incomparably rich culture.

Filipe introduced me to André, an elderly, self-effacing man with wise eyes and a broad knowledge of languages. In better days, André had taught high school French in the Portuguese speaking region of north Angola. But war had taken away his home, his family and his place of work.

André had a special way about him. Listening to him tell his stories in his soft, gentle voice, you forgot his well-worn clothes, battered shoes, filthy fingernails and sharp smell of perspiration. At these times, a different André emerged, a dignified man with a deep sense of tradition.

André promised to accompany Filipe on his forthcoming trip to the land of the Tchokwe and to help him identify authentic statues. We all addressed André as Patron, out of respect for his knowledge and age. André asked for no remuneration for his advice and we were all sure that he was the only one capable of preventing Filipe from being taken for a ride by those antiques artists. He assured us that he was not afraid of war, because the worst had already happened to him. But before setting off on the trip, he asked for some advance payment.

"I need this money," he explained, "to buy my way through police and army roadblocks. They don't get paid salaries, so they demand reparation from individuals daring enough to travel along the mine-riddled roads. They are no less poor than we are."

A few months passed since my meeting with André and Filipe. Some people said that they had simply diddled me out of my money, but, privately, I was afraid that André had been unable to withstand the hardships of the journey, or that their car had hit a landmine.

And then, one warm and humid day, the hotel's gatekeeper called the embassy's security guard and informed him that there were two 'very dirty' people here with burlap sacks. They refused to open the sacks and insisted that the ambassador had invited them!

André and Filipe came in, dusty, bleary-eyed, hungry and thirsty. They said they were afraid to hold on to their treasure for even another hour. We tore open the bags to reveal two Tchokwe royal thrones. Genuine thrones, without a shadow of a doubt.

André smiled a small, self-satisfied smile and said: "It was hard, very hard. But I kept my promise. Actually, the hardest part of this exhausting journey was the road-blocks at the entrance to the city. The soldiers very nearly robbed us."

They drank thirstily, ate a little food and hurried off to the tin hut in which they lived in a distant quarter of the city.

After a good clean, rub down and polish, the two chairs were given pride of place in the Embassy's reception room in the Presidente Meridian Hotel. They aroused the admiration of everyone who saw them. Every morning, I would stop to admire the chairs and surreptitiously stroke the beautifully carved wood.

In March, 1996, several members of the Kennedy clan landed in Angola, headed by former senator and US Attorney General, Robert Kennedy's widow, Ethel. Senator Kennedy, who was famous for his efforts to raise the status of the black community in the United States, was assassinated on June 5, 1968 by Sirhan Sirhan. Now, thirty years after his first visit to South Africa, the family had decided to set out on a special commemorative journey to the African continent. Robert Kennedy had dared to publicly and openly criticize the Apartheid regime in South Africa; now, the Kennedy family was taking the same route he had taken and were stopping at the same stations at which he had stopped. Luanda had been Kennedy's last stop before Pretoria. At that time Angola had been subjected to the fascist regime of the Portuguese tyrant, Antonio Salazar, who cruelly squashed any African movements struggling for liberation from colonial rule. Senator Kennedy had harsh words for the Portuguese governor of Luanda and, as a devout

Catholic, met black members of the Catholic clergy, much to the consternation of their white counterparts. In the years since then, the Kennedy family maintained close ties with the Catholic Church of independent Angola, provided scholarships and donated to charities. They owned a small oil refinery which purchased its oil from Angola, notwithstanding subsequent president Ronald Reagan's negative attitude toward the Marxist regime in Luanda.

Angola welcomed the Kennedys with open arms during their memorial journey to Africa. The American guests met the president, were invited to parliament and visited the Catholic University. Ethel Kennedy stayed at the American ambassador's residence and the rest of the family – 15 altogether – stayed at the hotel in which we lived. We met often and had long discussions on the tragic fate of Angola.

At night, the echo of nearby gunfire could be heard from the hotel; during the day, everyone suffocated from the heat, because the air-conditioning system had collapsed. We had become accustomed to the extreme conditions and we were happy to donate our cooling fans to the guests. Michael, the family representative responsible for the oil company, came to the embassy to thank us.

As soon as he entered the small suite that served both as chancery and residence, he fixed his eyes on the two chairs. "Tchokwe?" he asked.

"Tchokwe," I confirmed.

Twice a day, Michael would appear at the embassy and sit in the chieftain's throne, and from here he would talk at length about his vision for the future of Angola. We talked about the oil profit which was not seeping down to the people, about the curse of the landmines and the war that was never-ending. Michael Kennedy decided to leave American politics to other members of his family. He wanted to devote himself to Angola, and to the memory of his father. "I feel as though I belong here," he said and laid his hand on the arm of the throne of the King of Tchokwe. We agreed to work together.

On the day of their departure, I said to Michael: "These chairs are yours, a symbol of the deal you have struck with Angola and of our future work together."

He was beside himself with joy. "It's a deal," he said.

One day I had a perplexed call from the American Embassy: "Michael Kennedy has sent you a chair," said the voice on the other end of the line. What I received was a rocking chair, a registered exhibit, an exact replica of the favourite chair of his late uncle, President John F Kennedy. "The deal is alive and breathing," Michael had written on a scrap of paper.

Michael returned to Angola a few months later. The first mission we tackled together was the war on landmines.

In October, 1997 I received my last letter from Michael, "I am writing these lines from your chieftain's throne. I am hoping that it will provide me with some royal inspiration ... in all truth, these chairs are so beautiful, even against the background of an office building in Boston ... when I look at their wonderful craftsmanship, I remember our conversations about the landmines in Angola. We plan to organize a large conference next year at the John F. Kennedy Library to discuss the landmine issue. I'll be in touch. I am sure we shall do everything possible for Angola ..."

Two months later, on December 31, 1997, Michael Kennedy was killed in an accident that was one more link in the chain of tragedies that befell this very special family. His chieftain's throne remains, orphaned, in the Boston office building.

TG

M'Banza Kongo

M'Banza Kongo is a name that has been with me since I first fell in love with Africa. It is the name of the capital of the ancient Congo kingdom and appears on the very earliest 16th century European maps of Africa.

Even before Henry Morton Stanley uttered the immortal words, "Dr Livingstone, I presume"; even before the race was on to discover the source of the Nile; when only Ibn Batuta and daring Arab travellers were telling tales of Timbuktu, Portuguese seafarers were arriving at the large cape on the west coast of the continent, where the mighty Congo River flowed into the sea. In those days, the ocean was called 'Oceanus Ethiopicus' and the entire region was known by the Latin term, Nigritarum (the land of the black man). It was there that the kingdom (secret to white people) was discovered. From the big sea port, many thousands of African men and women were shipped across the ocean to work as slaves in the new continent of the Americas. The Congo was ruled by the first Christian king in Africa and Africa's first Christian church was built in M'Banza Kongo. Hundreds of years later, Pope John Paul II went there as part of his first visit to the black continent.

Many books have been written about the bitter fate of King Afonso I (1543–1506)—whose real name was M'Bamba N'zinga—and included heartrending descriptions of the trust he placed in the Portuguese sailors, his acceptance of Christianity and his journey to Lisbon, where he was held hostage until his death.

In this chapter, I shall tell for the first time the true tragic story of the descendant of one of his descendants, Crown Prince Monanga N'zinga. The date of his birth remains obscure, but the year of his death is well known: 1999.

I first met Crown Prince N'zinga at about the same time I met my colleague, Norwegian Ambassador in Angola, Ms Bjorg Leite. We had decided to join forces in an effort to save the ancient church of M'Banza Kongo. As enthusiastic students of local history, we wanted to take part in the Kongo people's struggle to restore the pride of their tribe to its former glory.

We thought that a good way to start would be by inviting several members of the tribe—dignitaries, academics and intellectuals—to a symposium. At all costs, we wanted to avoid too much involvement with professional politicians and told ourselves that we would meet, talk, discuss and galvanize a plan of action. The Norwegian ambassador even found a potential donor to fund the church renovations. But, of course, we soon discovered that our undertaking was no simple matter.

As befits an ancient African tribe with a fierce sense of tradition, each branch of the family claimed to be the real heirs of King Afonso I. Like all the ancient tribes in tropical Africa, the Bakongo passed on their traditions and history orally, from generation to generation, and we learned that the rift in the kingdom, which had begun dozens and even hundreds of years before, still held fast. What had started as a quarrel over inheritance involving a beautiful young queen, had, over the years and through generations, burgeoned into something much larger. The queen in question was Kimpa Vita, a priestess and founder of her own cult, who, like Joan of Arc, had experienced a vision that revealed her holiness. Following her vision, she set out on a mission to repair all the injustices in the kingdom, preached on the approaching doomsday and accumulated a large following. She changed her name to Dona Beatriz and her followers believed that she was a representative of the Christian God, who had, at last, responded to the pleas of the Bakongo nation. She succeeded in temporarily uniting the kingdom, before it was split once again by her heirs. The conflict, which has lasted for many a long day, shows no sign of being settled.

We learned, too, to respect the tradition of age groups, that it is unheard of among the Bakongo to invite young people from one family together with people of an, older generation from another family.

While we were still busily composing the invitation, rumours of the impending symposium had begun flying through town and village. A growing number of people arrived every day, claiming that their pedigrees entitled them to inclusion on the guest list and no matter how hard I studied my history books, I was unable to keep track of developments in the various African dynasties. Bakongo tradition, it appeared, is at least as complex today as it was 400 years ago.

"My family and I will host the symposium," announced Joseph, the distinguished elderly sociology professor. We thanked him profusely, aware of the genuine risk he was willing to undertake. But what we didn't know at the time was that in his hand he held a trump card. He was close to the Crown Prince of the Bakongo.

The security situation prevented the symposium from being held in the time-honoured way, beneath one of the sacred trees on the outskirts of town. However, every effort was made to reconstruct an authentic atmosphere in the professor's large courtyard and to ensure that everything was done according to traditional protocol. A fire was lit in the appropriate corner, the meeting's eternal flame. A group of youngsters was appointed to take care of the flame and they carried out their task in silence and with zeal throughout the long evening. It was clearly a great privilege.

Further away, in another corner of the garden, a fire burned under the pots of food. This was the women's job. The professor's wife oversaw the process and food was brought in by the many women who were taking part in the meeting, including distinguished members of parliament, housewives and a few grey-haired grandmothers. They were all dressed traditionally and what a magnificent sight it was to see African women dressed in their huge, colourful headdresses.

The guests arrived one by one and were ceremoniously led by the intermediate age group to the seats they had been allocated according to their rank and seniority. The older guests were seated near the eternal flame. Greetings were also exchanged in accordance with the status of each of the participants. It was a while before Bjorg Leite and I began asking ourselves if the discussion was ever going to open.

Suddenly, there was a drum roll. Everyone stood up—the Crown Prince had arrived. I saw a thin man, slightly stooped, dressed in a shabby suit. His demeanor held neither pomp nor majesty. He walked slowly, trying to identify faces in the dark, through the smoke from the fire. For a moment he appeared alarmed by the occasion. The crowd bowed down before him. We, too, lowered our heads.

I'm not sure if he even noticed us, two white women. He was too immersed in his own world, the world of the Bakongo. The guest of honour made an almost indiscernible gesture with his hand and the ceremony began. The prince spoke no Portuguese and the entire evening was conducted in the Bakongo language. We were provided with a whispered translation of the main points. The first to speak were the elders, who described the bitter fate that had forced them away from their homes and the graves of their ancestors. The spirits of their fathers called them back home. But there was war there and hunger, ruin and devastation. The others too, spoke of yearnings for their mothers' birthplace, which they had never seen.

By the time the prince began his speech, the fire had started to die down. Cautiously, the youngsters added twigs. No one made a sound. Even our interpreter had grown silent

"I have been here for many long years. The war is cruel to our tribe. The Marxist authorities had no respect for our tradition. They know that I can become king only after I have stood on the grave of my mother the queen. There in M'banza Kongo. And I am here, exiled from my homeland, my kingdom."

For the first time that evening, he turned to face us. "You, honourable ladies," he said, "you belong to the white race that conquered us, you have the power. Take me back to my home, save the great and noble Kongo kingdom."

Later, the hosts accompanied us to our car. This was not how I had imagined my meeting with Crown Prince Monanga N'zinga, heir of Nzimba N'zinga, Afonso I, King of the Bakongo.

The days went by and, with them, the meetings and the talks. Many and varied ideas were bandied about, some simple, like collating testimonies from the tribal elders in the villages, printing books in the Bakongo language, reinstating the old Portuguese-Bakongo dictionary, while other, more controversial, ideas were raised. According to the more militant among them it was time to wage a struggle to reunite the ancient Kongo kingdom and to undo the colonialist division of the tribes who were scattered across three countries, Angola, the Democratic Republic of Congo (Congo Kinshasa) and the Republic of Congo (Congo Brazzaville).

Sometimes the debate in their language would become heated and I had the impression that I could hear names such as Abraham, Isaac or Solomon being mentioned. In answer to my question, I was told that "these are names from the Book of Books. As you know, we are descendents of the Hebrews, and we consult with the Holy Book to decide on the right way to behave."

Ostensibly, they were united by a single simple idea, according to which they would all make a journey, led by the crown prince, to M'Banza Kongo, where they would announce the establishment of a Bakongo spiritual centre, the renovation of the ancient church and a call to all members of the tribe to contribute to the upkeep of their tradition. How easy is that? As the crow flies, the distance from Luanda to M'Banza Kongo is no more than 600 kilometres. Was it really necessary to involve foreigners in the organization of such a trip?

My colleague Bjorg and I knew that it was our job to provide a kind of international guarantee to this initiative. Ideology and tribalism are still firmly embedded in the stormy history of modern Angola and the Bakongo, who are associated with isolationism and uncompromising pride and which included known anti-Marxist activists.

The 1885 Berlin Conference was an important milestone in colonialism, when the ancient kingdom was carved up into three parts: one (Angola) was granted to Portugal, a second (now the Democratic Republic of Congo Kinshasa) came under the rule of the cruel Belgian King Leopold II and the third (the Republic of Congo Brazzaville) went to the French. Even eventual independence, which was granted separately to each country, perpetuated the colonial division. The international community and the Organization of African Unity decided that the only way to avoid tribal warfare in Africa was by honouring the colonial boundaries, no matter how arbitrary these might be. But this was not sufficient to put an end to intertribal struggles and violent conflicts. Throughout its pre-independence years, Angola suffered under a Portuguese colonialist regime of suppression and terror, headed by the right-wing fascist dictator Antonio Salazar, whose secret police, PIDE, cruelly persecuted anyone suspected of being a freedom fighter. And then, when Angola finally gained its independence in 1975, Luanda came under a Marxist regime, overseen by the Soviet Union and the communist countries of Eastern Europe. The PIDE was replaced by the East German Stasi and, during the long years of Marxist government until the fall of the USSR, the country was governed by a regime that banned all signs of tribalism and religion. The historic Bakongo kingdom and the Catholic Church of M'Banza Kongo became enemies of the revolution. Those Bakongo who lived in northern Angola were known for their support of the FNLA, one of three liberation movements who fought against Portuguese colonialism. In the independent state, the FNLA movement failed to win control of the government. It laid down its arms and some of its representatives were subsequently elected to parliament in Luanda. Quite a few of the Bakongo supported the central government and were even appointed to senior government positions.

When the Soviet Union collapsed in 1998, Angola, too, left the path of Marxist-Leninist socialism. Democracy began to bud and flower and parliament was no longer subjected to one-party control. But the burden of such a history is not easily lifted.

As representatives of liberal states, one of our objectives was to encourage the democratic process in Angola. We were not surprised, therefore, by the interest and cooperation we encountered among the Bakongo; we were surprised, however, at the depth of fear and suspicion within the tribe's traditional leadership. We were quite embarrassed by the fact that the Crown Prince's plea for help was aimed at us and not someone else.

We started by calling on the authorities to obtain official permits. The responses were hesitant. Although no one actually forbade us to organize the pilgrimage, the main official objection was, typical of Angola, security-based. Part of the province was still under rebel control, minefields were rife and made it virtually impossible to drive safely, and no commercial airlines flew to M'Banza Kongo.

One evening a terrified man came to my residence. "He's dead. Our Crown Prince is no longer with us," the messenger said.

We were on the way to the prince's home within minutes. The Israeli security officer decided that it would be best to warn the city governor that we were on our way to a quarter that we had never visited before. The messenger drove ahead of us in a rickety old car. The governor joined us in his jeep, accompanied by a car full of black-clad policemen, members of the special 'ninja' unit. It appeared for a moment as if we were on our way to the battlefield. That is how it was in those days in Luanda: a city at war, hidden enemies at every turn.

The further we drove from the familiar city centre, the darker it got. There were no street lights here, not even on the private electricity generators. The road turned into a dirt track, which turned into a sandy path. Instead of houses, we noticed tin huts and the skeletons of small houses made of bare blocks. Our car was unable to continue and we got into the governor's jeep, but had to abandon it, too. We covered the last part on foot; a strange, silent procession.

"Is this where he lives?" asked the governor in disbelief. "Here, in this miserable place? The Crown Prince of the great Bakongo Tribe?"

By now our way was lit by small oil lamps in front of the tumbledown huts. We had arrived in a different world.

People huddled together and silently made way for us. We arrived at the skeleton of a building made of blocks; doors without thresholds and windows without frames. Instead of a floor there was carefully swept sand. A woman sat, bent over and dressed in faded strips of cloth, near the opening.

"That's the widow," our guide whispered. We sat down on the ground beside her. "He so wanted to return to his homeland," she said with a resignation that was devoid of anger.

"He will," I said, "I promise you, all of you, that he will." I didn't know what I was saying to this sad woman and all the others who were crowding around her.

Later, our heads bowed, we entered the building. Wrapped in a sheet of African cotton pano, the slim body of Crown Prince Monanga N'zinga had been placed on a plain wooden board. A strange, sweetish smell hung in the air.

"We must make haste to bury him," said one of the mourners. "We have no money to pay for a place in a hospital morgue."

The governor promised that a place would be found for the body, at least for a day or two. I promised to pay. When we left the house, it filled with silent, standing people. A woman started to keen and the rest of the crowd burst into loud weeping.

The governor said he was willing to help and that it would be possible to conduct some kind of official ceremony in the offices of this remote and Godforsaken neighbourhood. He had probably never even set foot in this part of the city that was under his authority.

"We must hurry and return the deceased's body to his birth place," said the assistant governor, "or the Bakongo will go berserk, when they discover the conditions under which their king lived and died ..."

Heavy-hearted, we returned to our homes. I knew that time was short and that I was unable to fulfill my promise.

In a way that was mysterious and inexplicable, I suddenly knew what I would have to do early the following morning. I called the office of the Angolan chief of staff and asked for an urgent meeting. The adjutant didn't ask too many questions. Two hours later I was in military GHQ.

Chief of Staff João Batista de Matos looked at me coolly. "What's the matter?" he asked. Our relationship was one of mother and son and there will be more about that later. I realized just how audacious my request was, but it was too late. I stuttered at first, fumbling to find the right words. Then they simply tumbled out, including an abridged history of the Bakongo tribe and their Crown Prince.

"The Crown Prince is asking to travel to his home town, M'Banza Kongo?" he asked.

"Not the Crown Prince, his body. He is already dead," I replied and told him all about the previous night.

General de Matos looked at me in silence. "You've got white skin and a black soul," he said. "No problem. I'll arrange for a military plane to fly the body out tomorrow morning. You've got to see to a coffin, death certificates and any other relevant papers. There'll only be twenty-three seats in the plane. You'll be responsible for seeing that only close relatives go on board. By the way, you're not a close relative and I suggest that you give up your place to someone more worthy. You have nothing to do there." He stood up and we parted.

General de Matos was not a member of the Bakongo tribe, but like any true African, he knew that the prince had to be buried in the land of his fathers.

In the morning, Bjorg and I arrived at the courtyard in front of the neighbourhood offices. It was teeming with humanity. Thousands of people had flowed in from all over the city to see their prince on his final journey home. The governor had even erected mourning tents. The body was placed in an elegant coffin, but the army personnel insisted that it did not conform to military regulations, which meant the body had to be flown in a metal coffin. The family refused to open the coffin and to remove the body from it. We stood in the sweltering heat for two hours and waited. A compromise was reached: the elegant coffin accompanied by the mourners, would be taken, as far as the military airfield, where the body would be transferred to an official military coffin.

At midday we heard the noise of the engines and watched as the Russian military Ilyushin aircraft took off and made its way eastward to M'Banza Kongo.

Crown Prince Monanga N'zinga had to die before he could receive the respect reserved for kings, a state funeral and a guard of honour by the soldiers of the Republic of Angola.

TG

CHAPTER TWO

In the shadow of war

1960–2002. Fifteen years of struggle against a harsh colonial regime, and twenty-seven years of civil war with the ruthless intervention of global powers. We will never know the exact numbers of the victims, human and animal, in those dark years.

It is estimated that out of a population of 8 million people, 1.5 million were killed. Three and a half million internally displaced people, many of them women, children and the elderly, were reduced to living in extreme poverty in crowded refugee camps, in Angola and outside the country; hundreds of thousands of children were orphaned and deserted; many thousands more crippled, among them many landmine victims.

Many wild animals were slaughtered, hunted, and driven out of their natural habitats. A large part of Angola's wildlife did not survive the war.

Man and nature must now struggle together. The hope for a better future depends on a joint victory of the two, and on their ability to coexist in peace.

Mines

It is called the 'quiet soldier', or the 'silenced soldier'. It lies there calmly, waiting. Rain falls, the intense heat causes the ground to split; it continues to lay in wait. In elegant halls, sparkling chandeliers light up festive treaty-signing ceremonies in various capital cities in the world. Former enemies shake hands and promise, 'never again'. But it is of no matter. Rumours of peace have not yet reached this far-off piece of land, and it continues to lurk securely, waiting, hidden by the thick undergrowth. 'It' was here yesterday; it will be here tomorrow, too. Until it does what it is required to do ... the landmine.

The landmine is an explosive device that can weigh anything between a few grams and several kilograms. It can be made of metal or plastic; it can be large and cumbersome or small and lightweight. It can be manufactured in China, Russia, the USA, Israel or dozens of other countries across the globe. It is simple and easy to produce, inexpensive, effective and lethal.

Landmines are cheap to produce. According to the organizations that have undertaken the war on landmines, the cost of a single unit can range from less than a dollar each to about $150. But each landmine can cost as much as $1,500 to dismantle.

It has therefore become the ideal poor man's weapon. Against the nuclear bomb, the elusive aircraft, the smart, laser-guided bombs and the ballistic missile, the inexpensive little landmine more than holds its own. Its operator doesn't need to be a sophisticated pilot, or a highly trained technician. He doesn't even need to know how to read and write. With the simple drawings provided on the packaging, operating the mine couldn't be easier.

Nor is it always necessary to take the trouble of planting the mine underground. In countries with damp tropical climates and plenty of rainfall, the mines need only to be scattered around fields surrounding remote villages. The rain and silt will finish the job and the village woman setting out to tend her small patch will not even notice the 'soldier' lurking, just waiting for her to step on it.

The landmine does not distinguish between men and women, or between civilians and military. Children are the most frequent victims. Unlike the smart bombs, which are supposed to attack only pre-determined objectives, landmines are unpretentious and the people who lay them have no claims to accuracy or sophisticated planning. They have no need even to admit they were wrong.

The landmine is a weapon totally devoid of ideology. It has been used by the United States and the Soviet Union, Communist China and Apartheid South Africa. Everyone uses landmines in their war against everyone else, sometimes over the same scrap of land and in the same country.

I am so angered by the landmine because it does not obey the changing demands of its operators. Generals come and generals go, new politicians replace old politicians, but, from the moment it is placed in the ground, the landmine continues to lie in wait—a free agent.

There was much talk during WWII about minefields, well-defined, demarcated areas carefully detailed and mapped. Today, wars in the third world use no maps, but there are plenty of fields. The fields of naïve farmers, village schoolyards and remote churches. And, of course, airports, railways, roads and bridges. No longer wars between organized armies, but the kind of wars where anything goes.

Landmines make news. The fashion for condemning this revolting form of weaponry has drawn partners from far and wide. As if other kinds of weapons are any less reproachable. A few years ago it was decided, at long last, to make landmines illegal. An international charter was signed at a ceremony in Ottawa. According to the charter, it is forbidden to sell, manufacture, export or use landmines. The charter calls for the disengagement of the millions of landmines all over the world. The charter exists, but the large manufacturers have yet to conform to it. According to experts, the countries most plagued by landmines are Cambodia, Afghanistan, Angola and Mozambique. It is said that Angola has the largest number of landmines per capita and the highest percentage of child casualties. It is generally agreed that no one knows exactly how many landmines are scattered across the world today.

71

Angola's landmines hit the headlines thanks to the late Princess Diana, who spent 48 hours in this wounded country. One photograph of her in the company of a boy who had lost both his legs to a landmine explosion did more to raise awareness of the dangers of landmines than thousands of photographs of legless or armless children on their own. The entire world read reports and watched endless TV footage. But this is nowhere near enough.

The years I spent in Angola were years in the shadow of the landmines. No other issue concerned me more. It was my focus and, even when my tenure was over, I stayed on in Angola to contribute whatever I could.

During the last couple of years, so I am told, 30,000 landmines were removed and blown up in Angola. About ten million more mines remain in the ground. There may be more, or there may be less.

The statistics remain scary. Attempts to fight the 'epidemic' are limited; achievements are few and there are all too many failures.

TG

Kuando-Kubango

A threatening cannon and a colourful locomotive. The large cannon with its gun carriage was in the centre of a round stage, about half a metre high, with its muzzle slanted at an angle of 45 degrees towards the horizon. Opposite the cannon there was a small black steam locomotive with red wheels, decorated with red and white stripes. It looked like a toy. It was coupled to an open wagon and stationed on a small model of a stone bridge. On a sign fixed next to it, the word PRAÇA and the number 5017/P were written in red.

"This is the warrior monument," said General João Baptista Tchindandi, the governor of Kuando-Kubango province, pointing to the cannon. His eyes were shining. "Savimbi has placed it here, in the memory of Unita's warriors."

"And this?" I asked, staring at the locomotive. What can such a toy be doing in the middle of Jamba, in the midst of the battle ... and minefields? During the war, this was the central base of Unita, in the southeast corner of Angola, a zone that was referred to during the Portuguese colonialism era as 'the end of the world'.

"This?" he smiled mysteriously. "This is a special monument that Savimbi has erected in memory of his father, who was the first African stationmaster of a railway station, on the famous Benguela line. This is the number of his station."

A pleasant morning sun had lightened the day. We were strolling among the wooden shacks of what used to be Unita's headquarters. Nowadays, a unit of the Angolan army is stationed here and the Angolan flag flies in the middle of the base. It is a mixed unit of soldiers from both of the former rival armies. Between the wooden shacks and the trees, in front of the warrior monument and the train monument, you get the feeling of a peaceful morning walk in the kibbutz.

"Stop," Johan's voice interrupted my thoughts. He was the director of the demining company. "Do not walk any further. The mined area starts here."

"There." General Tchindandi pointed, musing, at an isolated shack in the midst of the mined area. "That was Savimbi's house." Tchindandi himself had served as a high commander in Unita forces. Everybody knew him then as General Black Power.

The horror stories I had heard about Jonas Savimbi, the clever and cruel guerrilla leader who had caused so much suffering to so many people, for so long, were running through my head. I recalled also the stories about the terrible hardships that his warriors had experienced in this very camp. The stories were incongruous with the painted wooden shack in the shade of the trees next to the colourful locomotive. The serene scene reminded me more of the stories of a little house on the prairie than of the dwelling of the rebelling guerrilla leader.

We arrived in Jamba by helicopter, the only way to avoid the minefields, and landed on a football field at the edge of the base. We were here to visit Luiana Reserve which is home to the camp at Jamba. We wanted to survey the reserve for signs of wildlife and to study the results of the landmine survey that Johan van den Heever and his South African demining company, Demining Enterprises International, had completed here.

The survey, supported by UNDP, the Swiss government and an international organization, Conservation International, was undertaken in 2003, within the framework of a comprehensive project of the provincial government of Kuando-Kubango and the central government of Angola. The defined objective was to create a corridor for the passage of elephants and other wildlife into southeast Angola, from northern Botswana, through the narrow Caprivi Strip of Namibia, along the Kuando River on the Angolan border. This way, elephants and other large mammals could renew their ancient migration routes, currently interrupted by borders, landmines, poaching, and war. It is part of an ambitious plan to establish a transfrontier conservation area around the Zambezi River basin, through the joint management of Botswana, Namibia, Zambia, Zimbabwe and Angola. This will enhance biodiversity conservation and the development of eco-tourism.

Although the elephants in Angola nearly became extinct during the war, there are still a very large number of elephants in northern Botswana, where they cause significant damage to the vegetation and the habitat. Wildlife also fall victim to human wars and to artificial borders and fences. The renewal of migration corridors is important for the region and especially for the conservation of the elephant population of central and southern Africa.

The demining project was the vision of Dr John Hanks from South Africa, an expert on elephants and transfrontier conservation areas. During the height of the war he presented the idea to Fatima Jardim, the then Minister of Fisheries and Environment. The mere thought of turning the Unita base into a centre for a transfrontier conservation area and thriving tourism project seemed completely unrealistic, the wild dream of a foreign professor who did not understand the reality of life in Angola. But, from Fatima's thoughtful look, I knew that she liked the idea. She would find a way to turn it into reality, when the right time came.

On National Hero Day, in September, 2002, several months after the war had ended, I received an urgent call from the director at the minister's office: "Quickly pack a bag for several days. You must be at the airport in Luanda in two hours. You will fly with the minister today to Kuando-Kubango province, to participate in an inauguration ceremony at a new border post and bridge with Namibia, over the Kubango [Kavango, Okavango] River."

After the formal ceremony we drove to Rundu, a small border town in Namibia, on the southern bank of the Okavango River. During the war, Rundu had served as a centre for covert meetings between army commanders of both warring sides, mysterious representatives of foreign countries that had supported this side or the other, mercenaries, and arms and diamond dealers. Rundu was used, more than once, as a base for organizing and equipping forces carrying out military attacks in Angola.

Nowadays it is a small, peaceful tourism and trading town. Along the main road, you can find a variety of shops selling everything, even cutting-edge electronic technology, fancy cloths and jewellery, as well as busy grocery stores. The shops are bustling and people come and go, pushing full shopping trolleys to their waiting cars. It looked very prosperous to me on that first visit, arriving from the 'end of the world' on the corner of Angola. Several years later I visited there again, arriving from Windhoek, the Namibian capital.

Somehow, it looked much less glamorous then.

On a journey that only takes five minutes by ferry, we go from Rundu in Namibia, the world of plenty, to Calai in Angola, on the other side of the river, a world of desolation, destruction and extreme poverty. During the war most of Calai's residents lived as refugees on the other side of the border, over the river, in Namibia. Even today, the lucky ones among them continue to make their living in Namibia, but most of the village residents are unemployed and struggle for survival. It is almost impossible to cultivate crops, due to the fear of landmines. At the time of our visit, the only way to get from Calai to Menongue, the province's capital, was through Namibia. Even the community's administrators and officials, nominated by the central government, lived in Rundu, and used the ferry every day to perform their duties in Calai.

The women of the OMA, the women's organization of the governing MPLA (Movimento Popular da Libertação de Angola), received the minister as she was disembarking from the ferry accompanied by the governor of the province at that time. Dancing and singing they approached the river bank, dressed in their colourful costumes of yellow headscarves, red T-shirts bearing the organization's logo, and dark pano skirts. As they were singing, an armed police unit, wearing blue uniforms, emerged from the opposite hill, performing a powerful war dance. The two troupes were competing for attention, enchanting feminine grace on the one hand; impressive masculine might on the other. The minister, the governor and the visitors joined in the dancing.

A serious debate began after the reception ceremony. The villagers presented a detailed account of the hardships they had suffered: extreme poverty, unemployment, a shortage of essential commodities and services, and the ever-present landmines. The minister listened thoughtfully throughout. Eventually she pointed at me and declared: "I brought with me a representative of the UN—she will help you."

"I cannot promise anything …" I murmured, but it was clear that the promise made on my behalf was stronger than my reservations. I presented to the governor and the minister the proposed programme for integrating the local communities for the establishment of a transfrontier conservation area.

Just five minutes away, across the border, tourism brought prosperity to the communities. Wouldn't it make sense to build a lodge or a restaurant on this side of the river as well?

One thing was certain: the area had to be demined first. Even the most adventurous of tourists, looking for a 'real experience', would not wish to travel through minefields.

Fatima Jardim requested that I promote the programme directly within the province. João Pessela, the Angolan consul in Rundu, offered to help. Things began to move. The project was approved by the relevant entities in the government and the province. A South African company was selected by open tender to conduct the preliminary landmine survey in Luiana Reserve. Everything was ready to begin.

But then the governor was replaced. Following the peace agreements, a new governor was nominated for Kuando-Kubango province. He was a former high commander in Unita's armed forces, General Black Power.

I requested an audience with the new governor and I was worried. Politicians tend not to continue with programmes initiated by their predecessors, especially if they come from an opposition party. His military nickname also sounded threatening. I did not rate my chances of an audience highly. It is usually difficult to get an audience with senior government officials in Angola and, when you do get a meeting, it comes after many previous cancellations and after waiting around for hours and hours in waiting rooms in the company of other disappointed people.

I was therefore very surprised when I received an invitation the next day to a meeting with General João Tchindandi, the new governor of Kuando-Kubango and former Unita commander, in the hotel which he stayed during his visit to Luanda. Moreover, several minutes after my punctual arrival at the hotel, I was received by a tall man with an impressive appearance, an elegant walk, and, of all things, wearing slippers. With a big smile he invited me to sit down and I explained the proposed programme to him. He listened with great interest and then asked for more details. From his questions it was clear that he knew the area very well. He told me about the large wildlife herds that used to roam in southeast Angola, years ago. He described the impressive elephant herds that were an integral part of his childhood. He was born and raised in the province.

"There are no elephant herds there now. No wildlife. Nothing. Only desolation and landmines," he said. But then he smiled and said: "They will be back. I know. The elephants and all the other wildlife will return to Kuando-Kubango. And with their return will come hope for the residents of the province. We must start immediately with implementing the plan. I will help in any way possible. You can count on me. First we must arrange a meeting in Menongue, the capital of the province, and go together to see the area, as soon as possible."

He was a general, a military man, and his attitude was practical and straightforward. Nevertheless, it was impossible not to feel the genuine love and concern he felt for the province of his childhood, and for its long-suffering inhabitants. The plan was in the right hands.

I followed the governor's actions in the media, as he moved, step by step, to improve the quality of life in his province. He cared especially for the remote communities and for the destitute refugees from other provinces and neighbouring countries, returning to the province after the war. Months later, I told him how impressed I had been by our first meeting and by his genuine concern for the inhabitants of the province.

He smiled: "Once we knew how to keep our tradition of mutual care in Angola. When the mother cooked the porridge," he demonstrated the action of stirring, "she used to work for hours, and then divided it all among the children. After all the children had theirs, there would be a little porridge left in the bottom of the pot. Only these leftovers she took for herself," he said, indicating the little bit between thumb and forefinger.

"I know that nowadays there are also other habits," he added after a short pause and sighed, "but I believe in our old traditions."

About a month after my first meeting with the governor, we visited Menongue, the capital of Kuando-Kubango province. We went there with John Hanks, Johan, and representatives of the central government. We discussed the details of the planned landmine survey in Luiana Reserve. General Tchindandi listened carefully and asked concise questions. Eventually, he gave details of the support that he and the provincial government officials, army and police officers, would provide for the operation.

"I am pleased that a South African company will help us with the mine clearing," he concluded the discussion. "After all, it was our friends from South Africa who helped us plant the landmines in the first place. It is only right that they will now help us to restore and rehabilitate our country."

That evening the governor invited us to a ceremonial dinner at his palace. The provincial palace usually serves to host the most distinguished guests from Luanda, ministers, senior government officials, ambassadors, and the like, on their visits to the province. Every day, when the governor returns home from the office, late in the evening, he first passes through the palace. It is there that those people who wish to have an unofficial audience with him gather daily. They usually come to seek help of some kind or another. Like a traditional African king, he receives them all, from the most senior army officers and government officials to the poorest from the most remote communities. Each one of them leaves with 'something' and a big smile.

Only after the last visitor had left, satisfied, was the table set and the dinner began. Tchindandi asked Johan about his demining work, how the surveys were carried out and how the landmines were removed. He chatted to John about the life and habits of elephants. The governor became engrossed with fascinating stories about the large elephant herds that used to roam the province years ago and about the other wildlife that were part of his childhood. The hours passed, and the atmosphere was pleasant.

It was late at night when Tchindandi asked: "What is the life span of an elephant?"

"Sixty years. No more," said John.

"No," the General countered with great confidence. "Elephants can live at least for a hundred years. Maybe more. I know."

"That's impossible," John was just as emphatic. "Their teeth get worn out and replaced every ten years, and their sixth and last set of teeth is worn out when they are sixty. Then they die of hunger. This information has been confirmed by scientific research." The elephant expert was certain, but so was the governor: "I believe that you are right, scientifically," he said with a smile, "and yet, I know that an elephant can live at least for a hundred years."

The next day we went for a short aerial reconnaissance over Luiana Reserve. Between the Kubango River, in the south, and the Kwando River, to the east, there is a large area of Miombo Woodland, which seemed almost completely devoid of wildlife. We managed to see only one alarmed duiker disappearing into the bush. Across the border, in Namibia's Caprivi Strip, we could see large herds on the move, elephants, buffalo, giraffes, and various antelope species. Most of the large wildlife in Luiana had been hunted out long ago, and the remaining few lived in constant fear of man.

Several months after his nomination, the governor established a small anti-poaching unit in Luiana Reserve, using demobilized soldiers from both armies, and a year later, in an aerial survey above the reserve, elephants, buffalo, various antelopes and even leopards were recorded. More wildlife has been reported from the area since. These observations have increased hopes for the future rehabilitation of the wildlife in southeast Angola.

After the survey, Johan and John went back to South Africa, and I returned to Menongue. The governor insisted that I stay at the provincial palace. In the evening, after dinner, once the last visitor had left, we spread out the maps and discussed in detail the results of the aerial reconnaissance and the landmine survey plan.

"Do you remember the conversation we had here the other night about the longevity of elephants?" Tchindandi asked suddenly.

"Yes, of course. Why did you insist that elephants can live at least for a hundred years or more, despite the explanations of the expert?"

"I told you that I was born here in the province," he responded. "But I did not tell you that my grandfather was a big king in this area. Several communities of Bushmen lived in the margins of his kingdom. They were the best hunters, and no one knew the habits of wildlife better than they. In my childhood, I befriended a very old Bushman. He taught me how to hunt with a bow and arrow and taught me about the wildlife. My friend and mentor told me about an old elephant bull that he knew. The first time he met this elephant was when he was a young child, and the elephant by then was already the oldest in the region. The old bull used to roam on his own, and he used to follow him. He respected the old bull, and followed him only to learn about his way of life. The elephant accepted his proximity and never tried to harm him. And so they became friends, the elephant and the child. When I met my Bushman teacher, he was a very old man. His elephant friend was still alive. He told me that this was the proof that elephants can live at least for a hundred years, or more. The expert may well be right, scientifically. But what I have learned from my old friend, who lived with nature and knew every stone, grass and insect, is irreplaceable. After all, the knowledge of the Bushmen has been accumulated over many generations of living in the bush, and science ..." He paused and then said, "Science is so young."

During the civil war, the Bushmen from southeast Angola were recruited as trackers, the infamous units of the South African army under the Apartheid regime, which supported the guerrilla forces of Unita. When the apartheid regime ended, the Angolan government was not keen to let them return home. They were forced to remain as refugees in Namibia and South Africa. Their traditional way of life was lost, and it was a short descent to poverty, unemployment and alcoholism. Against their will, and against their own good, they were caught in a war that was not theirs, and they became its victims.

"I want to right this wrong. I owe this to the Bushmen, my childhood friends," Tchindandi added after a few minutes of contemplative silence. "After the demining of Luiana Reserve, and when the elephants and the other wildlife have returned, our province will become the capital of tourism in Angola. Then I will also be able to offer livelihood opportunities for the Bushmen communities to return to. We will be able to offer them decent employment as wildlife rangers and tourist guides. No one could do this better than they."

The conversation went on as the hours passed unnoticed. When Tchindandi the child was old enough to go to school, he was sent to a mission and was taught by a priest, a padre. When he grew up he returned to the province, got married and had two children. He and his wife worked in the province as teachers.

When the war of independence in Angola started he knew that he must join the freedom fighters. As a member of a royal family from Kuando-Kubango he joined, naturally, Unita. A bullet wound in his leg, inflicted in an attack by MPLA soldiers in Menongue, only spurred him on to fight and he soon became a senior officer in Unita's army at headquarters, in Jamba. His wife Angela and his young children had to escape from the war zone, and sought refuge in her province. The communication between them was lost. Only following the first peace agreement, after sixteen years with no contact whatsoever, did he manage to find her. The children were by now already grown up. They found it difficult to believe that this person, of whom they had heard so much, this Unita general, was a real man of flesh and blood and their father.

The couple was finally able to live together again, and they had two more children. However, the peace was short-lived and the war began again, even more fiercely than before. This time Tchindandi and Angela decided not to separate. Despite the tough conditions, she and the children stayed with him in Jamba. I got to know her later. She is an exceptional character among the wives of Angola's rulers. She dresses simply and avoids official events. She lives in modesty in the province and continues to work as a teacher, a profession which she regards as her vocation.

Tchindandi avoided talk about his experiences during the war, but I had heard that he had a reputation as an admired, intelligent and courageous commander. When the civil war erupted he went on a long journey, crossing the vastness of Angola on foot, from west to southeast, over several months, in charge of accompanying a group of foreign citizens. They were captives of the rebel movement and he had led them safely to Jamba, Unita's headquarters in Kuando-Kubango, in the heat of the battles, while constantly avoiding the government forces. All of the captives survived, except for one who died of malaria, and they were later returned to their home with a senior minister on a government aircraft loaded with equipment demanded by the rebel leader. This was the only information I had about his military service, but I knew that he did not gain the nickname Black Power without reason.

After the peace agreements, as a former senior officer in Unita's forces,

Tchindandi was offered various attractive positions in the Angolan army, in the parliament or in the government. He insisted that the only position he was interested in was governor of the province of his origin, so that he could do his best to rehabilitate it and improve the quality of life for its citizens who had been subjected to the horrors of war for so long.

○○○

The landmine survey, to locate and mark the minefields in Luiana Reserve, was started soon after our meeting in Menongue. On the governor's instructions the survey team received full cooperation and support everywhere it went. The Angolan consulate in Rundu helped with all the necessary permits and authorizations, and with the logistics. Johan and his team travelled from village to village, visited all the army and police units, and interviewed anyone who could provide information. They recorded, mapped, marked and identified all known and suspected minefields in the survey region. During the process they found quite a few signs of the destruction and death that the mines had caused. Rusting remnants of vehicles, tanks and helicopters, were strewn over the land. Evidence on elephant skeletons suggested that animals were also victims of landmines; however, such reported incidents were scarce.

To their surprise, the demining team met very few mutilated mine victims, a common sight throughout Angola. Why here, in the minefields, were there so few victims?

The villagers had a simple explanation. Mostly people who are wounded here die before they can access adequate medical treatment. The journey to the province capital is not only long, but also strewn with mines. Anyone that is seriously wounded usually dies. Those who survive sometimes manage to get medical help in Zambia or Namibia, where they usually stay on as refugees.

After the landmine survey was completed and the report distributed and uploaded onto the Angolan government database, we revisited Luiana Reserve. We did an aerial reconnaissance over the reserve by helicopter, to learn about the survey's results, to look for signs of wildlife and to plan the way forward with the provincial government. We landed at Jamba and found ourselves in the headquarters' wooden shack, for a meeting with the senior commanders. We were invited to sit on large sofas. Someone turned on the TV in the middle of the room. The commanders discussed the landmines surrounding the camp and the region, while a children's programme on a Portuguese channel flickered in the background. The scene was somewhat surreal. A representative of the residents of Luiana community joined in the conversation.

"The landmines are less important," he said. "First we must deal with the acute poverty and the shortage of basic commodities."

The implementation of the programme for the rehabilitation of Luiana Reserve, here at the end of the world, suddenly seemed very far away. Maybe merely a wild dream.

"You must not lose hope," General Tchindandi told me when the plan seemed further away than ever. "The dream will come true. The large elephant herds will return to roam in Kuando-Kubango, along with other wildlife. The cannon and the locomotive of Jamba will turn into tourism sites. The inhabitants of the province will improve their quality of life, and even the Bushmen will return. This is how it has to be. You must only continue to believe."

I believe.

TR

Displaced

I arrived one day at a wretched camp for internally displaced persons on the outskirts of the central Angolan city of Huambo. A white man emerged from out of a large tent, unshaven, his hair unkempt, his dark eye sockets betraying a lack of sleep. His clothes were rumpled and he gave off a strong smell of ether. I didn't recognize him at first. Only when I came closer did I identify Dr Jean Claude. That is what everyone called him; I never knew his surname. He was one of the veteran members of the French organization Médecins sans Frontières—Doctors without Borders. We shook hands and kissed on both cheeks, French-fashion.

"When did we last meet?" I asked

"Where did we last meet?" Dr Jean Claude asked in reply.

We remembered that it had been fifteen years before, in a refugee camp near the point where the borders of Chad, Sudan and Libya converged. I was there as a journalist.

"You see," he said, "I'm in another country now, but I'm always in Africa and everywhere I go, every time the work is always the same work."

"Aren't you tired?"

"Tired?" he smiled. "Of course I'm tired. And desperate. As soon as things calm down a little in one spot—war breaks out elsewhere. There is no end to it. But there is no choice, if we're not here, these women and children will die." After a few moments of silence he asked me, "But you, what are you doing here? Aren't you tired of seeing these camps? In one camp the kid's name will be Muhammad; in the second, Ivan; in the third, the boy will be called Pietro. The names are different—the kids remain the same kids and the death is the same death. I'm a doctor, so this is my place. But you? You don't need this travelling circus to know what's going on here."

We took our leave of each other. Like our previous meeting, this, too, was brief.

I know nothing about the man; whether he was married, had a family, where he grew up, where he'd studied, what had brought him to his current situation. Dr Jean Claude reminded me of Dr Rieux, the hero in Albert Camus' book The Plague. Camus wrote about Algeria and his doctor, like Jean Claude here in Angola, was motivated by a heightened sense of responsibility, even though he was utterly disillusioned. The doctor in the book and the doctor in the field aroused in me a profound sense of respect.

On any trip to Angola a visit to an IDP (Internally Displaced Persons) camp is considered obligatory.

The displaced, in the professional jargon of international aid and welfare organizations, are known as IDPs, a cold, somewhat synthetic, term, aimed at distinguishing between them and refugees. Refugees, according to the official definition, are people who have been exiled across the border from their homeland; IDPs are people who are displaced from their homes and became exiled within their homeland.

Today, millions of IDPs and refugees live under appalling conditions in temporary camps that become their permanent homes. Their houses are canvas tents, clay-lined holes in the ground or plastic domes, all exposed to the elements in unbearable heat or bone-freezing cold, pouring rain or scorching sun. No running water, no sewerage, no electric lights, no privacy. There are a lot of women, children and old people in these camps, and very few men.

Of all the continents, the number of refugees and IDPs is greatest in Africa. During the 1990s, Angola held the African record with more than a million refugees and three million IDPs out of a population of twelve million.

Visiting presidents and their entourage- khaki-dressed, high-booted reporters and photographers and, especially, representatives of the various UN agencies and humanitarian organizations- all disembark from the white UN aircraft, climb into a United Nations SUV (also painted white) and whip up a cloud of dust as they drive off quickly into the hinterland. They go to the 'field,' take a turn, stop off beside a tent or two, have a peek inside, into the emptiness and human misery. They try to coax someone into saying a word or two, to show some sort of emotion. The cameras snap away, recording their horror, their shock, clicking their tongues, declaring that the situation is so awful, that they will do absolutely e-v-e-r-y-thing in their power … and then they have themselves photographed with a hand laid with exquisite pity on the head of an emaciated, pot-bellied African child. The world sees, hears and reads all about the tragedy, and gets on with its life. It is the same in Kosovo, in Afghanistan, in Iraq and always, always in Africa.

At first, the IDPs would run after the VIPs, hands held out, trying to describe the bitterness of their lives, expecting a handout. Later, most of them became indifferent. They have simply succumbed to despair. Only the children continue to run after the foreign visitors. They have nothing better to do. The soldiers and guards beat them off, often with a stick, as if they weren't part of their own nation. They do it under orders from their superiors, those overfed government officials, with their sweating, self-satisfied faces, who leave their air-conditioned offices only to take their guests to look at all this squalour—and to impress them to open their dollar-lined pockets.

As an ambassador, representing another sovereign state, I was sure that only after seeing things with my own eyes, would I be able to recommend to my government which of Angola's problems most required our urgent assistance. As a Jew and as an Israeli, I felt my solidarity might be even greater. Yet in time, as my visits to the IDP camps became more frequent, a profound discomfort started to weigh me down. What was I doing here? How had I become part of the 'humanitarian travelling circus'? Was it really necessary to visit dozens of IDP camps in order to know that the thousands living there were destitute, sick and hungry? Was I unaware of the fact that, so long as war continued to rage, the leaders continued to disregard the suffering of their people? The gunrunners and diamond smugglers were eating up everything. The UN was as ineffectual as always and the superpowers continued to look out for their own interests. It was easy enough to recognize that, under such circumstances, the number of IDPs and refugees would only rise.

On my return to Luanda after meeting Dr Jean Claude, I decided to go back to the IDP camp only when I had something concrete to offer. But I had no idea how hard it would be for me to stick to this decision. And, indeed, several months passed before I was to pay a return visit to the IDPs. The first hurdle, which was relatively slight, involved persuading the Israeli Foreign Office to offer real aid to the IDPs. As with most of the countries in the world, to the Israeli Foreign Office, Africa is at the bottom of its list of priorities. "No money," was the answer. Short and simple. The Israeli Foreign Office had no budget for aid to Third World countries. There was, however, a limited budget for professional instruction and training and for sending Israeli experts to developing states. In Jerusalem, the Africa Department is not held in great esteem, nor is a diplomatic appointment to an African state. All African countries have been categorized as difficult and anyone appointed to serve in one of them is promised a future posting to a 'normal' country, such as in Europe or the USA.

Nonetheless, many of those who were sent, almost in spite of themselves, to Africa, develop a powerful affinity to the continent. They forged something of a secret sect, touched with a mysterious love for the beleaguered continent and willing to continue working on its behalf even when their mission has been completed and they are back home. These people are the ones that can be relied upon to extend aid to African countries, refuting claims that Israel gleans no political or economic benefit from such aid. I was surprised to discover that the people in administration and finance, who were stern on the outside, were also generous. Thus, thanks to them, occasional, ex-gratia, sums of money were allocated for the purchase of equipment and medication for the victims of the Angolan tragedy.

But, in comparison with the millions of dollars donated by other countries, these sums were ridiculously low. It was important, therefore, for Israel's aid to be swift and effective, by reaching the hands of those who really needed it. And it was here that matters became complicated. Criticism of Africa tends to focus on the corruption that is rampant among the African states. I would prefer to discuss corruption among individual people. Although these can be found in every country on earth, when you encounter them in places that are as hunger-struck as Angola, the shock is especially great.

During my tenure in Luanda, I encountered a government minister who was one of these corrupt individuals. A tall man with gold-rimmed spectacles, he speaks several languages and is especially fluent in English, a rare thing in Angola.

He looks like a college professor who has stumbled into politics by accident; he used to be a favourite with representatives of the countries that provide aid to Africa. Within the diplomatic community rumours were rife that funds had been transferred to his office and never reached their designated destination. But until I actually witnessed what happened to a colleague of mine, the ambassador of one of the Arab states, I paid little attention to what appeared to me to be no more than malicious gossip.

My colleague arrived one morning in a highly agitated state at my office in the Israeli embassy and asked me to close the door. I had always enjoyed his pleasant nature and easygoing manner. Today he was different, as was the story he told.

"For several months," he said, "I have been arguing with my foreign office, until they finally agreed to send out a ship with three-ton containers of used clothing, and wheat and oil for the displaced people in Angolan camps. To me, this was a great achievement, coming at the end of my tenure here. We both know how our Foreign Offices provide us with daily reminders that the security and economic situation obliges us to devote all our efforts to our region.

"The ship docked a month ago in the port of Luanda. I informed the relevant Angolan authorities. The lady in the minister's office thanked me warmly and said that they would start immediately to arrange the tax forms, check the minister's schedule and then invite me and the local media to a ceremony at the port. I tried to tell her that I would like to hand over the donation at a ceremony at the actual IDP camp and not at the port. I asked if I would be able to choose the place where it would be possible to see the stuff being distributed among those poor souls. I wanted to go to the Bie province, where we have doctors volunteering at the camps. The lady told me not to worry. One ceremony would take place at the port and a second at one of the camps. And, indeed, one week later, I was invited to the port, where I found the minister and representatives of the local media. A crane unloaded the craters from the ship, but they remained unopened. The minister and I delivered brief speeches. As usual, that evening we were granted a three-minute news item on the state television channel.

"With a handshake and a pat on the back, the minister promised me that we would meet again soon in the Bie province and that he would arrange for me to be flown there in a military aircraft. I have been waiting ever since. Yesterday, I sent one of my embassy's Angolan workers to Roque Santeiro, the big marketplace on the outskirts of town. You can buy anything in that market and we're all afraid to go there. We needed some spare parts for one of our cars. The worker returned with the spare parts and with a few other items: used clothing made in my country, two sacks of flour, stamped with the legend that they were a gift from my country and three containers of oil, also our produce."

My friend and I sat in silence for a few moments. It was obvious that it was too late by now and there would be no ceremony at the IDP camp in Bie province and the camp's inhabitants, who desperately needed it, would receive none of that aid shipment. We agreed that it would be better if the ambassador did not report any of this to his Foreign Office; he had already told them about the ceremony at the port. They needn't know any more. The question we had to deal with was, should this nasty business be exposed and, if so, how?

The story was brought to the attention of the other ambassadors. Some of them advised their governments to cut back their humanitarian aid to Angola; and this is what happened. Others, like myself, believed that it was unthinkable for people to be made to suffer because of a crooked leadership and that other solutions had to be sought.

When Israel decided to send a half ton shipment of medicines to a region in Angola that had been devastated by war and also suffered from severe floods, I was determined to ensure that the goods reached their rightful destination. First of all I decided personally to obtain all the necessary waivers from the tax authorities, rather than to rely on the minister's office. It wasn't easy, but within a few days we were able to release the shipment from the airport customs office. Our diplomatic car made several sorties to the airport, after which the shipment of medicines filled all the rooms in our embassy and was well protected.

Only then did we contact the minister and inform him of the donation. His office proposed one ceremony at the airport, to be followed by a second ceremony at one of the IDP camps—of the minister's choice and according to the 'country's needs'. I thanked them and informed them that we wished to make things easier for them and that the shipment was already at the embassy. There was silence, followed by a brief consultation, after which we were told that the minister would be happy to participate in a ceremony the following week in the town Caxito, where a war-torn hospital was being restored.

We contacted UNICEF, the UN children's fund, and suggested transferring the medicines shipment together from Luanda to Caxito, so that their people could oversee the immediate distribution of medicines to the various departments. In the morning, we set out in a long convoy from the capital city. At the head of the convoy were the white SUVs belonging to UNICEF; the rearguard was taken by our embassy car, flying the Israeli flag.

At Caxito we discovered two bombed-out hospitals. One of them had been taken over by a private company and was being restored with the help of a large European concern that had been granted some fat contracts from the minister. The other, government hospital, which specialized in treating malaria patients, looked awful. Its walls were crumbling and its plaster peeling; it had bare, rusty metal beds, a feeble electricity generator and an empty, unequipped operating theatre.

The media and the minister's entourage were already waiting for the ceremony to begin near the rebuilt hospital, which showed obvious signs of advanced restoration. We saw clean wards, tidy beds and white-uniformed nurses. Our convoy drove past this hospital and continued toward the government hospital, where no preparations had been made for a ceremony of any kind and our arrival was received with great emotion. We started unloading the medicines. A few minutes later, someone from the Ceremonies Department rode up on a motorcycle to explain that we were at the wrong address.

In the end, the minister was obliged to take part in two ceremonies; one prepared in advance and the other improvised. That evening the state TV channel showed him speaking at both. The devoted UNICEF staff handed out anti-malaria pills to the patients at the government hospital and celebrated a tiny, candle-lit victory in a war that had no end.

TG

Death of an envoy

Alioune Blondin Beye died in the service of peace for Angola.

During the first years of my tenure at the Israeli Embassy in Angola, Beye headed the United Nations' military and civilian mission in the country. He was an old friend, whom I had met several years previously when he served as foreign minister in the government of Mali. When we met again, we fell into each other's arms like old friends. Dressed in the famous boubou, the richly embroidered robe worn by West African Muslims, Beye looked as if he had just stepped out of an etching by one of the 19th century's first travellers to the continent.

Since its foundation as an independent state, there has been a UN peacekeeping presence in Angola. Like everywhere else in the world, the presence of peace forces means that the region is in a state of war. In Angola, like elsewhere in the world, this presence is controversial. The blue berets arrive only after much blood—especially the blood of innocent women, children and old people—has been shed. Yet, when they arrive in a war-torn region, the UN forces usually lack the mandate to intervene.

The African countries—notably Congo, Angola, Mozambique, Rwanda and Sierra Leone—have all been honoured, if that is the word, with a record number of UN forces. During the 1990s, more than eight thousand UN troops from Zimbabwe, Bangladesh, India, Uruguay, Brazil and Jordan were stationed in Angola. France, Britain and Senegal supplied the supreme command to what was then the largest UN mission in the world. The cost of maintaining thousands of soldiers, and the cumbersome administrative system that accompanied them, came to about a million dollars a day.

No organization in the world is more bureaucratic than the UN. Everything happens at once and in a mish-mash of languages. The decision-making process is nerve-wrackingly slow. The UN headquarters in New York only encumbers the work in the field; everything is complicated, including the eternal need for consensus, the necessity to keep the permanent members of the Security Council satisfied, coping with their constant power struggles, manoeuvring among the complex ego games of the senior staff and to trying to coordinate the military traditions of each of the contributing delegations. Dealing with the system itself was always time consuming; valuable time that should have been devoted to the mission for which thousands of UN personnel had come to Angola in the first place—peacemaking—was wasted.

Nonetheless, what would we have done without those soldiers, called up from all corners of the world to serve in an unknown country, under foreign command and alongside fellow soldiers they don't know and whose language they don't speak? How many lives were saved due to their presence there? The UN presence in Angola was always a subject of debate and which continues to this day.

Alioune Blondin Beye had a special way of looking at his position with the UN. He believed that in a place where Africans were fighting each other, there must surely be a way to make peace among them, in an African way. His inspiration, as he told me on many occasions, came from the late president of the Ivory Coast, Félix Houphouët-Boigny. We both knew what he meant, since our first meeting had been in Abidjan, the Ivorian capital.

We both referred to Houphouët-Boigny as Father, or as the Grand Old Man of Africa.

Thus he was known by the young leaders of the French-speaking countries in western Africa, who habitually made pilgrimages to his palace in Abidjan and especially to his home village in Yamoussoukro. Anyone fortunate enough to receive an invitation to Yamoussoukro could expect to spend several hours in the company of the Old Man, not far from a lake in which sacred crocodiles swim calmly. Alioune Beye also sat there, usually choosing a slightly distant corner, listening and saying little.

There, in the relaxed atmosphere of his home village, Houphouët-Boigny was in his element. We listened to his stories, which almost always began with "That reminds me..." Each story took the form of a fable and we were expected to understand the moral. No instructions were issued, no orders were handed out and everyone was expected to decipher the meaning behind the fable. But if truth be told, it was hard at times to agree with him. Houphouët-Boigny had conservative opinions and, the older he got, the more attached he became to the past. He began to cloister himself in the reality of his tribe, the Baouléi and refused to adapt to the changing world. Nevertheless, there was something special in the fatherly way with which he gave us of his time and tried to share with us some of the wealth of his experiences, which made us love him even if we thought he was wrong.

Houphouët-Boigny had already died at a great old age by the time I met Alioune Beye in Angola, but we continued to call each other brother and sister. We saw ourselves as members of the kind of family that is gradually disappearing from the world. There was something extremely old-fashioned, outdated and ineffectual in the way this family was managed: the long conversations, the constant desire to do everything by mutual agreement, the exaggerated need to hide disagreements or even ignore them, the need to keep everything within the family confines. This, clearly, was not an ideal model for modern government. But the dated, conservative style imparted a sense of security and belonging. We used to quote each other one of the Father's better-known catchphrases: "Walk slowly, children, because we are in a hurry."

Few among us were blessed with the patience required by this wise saying and really did try to live by it. Alioune Blondin Beye was of those few. He wanted to manage the UN in Angola in the Houphouëtic way, the way of Houphouët-Boigny.

Another African former UN Secretary-General, Kofi Annan, had personally appointed Beye, an appointment that enjoyed widespread support among his fellow Africans. He did not disappoint them. Nonetheless, the representatives of the modern world were quite simply angered by the nomination. Beye's stubborn attempts at achieving compromises, his endless patience at meetings with the government of Eduardo dos Santos on the one hand and the rebel Jonas Savimbi on the other, his archaic speeches in old-fashioned French, his willingness to spend days and nights negotiating every tiny detail of the demands put forward by the hostile sides. To the Africans, this appeared quite normal; but the Americans and Russians often found it hard to digest.

Each side accused him of preferring the other. To Alioune Blondin Beye, that was the proof of his impartiality and objectivity and he continued to travel back and forth between the capital Luanda and the township of Bailundo, the bush headquarters of rebel leader Jonas Savimbi. Wherever he went, Beye made a point of personally shaking the hand of everyone present, smiling broadly at his counterparts, taking an interest in the health of the giant bodyguards.

This short man in a long flapping robe, shining ebony skin, a permanent smile on his face and an unfaltering faith in mankind, was happy with every sign of progress, however small. He was an eternal optimist, always believing in the best.

Strangely, though, Alioune Blondin Beye managed to infect the ambassadors of the USA and Russia with his optimism. Thus we were able to witness a rare sight: cooperation under UN auspices, between the world's two superpowers, who, throughout the Cold War years, had been fanning the flames of war in Angola.

The mutual suspicion between the two powers remained intact even after the fall of the Soviet bloc, but here in Luanda the unbelievable happened. Under the baton of a former cabinet minister from a remote African country, the two recent enemies started to work together to solve a crisis for which they themselves were largely responsible. In Moscow and Washington, the opinion was often that their ambassadors had lost their minds, perhaps because of the harsh conditions under which they were living. At times, they were recalled to their capitals for consultation, but they continued in their efforts to achieve peace.

The fighting abated a little, the government forces achieved a few victories, but the war was not over yet. Too many economic and strategic interests were involved. The rebel leader was smuggling precious stones to Western markets hungry for luxuries. These were blood diamonds. Meanwhile, Angola's central government funded its war with income from oil exports—black gold.

From the UN podium, distinguished representatives of world governments spoke in high tones about the need for peace, while each held on to its own interests. This, after all, is the real story behind most of Africa's wars today. The need for direct support from foreign governments is gradually fading. Instead, the wars are now funded by abstract elements—dubious businessmen, the unscrupulous emissaries of financial conglomerates, who work above and without laws. With their mercenary methods, they brought about the death of millions of innocent Africans. After several years of tireless work, Alioune Beye realized that even he, with his endless patience, could not overcome Savimbi's stubbornness. But he underestimated the dark powers that stood at the rebel leader's disposal.

Beye decided to embark on one more journey, a final effort to persuade Savimbi's supporters in Africa to cease their destructive activity. He was aware of his inability to fight what he coined 'the forces of darkness'. They were too strong. But he knew that the support of some African leaders for Savimbi was based mainly on the diamonds he poured into their pockets, and it was these leaders he now hoped to convince. He knew, of course, that even greater forces stood behind these leaders. But he was naïve and determined enough to try to persuade the Africans in the African way, the way he had learned from the Old Man. His objectives would involve Togo's President Gnassimbe Eyadema, and the Ivory Coast, the country of Houphouët-Boigny, which, in the past, had been one of Savimbi's most passionate supporters.

One evening, he took off, almost in secret, from Luanda in a small white jet, with the blue UN emblem painted on its side. We, his friends, believed this to be a futile mission. Savimbi was not about to relent, we told him. And his supporters—those who wanted the blood diamonds —were already corrupt to the core. He didn't listen. He wouldn't listen.

The plane landed in Lomé, capital of the Togolese republic, where he met with the dictator, President Eyadema. Shortly afterwards he took off for Abidjan, but he never arrived. The plane exploded and crashed into a lagoon a short distance from the airport. No message was dispatched from the plane's cockpit to signal any kind of mechanical malfunction.

It happened at night. A search began only the following day. French soldiers from the force stationed permanently in the Ivory Coast found the plane's wreckage. A French helicopter flew the soldiers together with representatives of the Ivory Coast government to the site of the crash. Relations between the Ivory Coast and Togo, on the one side, and France, on the other, had always been extremely close. The French left the inquiry in the hands of UN experts, who arrived at the site of the crash only four days later.

The mysterious crash of the plane in which Alioune Beye lost his life in 1998 bears a marked resemblance to the mysterious crash of another white plane: the one over Katanga, eastern Congo, in which UN Secretary-General Dag Hammarskjöld died in 1961. In each case, the wreckage and bodies were recovered and experts were called in from all over the world to study every detail and every broken piece of aircraft, but the efforts produced no results. It is worth asking if the term 'mysterious' in these two cases is not aimed at covering up the tracks of those who stand behind these evil acts. It is widely assumed that information exists, but that it is too sensitive. In the meantime, the UN continues to investigate these 'mysterious accidents'. Either way, the official reports and documents have yet to be published. It is reasonable to assume that they never will be.

The body of Alioune Blondin Beye was flown to the capital of Mali, Bamako. We took off from Luanda in a UN plane to attend the funeral. There we sat, surrounded by dozens of mourners, looking at the coffin, covered by a flag of Mali, not that of the United Nations.

Alioune Blondin Beye was given a state funeral within the means of his impoverished homeland. I sat next to US Ambassador Donald Steinberg in a giant marquee. The African sun was scorching. In silence, we followed the modest Muslim service.

"We are all to blame," Donald said in the end. "We shouldn't have allowed him to set out on that suicide mission. We knew he didn't stand a chance."

"But you knew he wouldn't relent," I said. "He was an African of the old school, believing to the end in the kind of discourse that led to a consensus that agreement can be reached after many hours under the sacred psalaver tree."

"Is this what you learned from Houphouët-Boigny?"

"Yes, it's the old way, which has become obsolete in our day and age. He could do it no other way!"

Four years later, in April 2002, after a lengthy manhunt through the thick African bush, an Angolan army unit disposed of Jonas Savimbi.

The mediator and man of peace did not live to see the end of the war. Savimbi died in a hail of bullets a long way away; and it was this that brought peace to Angola.

тg

CHAPTER THREE

The enchanted forest

Gorillas, chimpanzees, forest elephants, parrots, human beings, they all struggle for survival in the enchanted tropical Maiombe forest, but they do not always cooperate. The armed conflict threatens them all. The human suffering is endangering also the forest and its non-human inhabitants.

The Maiombe forest, stretching from the Angolan enclave of Cabinda and the Democratic Republic of Congo in the south, through the Republic of Congo, and up to Gabon in the north, forms the southwestern margins of the Congo River basin.

The Congo River basin forest, covering a large area in central and west Africa, is the second largest block of rainforest in the world, after the Amazon, with extremely rich and varied wild flora and fauna, including many endemic species. Even our closest relatives, the chimpanzees and the gorillas, occur naturally only in this part of the world.

Only when man learns to live in peace with nature and its treasures, and to take down political and artificial boundaries, will our species and other living beings survive side by side, even florish.

Where the forest ends

"Here the forest ends." The words were whispered. The scene before my eyes was horrific. The forest really ended here. Several giant tree stumps, stripped of their bark, their branches amputated, were lying on the barren sandy soil, a terrifying memory of the magnificent tropical forest that grew here until recently; a great nothingness, covering hills and valleys, spreading everywhere.

The Maiombe forest lies in the southwest of the tropical African rainforest of the great Congo River basin. It straddles four countries, from the Congo River in the southwest of the Democratic Republic of Congo (formerly Zaire), through Angola's Cabinda enclave, along the west of Congo-Brazzaville (the Republic of Congo) and north to southwest Gabon, where the Maiombe forest joins the other tropical forest systems of the Congo basin.

During my many visits to Cabinda province, I consulted the villagers in the forest about what should be done to protect the rich diversity of wild animals and plants. At our first meeting, the villagers said the forest in the two neighbouring countries was much more degraded by logging and hunting than in Angola. Nowadays, loggers and poachers from these two countries enter Cabinda illegally.

"Even if we stop hunting and logging," said one village head, the Soba, "the forest destruction will continue, and we will lose everything. The only way to secure the future of this part of the Maiombe forest is if all the countries that share it cooperate in its conservation."

This was how the idea of establishing a transfrontier conservation area for the whole of the Maiombe forest was first raised. The Minister of Fisheries and Environment, Fatima Jardim, was keen to promote the idea and asked for help from the UNDP, the United Nations Development Programme, to facilitate the initial contact with the neighbouring countries. At the minister's request, I arrived in Brazzaville, on a UNDP mission, to promote the concept of transfrontier conservation.

After several meetings with government officials in the capital, we went into the part of the Maiombe forest which is in the Republic of Congo, near the Angolan border of Cabinda. There were three of us: Mario, a representative of the Foreign Affairs Ministry from Brazzaville; Marcel, a teacher and UN interpreter; and me, a representative of UNDP from Angola.

We met the villagers and presented them with the plan for the development of a transfrontier conservation area. Like their Angolan neighbours, they also wanted to take part in the programme and protect the wilderness for their children and future generations. The three of us ventured into the forest to assess its status. Joseph, the chief of one of the villages that we visited, nominated two of the village hunters to accompany us as guides. He looked us over rather sceptically and then said: "The two men will be able to walk here all day. No problem. But this one ... a woman ... mundele [white] ... how will she walk in the forest?" The hunters nodded.

"I will be able to walk," I insisted. "Don't worry." We started out, but they seemed very concerned.

On the first day, Marcel tripped and sprained his ankle. The following day Mario suffered from heat exhaustion and became sick. Both of them could not go on beyond the third day. I wanted to continue walking with the hunters, but Mario refused to let me. He was responsible for my safety.

"No problem," said Joseph. "I will go with you to the forest tomorrow, and you, Mario, can stay here to rest, and feel confident that I will personally protect her." On the third day, three of us ventured into the forest: the chief of the village, one of the hunters, and me.

Walking in a tropical forest is not a very comfortable experience, especially in that mountainous region, where you go through steep ascents and descents. Here you cross a stream in knee-high fast-flowing water, and there a cloud of tiny midges sting your skin in an aerial attack and ornament it with numerous painful spots. Army ants climb on your body and torture it mercilessly. Small forest flies invade every orifice, and poisonous plants attack your ankles and arms. Every action is an effort, be it pulling your foot from the mud, hopping over the ground vegetation without falling, scrambling through thickets without getting caught in them, being careful not to step on the ants' routes, or protecting your face from swarms of biting flying insects. Within a short time your body is soaking wet—from rain, the moist vegetation, the streams, the mud and from sweat. Your feet continually slip inside wet shoes, and your shoes continually slip in the mud. Your skin is scratched, stung, itchy and burning, even inside your clothes.

Still, despite all this, what the eyes see and the senses experience is worth any inconvenience. The body is willing to forgive everything, in return for such spectacular sights, which fill the soul with supreme bliss. The forest, washed by the rain, always looks elegant and festive, from its ground vegetation right up to the canopy. The myriad colours, shapes, scents, the forest sounds, everything here swirls the senses as though you were hallucinating. Thousands of shades of green, dotted here and there with flowers in deep, hot colours. Small, picturesque streams add a touch of heaven to the forest floor, and overhead the parrots contribute a new and surprising hue to the forest canopy high above. The various palms, mostly along the rivers, are bewildering. Some look like poodles that just got out of the water, short and stocky with furry tops standing on end in all directions, while others look like washed and combed children, with their thin trunks and neat canopies. Some palms have fronds that resemble fox tails and some look like hedgehogs. But they all stand upright, proud, shining in the light as the rain drops slide slowly down their leaves.

A butterfly sits on my arm, sipping the moisture from my shirt; another lands on my shoulder. The third rests on my open palm. They flutter around me with their soft colours, beautiful and shining as fairies, but as quickly as they appear they vanish. The forest is so dense that at times it blocks the sunlight. After a few hours of walking, surrounded by this deep green, hidden from the sun, you start to believe that the whole world is a tropical rainforest. The whole world is full of these magnificent sights.

"What a privilege," a thought crosses my mind.

And then comes that awful whisper. The chief of the village says quietly in my ear: "Here the forest ends!"

We advance a few more steps and then the sun hits our faces. A desolate landscape of barren, sandy soil stretches in front of us. Tree stumps are scattered about, silent witnesses to what has happened here. Our eyes, having become accustomed to the soft shadows, are stricken by the bright, harsh and formidable sunlight. Our ears, having rung with constant chirping, twittering, whistling and trilling calls, amid the ceaseless creaking of the trees and the rustling of leaves, are suddenly deafened by the intensity of an awful and deadly silence.

A few more steps and the barren truth is revealed: the desolation has spread everywhere. Hills and valleys lie ahead without a single tree. Most of the forest has been felled. Only on the high mountain peaks, in the deep river valleys, in places inaccessible to machinery, small patches of the tropical rainforest remain.

We turn back quietly and return to the forest. A last safe haven for the myriad creatures that live here. A last piece of heaven, surrounded by the great nothingness that threatens to engulf it, too. Man-made.

T R

A journey in Congo

Guy had planned my first visit to the Republic of Congo (Congo-Brazzaville), and undertook to take care of even the smallest details.

My 'brother,' Guy Nestor Itoua, was a young diplomat in the foreign affairs ministry of Congo. I met him at a time when the idea of a transfrontier conservation area for the protection of the Maiombe forest was first mooted. We met at the Israeli ambassador's residence, during Guy's visit to Luanda while on a mission. There he felt at home, in the warm African-Mediterranean ambience, which is so different from the rather cold cocktail party atmosphere, typical of the social lives and homes of many foreign diplomats in Africa.

He was excited about the idea of establishing a joint conservation venture between Angola, Congo and DRC and had offered to help promote it, although it was not directly connected with his own diplomatic position. With his colleagues from the ministries of foreign affairs, forestry and environment, and from UNDP in Brazzaville, they had efficiently organized a comprehensive plan. The planned visit included meetings with government officials, UN representatives, environmental organizations and others, as well as field visits for the reconnaissance of the forest and the reserves bordering the Cabinda enclave of Angola, and meetings with the villagers there.

Guy met me at Brazzaville airport, clad in a suit and tie, as one would expect of a diplomat in his position. Instead of waiting with the other passengers in the long sweaty queues, typical of many African airports, he arranged a special reception, led me to the air-conditioned VIP room, and offered me a cold drink.

We went first to meet Mario Mackoloki, the government representative to our mission, and Marcel Kimbinda, the teacher and interpreter nominated as the UNDP's representative. The three of us were the core team, while Guy only participated in some elements of the visit, but took care of all of the necessary arrangements and co-ordination.

On the third day, we left the colonial-style hotel in the capital, and prepared for the field visit. That morning we had our last formal meetings with government officials. Then we had lunch at the residence of the UN representative in Brazzaville, with the American ambassador and the head of one of the leading international conservation organizations. During the lunch, which consisted of a selection of sophisticated Chinese dishes served on a specially designed revolving tray, with quiet classical music in the background, an intellectual debate developed around the theoretical question of whether it was possible and morally correct to deal with nature conservation in a country that is suffering from an internal conflict and a devastating civil war.

About two hours later we found ourselves on a short but exhausting flight in a small and overloaded plane. The Russian pilots looked like they had already had their daily ration of vodka. The engine rattled. The worn tires threatened to catch fire on each of the many landings. The already full plane became more and more overloaded with passengers, luggage, several loud and opinionated chickens, and one unhappy goat, all piled on top of each other. Steam rose from the sweating bodies. Needless to say, the air-conditioning was out of order.

We landed in Dolise, the capital of Niari province, adjacent to Cabinda. We decided to stay in a hotel that would be affordable to all of us. 'Hotel' may not be the correct term to describe the half-built construction on the brink of collapse. At least there was only one floor. There were several rooms, each furnished with a rickety iron bed, covered with a thin mattress with straw sticking out and a torn blanket. We had dinner at a local bar, with small crowded tables. We dined on grilled fish with fried banana, pestered by mosquitoe and all manner of insects. Some shared our meal, and others drank our blood for dessert. The evening air was hot, humid and oppressive. A squawking tape played local music. The conversation flowed pleasantly, although overly-loud, to drown out the music. Mario and Marcel told us about their families. I looked around and noticed that I was the only foreigner there. I thought with a smile about the diplomatic lunch. It seemed that many days had passed since then, not merely a few hours. For whatever reason, here I felt much more comfortable, and in my element.

We discussed our plans for the next few days. We had to get to the Maiombe forest to meet the villagers and reconnoitre that part of the forest with them to assess its conservation status.

"You should know," Mario said proudly, "it is not my job to walk in the forest. My work is in the office. I am a senior government official. I used to go to the office with a jacket and tie. Walking in the forest is the work of villagers."

Watching my blanching face, he immediately added softly: "But here we are all one team. We have a mutual objective—to promote this project. If you go on field visits I will of course accompany you. Don't worry. We will walk together."

After four days in the forest we were invited to a formal meeting with the administrator of the region. We arrived at his office, but due to the unbearable heat inside, the meeting was held outside in the yard. There were air-conditioners of course, we were told, but they weren't working at the moment. That is, they hadn't been working for several months. It was impossible to get spare parts. It all sounded very familiar.

We were asked to wait. We sat in the shade of a large tree, around a heavy wooden table, covered with a colourful tablecloth. We waited, and waited, and kept on waiting. Eventually the administrator arrived. He was tall and rather large, clad in a heavy warm suit, too small for his frame, a kipper tie knotted tightly around his neck, with sweat dripping from his forehead. The secretaries signalled for us to stand up in a gesture of respect, until the administrator took his place at the head of the table.

When he sat down he asked us to explain briefly the purpose of our visit. He was a very busy man, and still had many commitments that day. Mario gave a brief account of our programme and objectives, and of the planned project. He added some general references about the importance of protecting the Maiombe forest and its biodiversity.

When Mario had finished, the administrator responded. Usually, I have very little expectations of senior people's understanding of the importance of nature conservation, especially those who keep a formal appearance under any weather conditions. However, the administrator surprised me.

"I am very pleased with your visit here," he started his speech. "It is for a long time that I have been trying to promote the protection of the environment and nature in our region. I have explained to the residents that the consumption of bush meat, and especially ape meat, will bring these species, which are so important for our economic future, to the verge of extinction.

Some wildlife species are already extinct here. It now takes many days of walking in the forest to encounter animals that in the past were very common and easy to observe.

"If we carry on this way, what wildlife will we be able to show to our children when they grow up? What will they eat? What will they live on? We must find alternative livelihoods for the youngsters, so that they can stop hunting. When I served as an ambassador in other countries in Africa and people heard that here we eat apes and monkeys, they were astonished and they ridiculed us. I also warned our residents of the severe health hazards related to eating this meat. Maybe they will be more willing to listen to you, who come from afar."

The conversation flowed and we failed to notice the time until the sun began to set. We still had to arrange our travel for the next day. We thanked the administrator and started leaving.

"Please, wait," he said. "Before you go, there is just one more thing that I wanted to tell you. I want you to know that I have learned my understanding about the importance of wildlife conservation, in general, and of apes in particular, from my mother."

"In my early childhood, we too, as everybody else around here, ate meat of monkeys and apes, and it was considered a delicacy. One day, when my mother went to the river to wash our clothes, she returned home shaken and announced that no one would eat ape meat in her house any more. Later, after she relaxed a bit, she told us excitedly that when she was busy with the washing she saw a chimpanzee mother come down to the river, carrying her infant. The mother approached the water hesitantly, while the baby jumped down happily and ran towards the river. The mother hurriedly reached for his hand, and held it firmly, keeping him from falling into the river. She scooped water with her other hand, washed his face, and then let him drink. 'The chimpanzee mother treated her infant exactly as I treat you, my children,' my mother said. 'We will never hurt them again.'

○○○

The next morning we left for the coastal town of Pointe-Noire, a considerable distance away. There we met my 'brother', Guy. A friend of Guy's cousin had arranged, through another friend's uncle, a vehicle that we could rent cheaply. The friend of the cousin also booked rooms for us in a lovely little hotel, at a reduced rate. The hotel was owned, of course, by yet another cousin. It was so good to be part of the extended family. I invited everybody to dinner in an adjacent bar-restaurant, owned by another uncle of our family. The sole fish with the sweet fried banana melted in the mouth, and a pleasant breeze contributed to the good atmosphere.

The next day we went on to Conkouati National Park, about a six-hour drive away. It was the best-managed protected area in the region of the proposed transfrontier conservation area. The park warden, Gregoire Bonassidi, had been trained by an international organization, the Wildlife Conservation Society, by attending a special course for park rangers. He dedicated his life to the protection of wildlife, to fighting poachers, and to educating and raising awareness among the local population. Together with a young Belgian biologist from the same organization, he had established a special project for the protection of sea turtles along the coast in the park.

"The struggle for nature conservation," said Bonassidi with a deep sigh, "is daily and exhausting. We cannot fight the sophisticated commercial illegal hunting with our poor means. The uncontrolled logging also takes its heavy toll. And yet, we cannot give up. Every little victory justifies all the effort."

The world's first successful project for the reintroduction and integration of captive orphaned chimpanzees back into wild troops took place in Conkouati National Park. The project was established and is still managed by a tiny, stubborn French woman, Madame Alliette Jamart. She had received no formal education in this field. She was a shopkeeper in a small electrical shop in Pointe-

Noire, when one day she found a thin and miserable infant chimpanzee offered for sale by his poacher-torturer. Compassion for the suffering infant overcame her and she bought him. Only later she learned that it is 'kindhearted' foreigners who buy these orphaned chimps, 'to save them', that enable and promote this cruel trade in the infants of our closest relatives. She treated the baby and raised him, and she began to collect information and study the subject. In time, she received into her care several other orphaned infant chimps from people who had bought them and then found that the enormous task of raising them was way beyond their ability.

Madame Jamart decided that the only acceptable solution for saving her chimps was to reintroduce them into the wild. Nothing less would do. She wrote to many ape researchers, chimpanzee sanctuaries, and other experts. The advice she received was always the same: experience shows that it is impossible to successfully reintroduce chimpanzees that have grown up in captivity, into wild troops of their con-species. Wild troops of chimpanzees will not accept the introduced individuals and may kill them. Moreover, chimps raised in captivity have not acquired the life skills for survival in the wild. These skills are learned at an early age from the mother and other adult troop members. Although there are success stories of rehabilitated groups of chimpanzees raised in captivity and released into fenced areas of natural habitat or onto islands, previous attempts to introduce captive chimps into a troop of their own species in the wild had always failed. But a woman like Madame Jamart would not accept such advice to give up. She was determined to persist with her plan. Her chimpanzees would return to the wild, no matter what. It was the right thing to do for them, and she knew that she would succeed.

And succeed she did.

She has lived now, for more than a decade, in Conkouati National Park in an area designated by the government for her chimp reintroduction programme where she continues to lead the project. She rehabilitates the orphaned chimps, in small groups, with the help of volunteers. All are victims of the illegal pet trade. In choosing the group composition, she takes into account age, sex, personal likings, friendships and rivalries among the chimps The little infants are paired, whenever possible, with juvenile and sub-adult females who adopt them. When the chimps can demonstrate that they have mastered the practical and social skills required for their survival, they are released into the wild. Several individuals in each group are fitted with radio collars, so that their movements can be followed, their adaptation to the new environment monitored and additional food and medicine provided when necessary.

The most remarkable successes achieved by the project were the reintroduction of several young females, who were accepted and integrated into the wild troops. In the wild, adolescent and young adult females would normally separate from their natal troops and join other troops. The adult males happily facilitate their acceptance and willingly protect them from dissatisfied troop members, if necessary. In the same way, the young captive-raised females of the rehabilitation project were accepted into the wild troops. It was the first successful reintroduction of captive-raised individuals into wild chimpanzee troops.

"All the experts told me that I would fail. They all advised me not even to try to introduce my chimps into the wild, but only into enclosed areas," Madame Jamart told us. "When we succeeded, we thought that everybody would want to learn our methods. But this did not happen. Instead, they turned their backs on us. We were marginalized, and simply ignored. Our success has confounded all their theories, and they were not willing to accept it, especially not from a simple French woman with no formal education. Very few researchers have supported our efforts, and tried to help, or even to learn from us."

"If you had asked for my advice," I admitted, "I would have given you the very same response. From my experience with chimpanzees, I would have advised you not to try to release them into the wild, but only into an enclosed area. The reason for this is not only the risk that the wild troops would hurt them, but because these chimps have become so used to and dependent on human presence that they would always try to seek out people. When they grow up, they can be very dangerous to humans. How did you convince your chimps to live in the wild, without constantly returning to seek the company of people?"

Madame Jamart smiled. "Why waste too many words? You will see the answer with your own eyes. Come with me tomorrow to see them."

Early the next morning we spent about two hours in a small boat headed for the main island in the park, where the chimps had been released. The boat slid through the silky water, with the grey morning mist clearing slowly, revealing, bit by bit, a myriad forest colours, with a background symphony of bird chirpings, wildlife calls, and cracking branches, the sounds of the forest awakening to a new day. We reached the camp—several shacks comprising staff and volunteer accommodation, a kitchen, a laboratory, and an office. Everything was constructed of wood, thick cloth, poles, and nets, all simple, improvised, and built with a limited budget, but functional and comfortable at the same time. We went with two of the volunteer keepers to look for the chimps in the forest.

First, we met Derek, an adolescent female. She excitedly uttered friendly calls and ran to meet the keepers. Several other chimps followed. They all surrounded us. Bill, a juvenile male, caught the French volunteer by his leg, and would not let him go. These are ordinary scenes in chimpanzee sanctuaries.

Several hours later we returned to camp. The chimps stayed behind in the forest. This was less common than in other similar institutions. How had the keepers persuaded the chimps to remain behind, and allow them to leave? No captive chimp that I had met before would have accepted that without some violent protest.

We thanked Madame Jamart, and were about to leave for Pointe-Noire, so that we would be there in time for my flight back to Luanda later that day. The others had to return to Brazzaville. "No," she insisted. "That is not all. You must see two more females. Only then you will understand." "I would really love to, but we simply have to be back in time for the flight."

"No." She was emphatic. "You must see this. Even if you miss your flight, you will not regret it!"

Hesitantly and unconvinced I followed a volunteer veterinarian back into the forest. We soon met with two sub-adult females, around seven or eight years old. They approached the vet, and one of them held out her arm in a friendly gesture. The other one gently lifted the vet's coat, reached her hand into her trousers pocket and took out a small bottle. This was her daily vitamin drink. She drank the contents and returned the bottle to the volunteer's hand. The first adolescent held out her hand, received her bottle, drank its contents, and returned it too.

I was totally unprepared for what happened next. They both touched the vet's hand again, in a greeting, and then turned around and walked back calmly into the forest. No special persuasion was required. They simply felt confident enough to return to their own business, without demanding the company and protection of humans. They were ready to be released. Madame Jamart was right. I really had to see this with my own eyes, to believe.

Now we started the race back to Pointe-Noire. We had not given up on reaching the flight in time. The boat trip back seemed longer and less enchanting. From there, all the way back with the rented vehicle, we sped along as fast as the potholed road would allow. I was tense. Guy was smiling. "Don't worry," he said. "We'll get there on time. Everything will be all right. That is how things work here. You will see." And then we reached the wide river, and stopped.

To cross the river you have to use the motor pontoon. Vehicles drive onto the pontoon on one bank, and the pontoon operator takes it across to the other, but now the pontoon had been abandoned on the other side, and the operator was gone. What to do?

Two children in a small dugout canoe were trying to fish in the river. "The operator has taken a break and gone to his village, on the other side," they said indifferently. "He will be back in about two hours."

"Two hours?"

"Maybe three," they mumbled and calmly continued to fish. "Unless someone can go and call him."

All seemed lost and I fretted over my flight, but then I saw Guy skillfully rowing the boat. He had paid the children, borrowed their canoe, rolled up his sleeves and quickly rowed across to look for the pontoon's operator. He stood at the back of the canoe and rowed with remarkable speed and balance. I rubbed my eyes. Was this the same Guy that I was used to seeing only in a suit and tie? Ten minutes later he was back with the operator.

"How did you do that?" I asked with obvious admiration when we got to the other bank and were again speeding towards the city. "What? Ah, that?" he smiled. "I grew up in a fisher village. I rowed boats throughout my childhood. It is not a problem at all."

Despite all our best efforts, we arrived at the airport in Pointe-Noire an hour later than the flight's scheduled departure time. I started thinking feverishly about what to do next. A colleague would be waiting for me in Luanda Airport and the next day I was due to participate in an important meeting at the ministry. My UN travel permit would expire today, and so would my Congo visa. I would, of course, also forfeit my plane ticket.

But Guy was all smiles. "Everything is in order," he said calmly. "We are just in time."

"But the flight was due to leave an hour ago," I was not as calm as he was.

"Yes, but it is delayed. We'll still make it. A friend of my cousin will help us."

The police commander at the airport was a friend of a friend of the cousin, the pilot was another cousin, the customs officer was his nephew. It seemed that all the key positions around here were somehow occupied by 'our' family. I landed in Luanda that same night.

TR

A dream

The deep thrumming of the tom-tom at the church woke me. The sun was rising. Tom-toms are still used here as a means of communication, and for calling the faithful to their prayers.

The women of Buco-Zau, a small township in the centre of the Cabinda enclave, in the heart of the Maiombe forest, gathered for their daily prayers. They arrived at the church from all directions, tall, lean and remarkably beautiful, wrapped in colourful pano skirts, and with multicoloured cloths tied to their heads. Some of them carried babies tied on their backs. Others had toddlers in their arms. They welcomed the rising sun at the churchyard with their captivating song and a dance to the drum and rattle of a tambourine. From there they dispersed to their daily labours in small groups, some in the fields of the villages nearby, others in town. Three goats ambled lethargically down the street and then stopped for a rest in the middle of the main road. A fourth goat joined them, bleating. The morning chirpings from the awakening forest mingled with the crowing of the roosters from the township.

Lightning suddenly rent the sky, followed by thunderous claps, and a sudden rain shower washed the streets and the surrounding forest. Then it stopped as quickly as it began and the sun was out again. The washed palm fronds glistened, seemingly poised to shake the raindrops out of their manes. Fresh scents filled the air. It was a new day in Buco-Zau.

We walked into the dripping forest as soon as the rain stopped. Two hunters from a nearby village went with us, André Bumi the Soba, and his son, Celestino Mbumba. We walked with all our senses alert, jumping with every rustle of the leaves. I was told that this was the first time in more than twenty years that a permit had been granted to a foreigner to enter this forest, let alone a woman. Only the local residents, the government soldiers and the loggers, accompanied by whole armies of security men, were allowed to walk in this forest.

The war between the government forces and the local separatist movement in Cabinda province was still at its height that year, in 2000. The rebels were members of the local communities and they knew every inch of the forest intimately. They kidnapped foreigners who worked in Cabinda from time to time and used them as hostage for ransom, while at the same time trying to raise international awareness of their cause. Shortly before our visit, the story of a Portuguese hostage had hit the headlines. He had just been released after being held in the forest for a year by the rebels. At his release he weighed about half his original body weight. Personally, I prefer a less drastic slimming regime.

To enter the Maiombe forest on foot, we needed the approval of the provincial government, the army and the police. I arrived in Cabinda equipped with a letter from the Minister of Fisheries and Environment to the governor, asking for his support in developing the Maiombe forest biodiversity conservation project and for his help in ensuring my safety. On our first drive to Buco-Zau with the project team members from the provincial government and the local organization Gremio ABC, the road from the coastal capital of the province to the township in the centre of the forest was guarded by armed soldiers positioned at regular intervals along the road.

To enter the forest itself we also needed the verbal approval of the villagers. We asked to meet with the Soba, the local traditional authorities at the villages around Buco-Zau and Inhuca to the south. The municipal administrator assembled the Soba in the jungo, the shed where debates are held. The Soba arrived accompanied by youngsters from their villages, some of whom, I was told, might have been rebel militia. We didn't ask. The Soba and their parties took their places in the shed. The women and children gathered around.

We started off by presenting the project goals. We discussed the various long-term advantages and potential benefits to the residents if the forest, its vegetation and wildlife were protected. We mentioned the global conservation importance of some of the species found here. We talked mainly about the apes in the forest, the chimpanzees and the lowland gorillas, our closest relatives. We asked for the approval of the Soba for our work in the forest, and we asked for their protection against the rebels, so that we could promote this conservation programme together with the villagers.

After our presentation, the Soba said they had to discuss the matter among themselves before giving us an answer. Only Soba participated in the debate.

We waited anxiously. After about an hour or so, the Soba returned to the shed. One of them began by saying that they had all reached a decision and that he had been selected to deliver it.

"I will speak in Fiote, our language." He indicated that a representative of the provincial government would translate.

"What you said is true," he said. "We know that the number of wild animals in the forest is declining. Once there were only a few hunters here. A hunter could leave his home in the morning, and return a few hours later with enough meat to support himself, his family and the entire village for several days. Nowadays he must travel for many hours and even days, to get the same amount.

"You are right. If we do not reduce the hunting now, it will not be long before the hunters will be obliged to walk in the forest for weeks and months without success.

"The problem is the famine, the poverty, the unemployment, and the armed conflict. We do not have other livelihoods. To hunt less we need assistance with the development of alternative income sources. Meanwhile, we suggest that the hunting will be prohibited in the area that was designated as a forestry reserve during the colonial era.

"We also accept the idea that we should stop hunting chimps and gorillas. Eating ape meat was never part of our culture here. We started to hunt them only because of the demand for their meat across the border. It is not a problem for us to protect them. But not elephants. Elephants are our enemy. They cause serious damage to our meagre crops, and we must fight them.

"You also need to know that we are not the only ones around here who hunt wildlife. Poachers from both of the neighbouring countries infiltrate Cabinda illegally. To protect the Maiombe forest within Cabinda, the borders must be guarded. The government soldiers serving in the forest hunt here as well. You have to talk with them.

"The project is important to us," he concluded. "We ask that you will support our efforts to protect the forest, and to develop alternative livelihoods, so that when peace comes we will be able to benefit from tourism as well. We have decided to help you. The hunters will show you the way in the forest, and will protect you and keep you safe from danger. Don't worry. No one will hurt you."

The meeting went on. Many of the residents had questions, ideas and suggestions. They delved into their memories for examples from their own experience and knowledge of the forest animals, and I also told of my own experiences of the human-like apes, monkeys and other wild animals that I had encountered through my work in other places, both in the wild and in captivity.

We returned to Buco-Zau. The sun was setting in flaming clouds. The men's church choir accompanied the falling of the night with deep, soulful, penetrating singing. The noisy arguments of the birds, as they roosted for the night in their multitudes, finally concluded with the last few chirps. The silhouettes of the palms blurred slowly into a dark moonless night that wrapped around the township and the forest, along with their inhabitants. Now, there was only the soft sound of a light rain, a swooshing bat, and quiet flowing chat of women in the street.

The next morning we ventured into the forest with the two hunters, André and his son Celestino. We followed gorilla spoor, searching for fruit remnants, flattened lianas, faeces and footprints. After several hours of slow progress through the thick vegetation, we reached a small clearing.

"Look up," whispered Celestino.

In the canopy of a tall tree we saw a troop of red-tailed (white-nosed) guenon monkeys feasting on ripe fruit. A young male noticed us and uttered a shrill alarm call. Within seconds they had all dispersed into the other nearby trees and disappeared from our view. It was typical behaviour of wild animals that had learned to be wary of humans.

I tried to locate the escaping monkeys with my binoculars. Suddenly we heard deep grunting sounds from within the thicket. "Umm … umm." It was a gorilla's characteristic groan. We stopped breathing. There was a moment of silence, and then we heard an unmistakable sound: a gorilla beating his chest.

Celestino signalled to us to get down, and we advanced slowly, crawling on our hands and knees, and at times on our bellies, while he was clearing the way with swift machete swipes. The gorillas now sounded much closer. We hid in the thicket and Celestino created a small opening in the lianas with his knife, through which we could watch. He pointed to a tree.

About twenty metres from us two adult female gorillas were sitting on a big, high horizontal branch. One was young and heavily pregnant, and the other old, with a pockmarked face, and thin hair. She had a deep and ugly scar around her right hand, which seemed paralyzed. It was probably the result of an old injury caused by a snare.

"The real traditional hunters never leave traps without frequently checking them," Celestino told me later, on our way back. He was collecting snares he found on the ground or attached to vegetation. "Only the commercial hunters do that," he said "those who do not care about leaving trapped animals to suffer and die slowly, and in vain, without even collecting their carcasses."

The two gorillas groomed each other's fur and grunted softly. Then a third female appeared and climbed onto the same branch. She had a tiny infant clinging to her belly and started grooming him with great attention. The baby, cradled in the security of her huge arms, lifted his head from time to time, watching the world with large, round and bewildered eyes. Another older female, a bit rounder, started to climb the tree with some difficulty. She reached a lower branch and sat on it, scratching her head.

We could hear the male's deep grunts from the forest floor. He was hidden from our view in the thicket, but we heard him beating his chest several times. Then he started to break branches. The female on the lower branch started hitting her chest and the tree alternately, a sign of agitation. We thought that they may have noticed our presence and we moved a little distance away so as not to disturb them.

That evening Gabriel Muel, the administrator of Buco-Zau, invited us to his home.

"Now I know with certainty that your programme is going to be successful," he said. "I have lived here all my life, for more than fifty years, and I have never even seen one gorilla. And you, on the first day in the forest, have already seen a whole family. I have no more doubt that God is with you. I can understand that," he added. "Not many foreigners would join us here, in these difficult times of war."

I returned to the Maiombe forest many times, to Inhuca, to Buco-Zau, to the villages, and to the thickets. Together with the ministry, the provincial government and Gremio ABC, we continued to promote the programme for the protection of the Maiombe forest and its biodiversity. At every visit we met the Soba and the villagers and consulted them. The meetings usually ended with the exchange of personal forest and animal stories.

During one of our visits to Inhuca an elderly woman stood up. Her name was Donna Rosa Bwanga, and she told us her story. She spoke in the local language, Fiote, and her words were translated into Portuguese by Chicaia, from Gremio ABC.

"During your previous visit here you told us stories about gorillas that you knew, and about their behaviour and their great resemblance to us. On that same night I had a dream. In my dream a gorilla came to visit me, dressed in a suit and tie. He started to talk with me and he asked me to tell my husband that he must stop hunting apes, since the man and the gorilla belong to the same family, and we must not hurt our relatives. He even asked me to pass on his words to all the other women in the village, so that they could also persuade their husbands not to hunt apes any more.

"I was disturbed by the dream," Donna Rosa told us. "When my husband woke up in the morning, I told him what had happened and he was also very moved by it. There and then he decided never to hunt again. Since then we do not eat any more bush meat at home. We have started to cultivate bananas, and slowly, slowly we have become among the most successful banana growers in the region, and our own quality of life has improved considerably."

All because of a dream.

T R

Bitter sweet

Sweet or bitter? Bitter or sweet? This is Angola. Bitter turns into sweet and sweet into bitter and all in one strange mixture. But here nothing seems strange. Everything contains its own contradiction, and the contradiction is the thing itself.

It all started with a cough.

Three of us ventured that day into the Maiombe Forest in Cabinda: the traditional hunter David Messo, Agostinho Chicaia of Gremio ABC, who had participated in the project since it began, and I. We were looking for the forest animals. We wanted to photograph the chimpanzees, the gorillas, the forest elephants, the parrots, and whatever else we could find. We walked for several hours on a narrow road through the dense tropical forest, washed by fine but constant rain.

The whole way I was seized by a persistent cough that would not stop. I tried my best to suppress it, but it was no use. Every few minutes the still air was filled with annoying noise from my irritated throat.

David was losing patience. "You must stop with that horrible cough," he reproached me. "Otherwise we will not photograph anything today."

He stopped for a minute, checked the area and then turned around and started marching with deliberation, straight into the dense thicket. Chicaia and I tried to keep up, while struggling with the thick and prickly vegetation and getting bruised, scratched and wet, while I kept on coughing. Eventually David stopped near a reddish tree. With a swipe from his machete he chipped off a small piece of the bark and handed it to me.

"Chew," he commanded. I chewed. "Uuuuuuuugh!" I have never before tasted anything as bitter. It was disgusting. I wanted to vomit. "Calma, calma, relax," he said with a big smile. "Now quickly drink a gulp of water." I obeyed. One gulp. I wasn't ready for the surprise that followed. A wonderful taste, sweeter than honey, spread in my mouth, caressed my tongue and stuck to my palate. I spent the rest of that day walking in the forest, chewing bits of the bitter bark, and immediately washing my mouth with water, enjoying the sweet-sweet taste. My cough would not let up and we did not see any animals that day. But this enchanted forest, where bitter turns into sweet with a little drop of water, had captivated my soul.

I recalled this incident when Agostinho Chicaia and I went to meet the soldiers of the armed forces of Angola (FAA) stationed in the Maiombe forest. The Angolan army kept a heavy presence in Cabinda, and in the forest, because of the struggle between the government and the separatist rebel movement, FLEC, which was fighting for independence from the enclave.

The little enclave is rich in natural treasures. The wild fauna and flora there are not any less important than the abundant polluting oil and minerals, or the politics, but they are destined to exist in their shadow. This ecological system is part of the Congo basin tropical rainforest, one of the most important, species-rich ecological regions of the world. The Maiombe forest forms the southwesterly margins of distribution of many endangered species, including chimpanzees and lowland gorillas.

The local residents told us that poaching by the army soldiers was among the biggest threats to wildlife. They said that the soldiers received rations and therefore they had no justification to hunt wild animals for their subsistence. They claimed that there were even some armymen who cooperated with the illegal hunting and wildlife trade networks.

The provincial government officials had advised us to meet the army commanders and soldiers in Cabinda. We were worried about that. Previously, when we had encountered the army in the forest, it was not always under the most pleasant of circumstances. More than once we were stopped by armed soldiers manning roadblocks.

Accompanied by officers nominated for this task, we embarked on a comprehensive awareness campaign among the armed forces serving in the Maiombe forest. Over several weeks we visited most of the army units. We told the soldiers, who came from different provinces of Angola, and who were used to a different natural environment and different animals, about the special wildlife of the Maiombe and about the rich biodiversity of the tropical rainforest. We used the same arguments we heard from the Soba and the villagers.

The army commanders supported our campaign and asked the soldiers to take part in the protection of these treasures. They, who were tasked with protecting the security of their country, also had to protect its rich natural heritage. It is common knowledge that oil is a non-renewable resource, while eco-tourism, which is a rapidly growing industry in southern Africa, may become an important future source of income for the people of Cabinda, and for the entire country. We also emphasized the health hazards related to hunting and eating monkeys, especially apes.

"But the wild animals are dangerous even if we do not hurt them," some soldiers claimed. "During patrols in the forest, when we are looking for the rebels, if we encounter large animals, we shoot them instantly, so that they will not harm us."

Some even added horrifying descriptions of aggressive animals which they said had attacked them. These were the sort of legends that are weaved around the campfire after patrol, when soldiers try to impress each other with their heroic tales. Needless to say, stories of that kind do not contribute to the health of wildlife, as the listeners thereafter tend to become trigger-happy when they encounter animals in the forest. To overcome the terrifying images of the animals in the soldiers' minds, we concluded every meeting with real stories about the many human-like characterisics of chimpanzees, gorillas, elephants and others.

Chicaia had a great idea. He suggested that after the awareness session with each unit, we should establish, among the soldiers, 'a Club of Friends of Nature'. Every club member would make five commitments:

I am a friend of nature.

I protect the forest and the wildlife.

I refuse to buy or to sell wildlife or any product made from them.

I do not eat bush meat.

I pass on the word.

Joining the club was voluntary, and there was no reward offered to those who joined, nor any sanctions against those who did not.

After a long talk with the first group, we presented the idea of the Club of Friends of Nature to them. There was silence. They looked at us expressionlessly. We did not know what to expect next. Would they ridicule us for suggesting they stop hunting and eating bush meat, would they castigate us, or would they, or at least some of them, want to take part in nature conservation? Long minutes passed.

Eventually one of the soldiers broke the silence. "So those who join the club must not eat monkeys?"

"True."

"And antelopes too?"

"Correct."

"And even snakes?"

"Yes."

He contemplated for a minute and then said: "Ahmm… so… it is like, er, quitting smoking or drinking?"

"Yes. Maybe. It is similar, but the goal is different," I tried to respond.

"Aha," said another soldier. "It is like joining a church. A church for nature conservation. Isn't it?

"I want to join this church," he added immediately. "I want to protect the forest animals. Where do I sign?"

At first only about a quarter of the soldiers joined up, but they tried to persuade their comrades. On our second visit to the army units about a year later, the number of the club members had increased to several hundreds, about three-quarters of the participants in the awareness sessions. The soldiers asked for membership cards, which they could carry in their shirt pockets. A private donor, Martin Davies, volunteered to print them, and each club member signed the 'five commandments' on his personal membership card.

In the group photos taken of each one of the ten Clubs of Friends of Nature, the soldiers in the Maiombe forest are seen proudly presenting their membership cards. All of the commanders of the units volunteered to act as the respective club coordinators, and even the chief commander of the army in Cabinda registered as Member Number One, while the provincial governor joined as an honorary member.

Here, in this forest, the bitter and the sweet coexist.

T R

Massamba

Such a frightened infant chimpanzee. Little Massamba was sitting on the ground, his little body shivering and his hair standing on end. He wrapped his thin arms around his skinny belly and stared, terrified, at the group of people surrounding him, uttering weak cries of distress.

I have seen many traumatized baby chimpanzees in captivity, but Massamba's terrified expression was heartbreaking. These babies, which now live in zoos and in sanctuaries for orphaned chimps, were caught in the wild and have experienced horrific traumas. Often they have witnessed the violent killing of their mother and other family members, been kept in tiny cages, starved, held in chains and tortured.

The life of an infant chimpanzee in the forest can be happy and carefree. The mother protects him, carries him with her when she travels through the forest, first on her belly and later on her back, breastfeeds him in the first years of his life, and later helps him to find food. At night he sleeps in the nest she has prepared, protected in her arms. She teaches him all the skills that he will need to survive in the forest, and how to get on and to socialize with the other members of his troop. His older brothers and mainly his sisters help to carry him around and raise him. The adult females groom him, and the adult males protect him. When he is old enough to leave his mother for a while, he spends time playing with other infants in his troop and with older juveniles.

The capture trauma is severe. The baby often witnesses the slaughter of his mother. He hangs onto her dead body, whimpering. In an instant he loses his whole protected existence, his mother, his troop, and the forest. He is thrown into a strange, incomprehensible and cruel world.

This is what had happened to little Massamba, when he was about a year old, in the Maiombe forest in Cabinda. Within the framework of an awareness campaign with the provincial government of Cabinda, we gave talks to army soldiers in order to sensitize them to the importance of the forest conservation. We had visited a unit stationed near the village of Massamba, in the municipality of Belize, in northeast Cabinda, near the border with DRC. After the awareness session, the soldiers told us about a poacher who kept an infant chimp at his home in the village. They offered to show us the place. Near the poacher's cabin we found the little frightened chimp, with a rope tied around his waist. The rope had cut deep into his flesh, and it was evident that he was suffering great pain. The poacher ignored the baby's suffering and heartbreaking whimpers and had mercilessly pulled the rope tighter, cutting deeper into the wounds.

Jorge, the local representative of the Forestry Department, which is responsible for the enforcement of the forestry and conservation laws, and Major Antonio Kitongo, the army commander of the area, interrogated the poacher. He knew that the hunting of chimpanzees was illegal, but that the law allowed a person to protect his crops. The poacher claimed that he saw a chimpanzee approaching his cassava field, and he fired a shot to chase her away. Then he found out that she was carrying an infant. When he shot, he argued, the mother panicked, threw her baby to the ground and ran away. He only collected the deserted infant in order to take him home to save him, so he said. The obvious lie and the baby's suffering caused me to lose my temper, and I interrupted the interrogation.

"The story about a mother chimpanzee that throws her infant to the ground, in the face of danger, and runs away, cannot be true," I said. "You had better tell us the truth."

"The lies only implicate you more," Jorge said.

Meantime, the soldiers had gathered around the miserable baby. They crowded round, armed, in a threatening silence, observing the scene with the villagers looking on. The poacher started to stutter. "Eh ... well ... it was not exactly so ..."

Eventually he told us what had happened, and others have completed the story. He was hunting chimpanzees, to sell them for the bushmeat trade. It was not the first time that he had done that, and he was not the only person in the village for whom it was a livelihood. If a live infant is also caught, it has an added value. It could be sold at a good price to pet dealer networks across the border.

The poacher saw a large chimpanzee and shot him. It was an adult male. He uttered one scream and died. The poacher thought that this chimpanzee was roaming on his own, and he approached to collect the body. But then he heard an awful scream from some distance behind him. He turned around and saw a female approaching him threateningly from behind a tree. When he tried to move towards the body of the male, she screamed again and moved another step forward, with her hair standing on end. He aimed the gun at her and shot. She died instantly and fell to the ground.

The poacher collected the male's body and then returned to collect the female's too, happy with his bounty. He would have a lot of bushmeat to sell. Only then did he notice the baby clinging to his dead mother's fur, holding onto her with all the strength of his little fingers and toes, and crying his heart out. The poacher forcefully tore the infant from his dead mother's body, tied a rope around his waist, and dragged him to the village. Whenever the baby tried to resist or screamed, the poacher pulled the rope tighter until it cut into his skin, creating a wound so deep that the toddler's bones and internal organs were exposed. The poacher kept the baby outside his cabin for several days, tied up, lonely, wounded and terrified. From time to time he threw him a banana or other fruit. He planned to sell him across the border to pet traders, and hoped to be well rewarded.

Jorge decided to confiscate the infant chimpanzee and to fine the poacher. But what should we do with the baby? We were in the middle of the awareness campaign for the army soldiers in the forest, which had taken months to organize and obtain all required authorization. There is no wildlife sanctuary or a descent zoo in Cabinda, or, for that matter, anywhere in Angola, and raising a baby chimpanzee is an extremely difficult task.

"I will take him," said Major Kitongo decisively. "I will take care of him at my home with the help of the unit's soldiers, until you will find a better, permanent place for him." I promised that immediately upon my return to Luanda I would start searching for a good place in one of the existing chimpanzee sanctuaries in

Africa. These institutes specialize in the rehabilitation of orphaned chimpanzees, raising them in natural conditions and, most importantly, in the company of their own species.

But the problem was more complicated. The village and the army camp were in the forest, and the only dirt road leading to them was flooded. About seven kilometres from the village there is a large stream with a rickety wooden bridge over it. In the rainy season the water is so high and the flow rate so fast that it is impossible to cross the bridge with a vehicle. To get to the army camp we had left the vehicles near the river, including the army's all-terrain Unimogs. We had proceeded on foot, crossing an improvised narrow bridge and had walked for about two and half hours, along a narrow path cut through the forest.

How could we return all that way through the forest with this terrified infant? After the terrible experience he had had at the hands of humans and with the great pain that he was suffering, he would not let anyone get near him. When anyone tried to touch him, he first shied away and then screamed and tried to bite. If we tried to carry him, against his will, he might have escaped and, alone and injured, he would not have stood any chance of survival. But we could not leave him with the poacher. He was malnourished and needed urgent medical care. Besides, we were certain that if we had left him at the village, the poacher would immediately sell him off to illegal pet traders across the border.

"No problem." I suddenly heard behind me a quietly confident masculine voice. "I will take him to the vehicle. He won't escape."

I turned around. To my astonishment I saw the baby chimpanzee cradled in the strong arms of a tough soldier, with wrinkled uniform and a wild look. We had been so absorbed in the discussion that we did not notice that the soldier, Joaquim Coimbra, had approached the little chimp and started caressing him gently.

Slowly but surely he had gained his trust, and then he had lifted him to his chest. The baby struggled at first, trying to bite, scratch and escape. But the soldier held him firmly and close to his chest in one arm, and continued to caress him softly with his other hand. The baby began to relax. He submitted to the calming touch, and his terrified look subsided. His tense expression faded away, and now he looked at the soldier with trusting eyes. The soldier's tough expression softened as well, and his eyes were filled with compassion.

"I will take him," he said again. "I will take care of him." The baby chimp shifted his position in the soldier's arms, and looked relaxed and more confident. He held the soldier's shoulder strap tightly, and would not let it go. When another soldier tried to approach and touch him, he wriggled, snuggled into Joaquim's arms, tightened his hold on the shoulderstrap, and looked up into his protector's eyes.

After a short discussion it was decided to call the baby Massamba, after the place where he had been found. That way, when he was moved to a sanctuary somewhere else in Africa, everybody would know where he came from. "It is important that wherever he ends up eventually, people will know that this chimpanzee was born in our Maiombe forest, here in Cabinda," the soldiers agreed.

We went off on our long journey to the central army base in Belize, where we were hosted at a small urban centre, at the home of the municipal administrator for the awareness campaign in that part of the forest. We walked in a strange sort of procession, with Major Kitongo in the lead, accompanied by several soldiers. They were then followed by Joaquim, carrying little Massamba in his arms, and surrounded by the unit soldiers who were guarding him and his little companion. Massamba was completely relaxed and watched quietly and with great interest all the way, staring at his soldier with admiration from time to time, and never letting go of the shoulder strap. The representatives of the provincial government and I followed behind, and several armed soldiers protected our band at the rear. Several dozens of the villagers, who wanted a lift to Belize, had also joined us.

We walked for around two hours along a narrow forest path, until we reached the wide stream and crossed it. There we found the vehicles awaiting us and went on to Belize, with the army vehicles in front and at the rear. In our pickup truck, in the middle of the caravan, Joaquim and Massamba sat huddled, looking at each other with affection.

"You must be a good man," I said to Joaquim. "Massamba knows why he picked you. It is no coincidence." But I could not get another thought out of my mind. Would I still have thought that he was a good man if I had met this wild-looking, tough and armed soldier at one of the road blocks?

"Yes," said Joaquim, with a serene expression. "I really am a good man." He contemplated that for a few minutes and then said: "I will never eat chimpanzee meat again. Now I understand." His hand was caressing his little protégé.

We hurried to the clinic of Belize. The young doctor there had never treated a chimpanzee (or any other animal) before, but he was happy to try. The treatment was obviously painful and unpleasant for Massamba, and he wriggled and tried to bite everybody, especially the doctor. Joaquim held him firmly, and only then did he submit to the injections, the disinfectant and the stinging iodine spray. At the small market we bought some special porridge powder for babies, enriched with vitamins and minerals, a feeding bottle and bananas.

Joaquim took Massamba to the commander's home and remained there for several months, helping to take care of him. Major Kitongo raised Massamba in his house, and soon he became a full family member. He slept in the house, ate with the family, and was loved and spoiled by all the household residents and visitors, and especially by all the unit soldiers, who shared the tasks of nurturing the chimp under Joaquim's watchful eye.

As soon as I returned to Luanda I started looking for a permanent home for Massamba at one of the sanctuaries for the rehabilitation of orphaned chimpanzees in Africa. Most of these sanctuaries were already full with the many rescued survivors of the cruel baby chimp trade.

These orphaned infants are usually sold by the pet traders to unsuspecting foreigners, whose hearts are captivated by the charm and the distress of these human-like babies, and they try to raise them. They may believe that they are saving the poor thing, but fail to understand that by buying the infant they only encourage the poaching of others, and the killing of their species in the wild. At about four or five years old, the chimpanzees become too big and strong to keep at home, and two to three years later they can become violet toward humans.

There are people who have raised chimpanzees at home as their own children, but when they grow up and become dangerous they have had them killed.

Others build small cages for them, where they spend their lives behind bars, lonely and in an unbearable boredom for such an intelligent species. Some lose their sanity. Some get sent to zoos. Only the lucky ones find their way to the sanctuaries and wildlife orphanages. Chimpanzees can live for forty or even fifty years, and those caught in the wild and sold as infants are often doomed to a miserable existence for the rest of their lives.

Eventually, a place was found for Massamba in Sanaga-Yong sanctuary in Cameroon. The founder and director of the sanctuary, Sheri Speede, an American vet, agreed to help rescue little Massamba. She was assisted by two American philanthropists, Victoria Buesing and Steven Bernheim, who covered all the costs.

Massamba's journey to Cameroon was a rather complicated operation. He was the first chimpanzee ever to be confiscated by the Angolan authorities and transferred for rehabilitation to a sanctuary outside the country. Special permits were required, but no one dared to sign them. It was six months after his confiscation from the poacher before Massamba could finally be on his way to his new home. Major Kitongo, the army commander who took care of him at his home, and officials of the provincial government, accompanied him. At the end of a long journey on potholed roads from Cabinda to Pointe-Noir in neighbouring Congo, they met a volunteer from the sanctuary, who travelled with him on the flight, and then on the long drive to Sanaga-Yong. Sheri waited for him there, bringing with her an opportunity for a new life.

Again in the tropical forest. Again in the company of his own species. One soul was saved.

T R

A green turtle caught in a fisherman's net, about to be released.
Photo: Tamar Ron

An olive ridley caught in a fisherman's net is released back into the sea.
Photo: Tamar Ron

Agostinho learned to read. On the Marginal of Luanda.
Photo: Tamar Ron

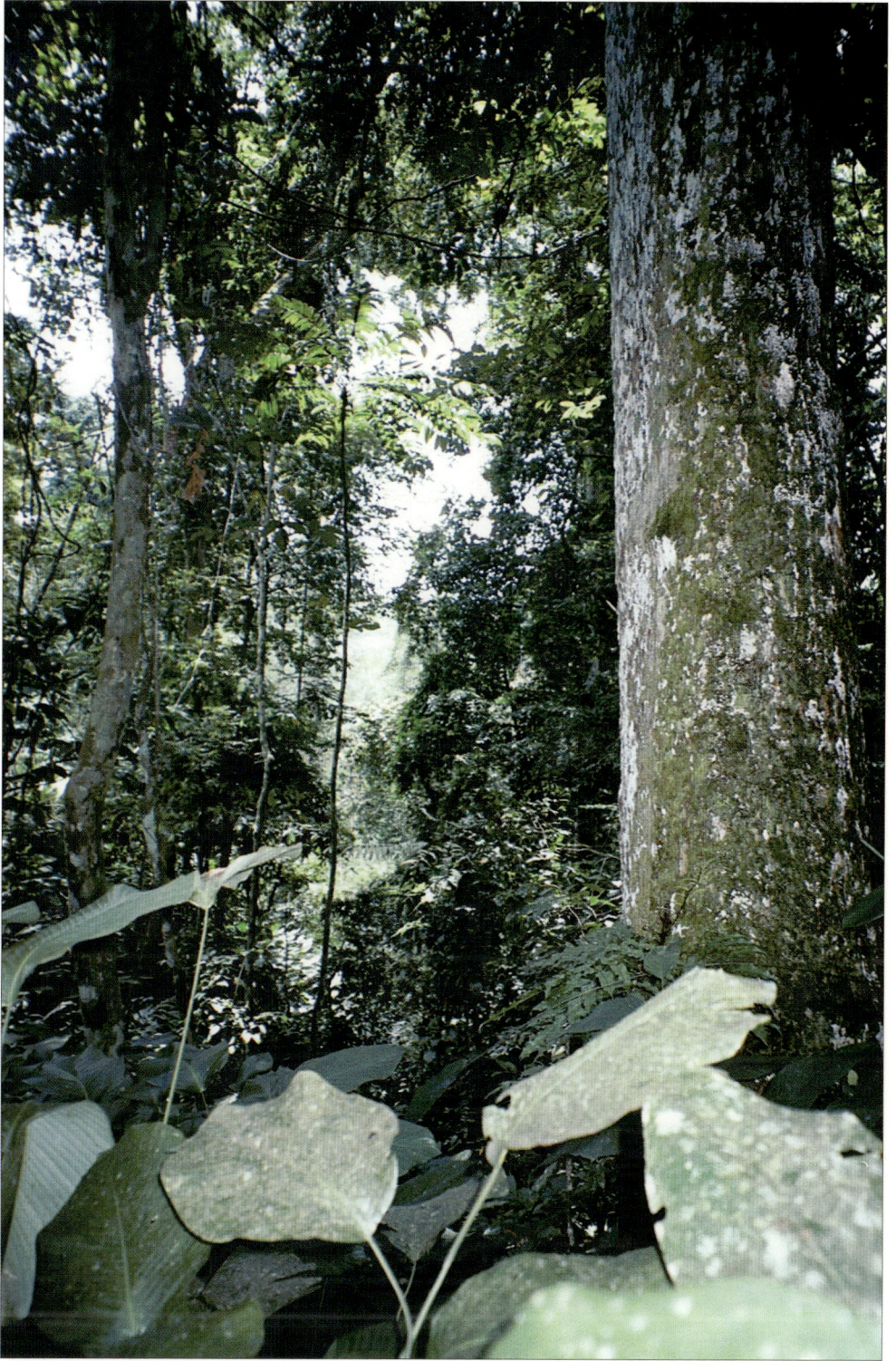

The tropical Maiombe Forest in Cabinda Province.
Photo: Tamar Ron

A poster created for awareness campaigns in Angola.
Photo and design: Tamar Ron

ME ...

A meeting of Sobas in the Maiombe Forest.
Photo: Tamar Ron

Bottlenose dolphin.
Photo: Tamar Ron

The illegal pet trade. This chimpanzee was hunted in Cabinda and sold in Luanda as an infant.
Photo: Tamar Ron

Fishermen on the Atlantic coast of Cabinda.
Photo: Tamar Ron

Baobab.
Photo: Tamar Ron

Cabinda.
Photo: Tamar Ron

Children of Buco-Zau in the Maiombe Forest.
Photo: Tamar Ron

A Friends of Nature Club.
Photo: Tamar Ron

Common dolphins.
Photo: Tamar Ron

Elephants in northern Botswana.
Photo: Tamar Ron

In the shadow of war.
Photo: Tamar Ron

Kuando River.
Photo: Tamar Ron

Above and below: Little Massamba, a pet-trade orphan survivor.
*Photo*s: Tamar Ron

Fishermen in Cabinda.
Photo: Tamar Ron

Sobas meet in Bola Cachasse, Cangandala National Park.
Photo: Tamar Ron

One of the Friends of Nature Clubs of the Angolan Army in Cabinda.
Photo: Tamar Ron

Pilot whale with bottlenose dolphin.
Photo: Tamar Ron

Landmines, beware!
Photo: Tamar Ron

Tamar Ron and the Soba, André Bumi, in the Maiombe Forest.
Photo: Agostinho Chicaia

The forests of Angola are being harvested for charcoal.
Photo: Tamar Ron

Projects in Cabinda are developed with the communities.
Photo: Tamar Ron

Sula (gannet).
Photo: Tamar Ron

Common tern.
Photo: Tamar Ron

The Tchokwe chieftain's thrones.
Photo: Tamar Golan's collection

The train monument, Kuando-Kubango.
Photo: Tamar Ron

The Unita warriors monument, Kuando-Kubango.
Photo: Tamar Ron

Maiombe Forest, Cabinda.
Photo: Tamar Ron

Tamar Golan and her first friend
in Angola—Benvinda Barbosa.
Photo: Tamar Golan's collection

Reminder of war.
Photo: Tamar Ron

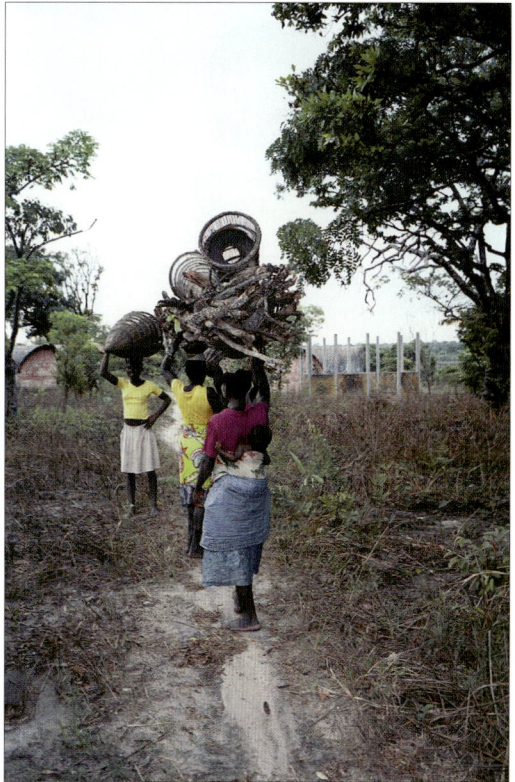

Women carrying fishing traps and wood for fuel.
Proverty and loss of biodiversity are interlinked.
Photo: Tamar Ron

War remnants and new villages in Kuando-Kubango.
Photo: Tamar Ron

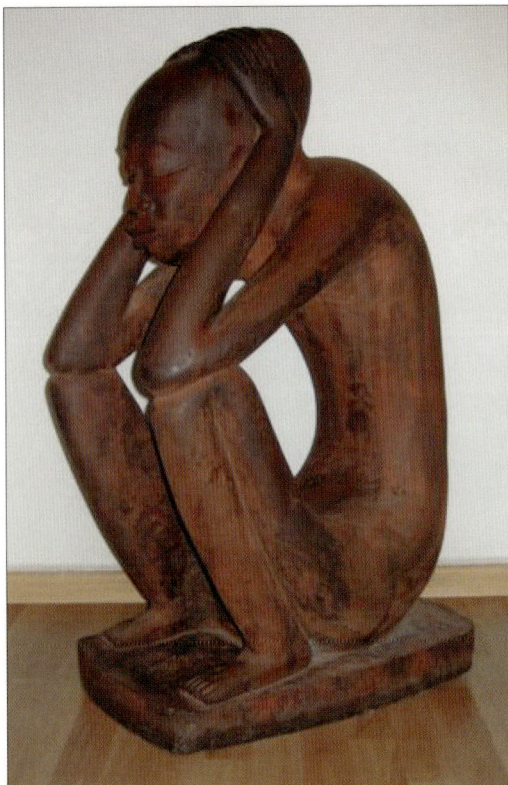

Pensador, the thinking man, an Angolan symbol.
Photo: Tamar Golan's collection

Palanca negra, the black giant sable.
Photo: Brian Huntley

Menongue, Kuando-Kubango—life goes on in the shadow of war.
Photo: Tamar Ron

Kuando River in Luiana Reserve, Kuando-Kubango.
Photo: Tamar Ron

Elephants and other wildlife have started returning to Luiana Reserve in Kuando-Kubango.
Photo: Tamar Ron

The humped dorsal fin on the rounded back of the Humpback whale.
Photo: Tamar Ron

The border between Angola and Congo along the Maiombe Forest. The forest is clearly much less degraded on the Angolan side (in the background); therefore cooperation between the two countries in protecting the forest is essential. *Photo*: Tamar Ron

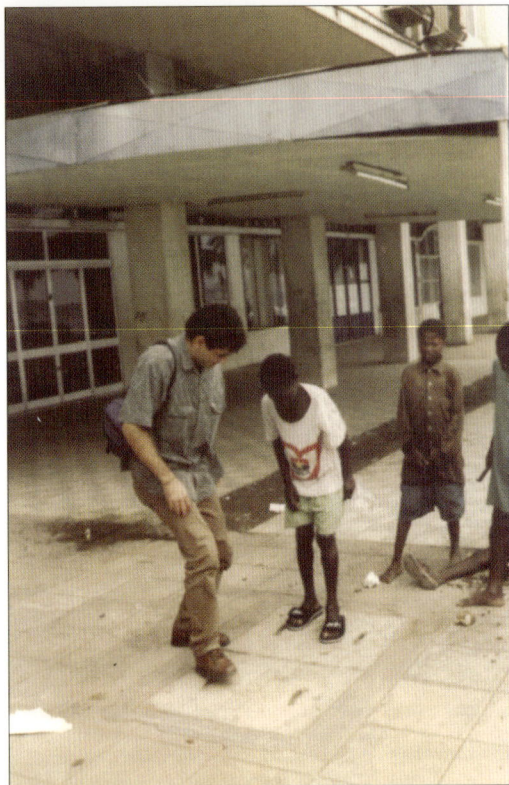

Antonio and Roni.
Photo: Tamar Golan's collection

Antonio and Vazia.
Photo: Tamar Golan's collection

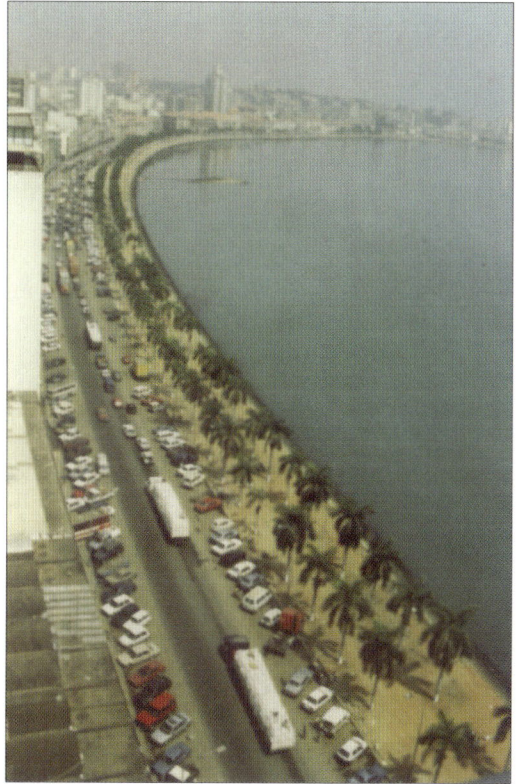

The Marginal of Luanda.
Photo: Tamar Golan's collection

The consequence of war—poverty and destruction.
Photo: Guy Raivitz

The border post into Angola in the Maiombe Forest, a real natural treasure.
Photo: Tamar Ron

CHAPTER FOUR

Children of the Marginal

Children are the future, or at least they are held to be. In Angola there are many children who have no future, children who are the reminder of the past and the present of war, cruelty and despair.

Children who were torn from their homes and villages are left to their destiny in the streets of the big cities, where they live in cardboard boxes on the pavements, or in underground sewage systems. Deserted orphans wearing rags; young mutilated victims of the landmines that were spread across the country; street urchins and little thieves, hiding in every corner, living in gangs. They were mostly boys; young girls were usually better protected by their families, but at times they were seen selling their bodies for a meal.

Even when the street urchins manage to gather enough food for their survival, malaria and other diseases ruthlessly wrack their thin bodies. Most adults treat them with revulsion, fear and abuse, rather than with compassion.

Antonio will never grow up to be a man. Neither will the boy whose body was left under a filthy blanket, on the Marginal, Luanda's prestigious esplanade.

A child on the Marginal

I remember the date very well. It was September 11, 2001, a terrible day engraved in the collective memory of the entire world. That day, in Luanda, a group of shocked Israelis had gathered to watch the horrific images from New York on television. Later, that evening, I returned home, walking as usual on the Marginal, Luanda's esplanade.

A small parcel wrapped in a dirty blanket was lying on the road. A group of people had gathered around it. I approached. It was a child, one of the street children who lived on this part of the Marginal. It was a boy. I recognized his face, but I never knew his name. He had been run over by a car and died on the spot. The driver sped away, and did not bother to stop. Some people came to see what happened. Someone threw a dirty blanket over the body. They discussed what to do with 'it'.

One child. One of thousands of street children in Luanda. A small and thin boy, dressed in rags. A child who had lived and died as a feral cat. There was not even one person to mourn for him, or to claim his body. The body was lying on the side of the road, wrapped in a filthy blanket, and a few people were discussing indifferently what to do with it. What should they do with the body of a small child that nobody wanted. Not in his life, not in his death.

In the days after, the horrifying images from New York were being replayed, again and again, on all television channels. The thousands of casualties, the Twin Towers collapsing, the destruction, the terror, the death, the tears. Again and again. Only one image ran in my mind: one small and thin boy. A body under a dirty blanket. No one claims the body. No one cries. One little child. One of thousands. Again and again.

T R

Antonio's smile

Antonio.

My great love. My grief.

Like the lives of so many children in Angola, the life of this child was cut short in a moment; bare-footed Antonio, with his burning eyes and a smile to melt the hardest of hearts. Antonio couldn't read or write, his birth had not been registered, he never even told us who his parents were. He was one of thousands of abandoned children—the greatest victims of the war. For a moment, that smile, which flooded his face with an ethereal light, would touch your heart, tweak it—and fade away.

I met Antonio in July 1995 through Roni, our Luanda embassy's first security officer. The Israeli Embassy opened twenty years after Angola won its independence. The civil war that had broken out on the day independence was declared was still raging and the resulting devastation was reminiscent of Europe at the end of World War II, except for the deep red skies at sundown and the pouring tropical rains in summer.

It was difficult to find a house or an apartment in Luanda that was not damaged or completely abandoned. We took up residence in the Presidente Meridien Hotel; a temporary situation that was to last more than two years. But even the hotel's French management was unable to overcome the lengthy power and water cuts, the lack of spare parts for the elevators and air-conditioners, the giant cockroaches that scampered around the rooms and the mosquitoes, eagerly feasting on the unfortunate, perspiring guests.

Outside there were nightly shoot-outs from every direction and large groups of children dressed in worn, tattered clothes aimlessly roaming the streets. Wealthy European visitors shook off the young street beggars who would then force their way into cars parked in front of the hotel and make off with whatever they could lay their hands on. Our security officers ordered me to avoid going out at night and

Roni, who acted as embassy security and as my personal bodyguard, permitted only short journeys to official receptions and diplomatic dinners.

The embassy operated from one of the hotel's suites; next door was the security officer's room. The bedroom was my own private territory. The salon served as a dining room, office, communications room and the official reception room. On evenings when the power was on, Roni would leave me alone in the suite and go downstairs to 'check things out.' When there were no lights, he would sit in the dark, laying in wait for anyone who dared come anywhere near our floor.

Like many young Israelis who had completed their military service in the elite units of the Israel Defence Forces, Roni had spent several months backpacking and trekking. He had been to Brazil, where he had picked up enough Portuguese words to be able to communicate in Angola, a former Portuguese colony.

One morning, Roni asked me to pack a few sandwiches for him in the hotel dining room. "I have a new friend and he's hungry," he explained. "His name is Antonio and he's the most delightful kid I have ever met." It's a little embarrassing to take food out a hotel dining room but it soon became our habit.

Dozens of children gathered around us whenever we stepped out of the hotel. Roni was usually alert and prepared for any threat, but after only a few days, I heard the children call him: "Amigo! Amigo!"

Roni smiled and walked over to a small boy, who was standing shyly a short distance away. "Antonio. Everything okay?" Antonio barely dared to raise his eyes as he muttered, "Thank you, thank you, amigo." He received the small bag of sandwiches. The other children remained behind, hopping after him in delight.

"Do you know what happened the first time I brought him a sandwich? He waited for me to move away and then he called all the other kids and shared out the food. He wouldn't eat it by himself! Do you see now why I am always asking you for more sandwiches," Roni told me. "That kid will never run off to a corner to eat alone. He shares the little he has with all his friends."

Roni, who had been a group leader with the Israeli youth movement Hano'ar Ha'oved, had experience with street gangs and knew how to win children's trust. Every evening he went down to the street to 'check things out'.

Some time later, a senior officer in the Angolan Defence Ministry told me that he had seen Roni in action one evening. The following day he reported this to his superiors. "Now I understand," he told me, "why the whole world is so in awe of the Israeli intelligence system. They even know how to handle the street urchins. We ourselves ignore them, or just shake them off, but the Israelis ..."

It is not easy to explain the effect Antonio had on us. Our heavy workload kept us busy and we were involved in all kinds of issues, but we still found ourselves organizing our schedule around the 'kid'. First thing in the morning we'd go through the sandwich smuggling ritual in the dining room, then we would go out to check that he was still alive after the previous night's gun fights. In the afternoon, we would search for him in front of the hotel to see if he and his friends had enjoyed their food. They all called to Roni—"Amigo, Amigo"—until they were chased off by the hotel security guards. In the evenings, Roni went down to see them and the children took him to their hiding place, the unfinished skeleton of a smart office building, where construction had been stopped by the outbreak of war. Stinking remains of food were scattered all over the floor, together with rags that had once been clothes, stolen radio parts and cardboard boxes in which to sleep. There was also a small communal box in which the children kept the cash they had collected from cleaning cars and from picking pockets.

Time passed quickly and we had already begun handing out soap and towels. The children dipped themselves in the foul waters of the lagoon in front of the hotel, which they referred to as 'bathing'. Antonio's eyes began to shine with greater intensity. He, the smallest and weakest in the group, had become their prince.

Late one evening we smuggled him into our 18th floor embassy. The mission was to give him a real shower. Antonio stepped into the shower stall and stood under the warm running water; he stood and stood and stood. Was it just our imagination, or was he actually singing?

The day came for Roni to leave Luanda on his way to other assignments in Israel and elsewhere in the world. We had several long conversations in which we discussed Antonio's future. I asked Roni what he thought was more important: security service on behalf of Israel, or making use of his very special talents to secure the lives of war-damaged children in Israel and Angola? We even toyed with the idea of the state of Israel establishing a home for war orphans in Luanda, where Roni could put to use all his unique methods. Of course, Roni chose service on behalf of his country, but he kept in touch and every telephone call from him began with "What's happening with Antonio?"

Roni's farewell gift to Antonio was a pair of sandals. The hotel's guests, the security guards, police and soldiers at the entrance watched as the Israeli armed officer went down on his knees and fastened the plastic sandals to the feet of the small, skinny street urchin. He straightened and, to the cries of the children - "Amigo, Amigo" - and to the applause of the watchers-on, we set out tearfully for the airport.

Roni's replacement had not been trained in Israel to deal with child war victims. On the other hand, he had been warned that Angola was an especially difficult country to serve in. A cruel civil war was raging; there was uncontrolled gunfire in the streets, violent crimes, a lack of essential commodities and irregular communications. But he, too, was quick to adjust to this reality—and to the children. More important, the guards and security personnel outside the hotel had also become used to this reality. Our children and, especially, Antonio, enjoyed 'diplomatic' immunity. Antonio, the boy with the big smile, had a way of penetrating even the hardest of hearts and raising the level of humanity and tolerance.

This went on for almost two years. Antonio and the children grew and people told us that they were taller and plumper than other street children. The gang enjoyed special status, was less susceptible to harm, but continued to live on the street, like so many others. We realized that the difference we had made to their lives was neither momentous, nor real.

In the meantime our long-awaited residence had been located. It was an apartment that conformed to Israel's strict security rules and overlooked the breathtaking view of the bay of Luanda. We were happy (if not without reservations) to leave the hotel that had been our home for two years. Although the management had done its best to make our stay as pleasant as possible, a hotel is still a hotel. The embassy offices remained there, on the 18th floor, until such a time as suitable premises were found for them, too.

The children followed us with their eyes as we made our way out of the hotel with our possessions. The first night in my new comfortable residence that smelled of fresh paint, I found it hard to fall asleep. Antonio was out on the street.

In the afternoon, one of the Angolan bodyguards, Vazia, picked him up in the car. Vazia was the Angolan security officer at the embassy. His real name was Baumano Samutela, but had been nicknamed Vazia—'empty' in Portuguese—by his former colleagues in the policeforce, since his pockets and his belly were all too often empty.

The boy was excited. He had never been in such an elegant car before. He was used to hanging onto the backs of lorries as they drove out of the port; this was great fun for him. I asked him if he wanted to come and live in my new home. He muttered something. Vazia told me he "would talk to him later. Right now he's too excited." Vazia and I had developed a warm relationship. He was one of the three Special Unit policemen allocated to me on the night that Israeli Prime Minister Yitzhak Rabin was assassinated in Tel Aviv, on November 4, 1995. From that day on, until the end of my tenure, we never parted. Vazia was a wonderfully silent man. He was a man of rare courage and profound integrity. I trusted him and consulted with him often. He said little—and I understood.

That evening Antonio ate his first real meal at a properly laid table in our spacious new kitchen. The entire staff knew him already. I left them alone, to talk in their own language, to help him get acclimatized. He found it hard to eat; he tried to use a fork and a knife and in the end used a large spoon. Vazia said that Antonio was not familiar with 'white people's' food. Later, he was taken to the bathroom. It was the real thing. The hot water flowed and flowed over his body. He played with the soapsuds and didn't want to get out. The second shower of his life.

Vazia said that it was the shower that had persuaded Antonio to agree to come and live with us. Not the food, not the clean clothes and not even the large bed with clean sheets.

The days passed; days of supreme pampering. Antonio would get up late, eat as much as he wanted, and take five showers a day. We were slow to notice, but soon it was impossible to ignore: Antonio was smiling less; his eyes were downcast. He wasn't happy. We saw him sitting by the large windows overlooking the bay toward the sea. But Antonio wasn't looking at the expanse of the ocean in front of him; he was too busy trying to see what was happening below, in the street.

One morning, he barely touched the warm sweet breakfast porridge that our lovely cook, Julia, had prepared for him. Julia was the epitome of the plump, warm-hearted mother type. She stroked his head and asked, "Would you like to go out?"

Antonio's eyes lit up. "I want to see my friends," he said. Julia came and told me, "He has to go out. He's missing his friends. They've been together for so many years!"

We told him he could go out. After all, his new home was not supposed to be a prison. It was obvious that he was holding back.

"What's the matter?" Julia asked.

"If you haven't thrown out my breakfast porridge," he said, "the one I didn't finish eating, I'd like to take it to my friends. To my amigos."

The food was prepared and quickly packed and Antonio disappeared for a moment. When he reappeared, he was dressed in the same rags he'd been wearing when we brought him home.

That kid taught us a thing or two.

TG

That kid taught us a thing or two

Antonio was unable to part from the other children. He was one of them and they were his life. The only thing that group owned, the one thing that no one could take away from them, was their freedom. They were free to do anything they wanted, whenever they wanted, wherever they wanted. They had become a single body, of which each member was a different organ. Yes, at times quarrels would break out among them, but when it came to facing the world, they always presented a united front. To these boys the world was more often than not a hostile enemy, dangerous and menacing. Did they remember different times from their past? Had they experienced better, sweeter days in their lives? If they did, if they had, they never said.

Antonio was alarmed by the new life we offered him. Although he didn't really know how to handle it, he was also attracted to it, as if by a magic cord. A few days after he had left, we saw him from a distance. He hid, ashamed. Scared. He was sure that he had done something wrong. When we sent Vazia to him, he ran away.

Vazia told one of the other children to let Antonio know that he wanted to speak to him.

"Did he steal something from the house?" asked the boy.

"Not at all. Nothing has been stolen," Vazia replied.

"Is the ambassador angry with him? Does she want to hand him over to the police?" the boy insisted.

"No, the ambassador loves him," Vazia said. "She asked me to tell him that he can come to visit, if he likes. You all know I would never hand you over."

That evening the children accompanied Antonio as he 'gave himself up' to us. Upstairs, on the ninth floor, no one said a word. Antonio was given a towel, his clean clothes were laid out in the bathroom and his food was placed on the table. As if nothing had happened.

Antonio smelt good as he stepped out of the bathroom, his hair shining wet and his wonderful smile lighting up his face. We hugged and kissed him.

We learned to share Antonio. He was at once the street kid who belonged to his gang of friends and he was also our child. We left it to him to decide.

It wasn't easy for him. He asked to be taught to read and write and we provided him with a notebook, a book, a pencil and a teacher. He found it very hard to conquer the alphabet. He couldn't concentrate. His body was in a state of restlessness, constantly on the alert. Every sound from outside would cause him to leap from his seat. His progress was slow.

To keep himself occupied, he tried to help with the household chores, until he discovered television. This child, who had only just mastered the alphabet, exhibited an amazing talent for operating the TV, manipulating the satellite box and the video and in no time, he had developed a special talent for the game Tetris. He would sit for hours watching movies in languages from worlds of which he had no knowledge and insisted that he understood everything.

Antonio soon made friends with the diplomatic community and political elites in Luanda. He was handsome, well-mannered and bashful; he was also clean and well-dressed. The distinguished visitors to the residence enjoyed greeting Antonio as they came and left, asking how he was and saying, "what a charming child; how good it is that someone is doing something for those poor children".

There were also those who found it necessary to point out in a somewhat critical tone that they had seen Antonio out on the street with his gang of dirty friends. "Do you know how dangerous they are?" they would ask.

Antonio's gang was of considerable concern to us. Not only because their lives were so harsh, but because we could sympathize with Antonio, who was torn between two worlds. We wanted to house them all in one of these homes established by international voluntary organizations and churches in Luanda. How could we not feel grateful to those youngsters from Ireland, Holland, Denmark or Sweden, who had come to Angola for the sole purpose of helping the abandoned orphans? With a low budget, consisting of funds provided by good-hearted people in Europe, they collected mattresses and blankets, cooked hot meals, taught the alphabet and organized group games.

142

We invited the kids and introduced them to one of the foreign benefactors. They were happy to come, to drink something tasty, to eat cakes and to listen. We thought they had been persuaded. The next day we drove them to one of the street children's homes. Three days later they were back on their regular pitch. They mumbled some kind of explanation. They had apparently encountered children from a rival group, or simply gotten involved in a fight. Later we heard about a Spanish Catholic priest who worked wonders with children at his home. He, too, was happy to come to the embassy to meet our group, but the story repeated itself, although this time they stayed for a whole week before returning to the street.

"It doesn't surprise us," explained a young Irish volunteer. "It's only the weaker kids who stay on at the home at night, to defend themselves against stronger ones. The others come here for a few hours at a time, mainly when they're hungry, and then return to their own war zone, the street. The atmosphere of war has become an integral part of their lives. Every day we witness and hear about adults— soldiers—killing each other on the battlefield. The kids have their own gang wars in the streets. Your particular group feels itself strong and is keen to show off its power."

"Are you hinting that it is our support that causes them to refuse to come to your shelter?" I asked.

"Possibly. They feel protected. Chosen children. But the same happens with children who come to us beaten and weak. As soon as they recovered and put on some weight, most of them go back to the streets. Outside, what awaits them is war, cruelty and injustice. But we don't have any real substitute to offer them. Still, we give them a few moments of security and happiness. And that's something. Only in the movies, where the ending has to be good, does the poor orphan turn into a happy member of his new family. Here in Angola it's not like that. We're not living a movie."

There was nothing I could say.

A month later I travelled to Kinshasa, the capital of the Democratic Republic of the Congo. There, too, I served as Israel's ambassador.

The staff in Luanda continued to care for Antonio, food for the gang of children was assured and Antonio, who accompanied us to the airport, took his leave with a smile that was full of light. He even placed a shy kiss on my cheek.

The telephone rang early on Sunday morning. It was a call from Luanda: Isabel, our devoted secretary and Stella, our dear housekeeper. As usual, the line was bad.

"It's Antonio. Antonio. He was murdered during the night!"

A story emerged, out of all our tears. So simple, so banal. On Saturday night Antonio was bored sitting at home with Stella and watching television. He went down to meet his friends. Together they found their way to a miserable kiosk not far from the building. Antonio had some pocket money and he ordered Coca-Cola for his friends. A uniformed armed guard or policeman, maybe even a drunken soldier, signalled to the children with his rifle that he wanted to sit on the bench they were occupying. Antonio didn't move fast enough; he was the 'ambassador's son', after all. From a metre away, the drunk shot Antonio in the chest.

The kiosk owner quickly closed up. The drunk went home. Antonio's body was thrown up against the door, in the mud. The children returned later to see what had happened to Antonio. They found him, but didn't know what to do with their dead friend. At dawn they hurried to my residence, woke Stella and told her. To them, we were Antonio's family.

One of the children told Stella that once, a long time ago, Antonio had told him that he had a cousin or of some sort, in a poor part of the town. They had gone to visit her. The relatives were very poor and Antonio had given them a little money and an old radio. He told them that he now had a mother, an ambassador. They were all very glad. The boy led Isabel and Stella to the family.

We buried him in his favourite new clothes and his white sneakers. The rest of his clothes and his new watch we gave to his cousin. She told us that she had another young relative at home and that they lacked food.

We located Roni a few weeks later, in some distant part of the world, and told him what had happened. There was a long silence on the other side of the line. "If only I'd stayed. If only ... "

TG

On the street

Antonio's gang of friends remained on the street. They were filthy, bedraggled and terribly thin, but all had a rebellious spark in their eyes. When I stepped out each morning on my way to work, they stood silently, watching me and, when I returned home, they sent me smiles from afar. Waiting. For what?

One morning when the rain was especially fierce, I saw they were wet and shivering. I rushed back home and told Julia to "prepare some food and take it down to them". There was no need to explain who 'they' were.

Julia, the best of women, our plump and kindhearted embassy cook, smiled. "I'll do it immediately, right away."

I understood then that they all, the children in the street and the embassy staff, had been waiting for this moment. They had said nothing. As in other places in Africa where suffering is the order of the day, in Angola the black man adopts a mask when he meets the white man. But his eyes see everything, know everything.

When I returned from work that evening, we all sat around the kitchen table to discuss the best kind of food to provide the children. There was a family atmosphere. Borges, the embassy chauffeur, the oldest and most senior member of the embassy staff, said gravely: "I know you would like to feed the children the same kind of food as is served in your residence. But you would be making a big mistake. The kind of food they need has to be highly nutritious and they prefer to eat our own traditional food. I'll get food additives from the welfare organizations and then get the mandioka powder that we love from the big market. Of your kind of food we only need milk and sugar. You've spoiled us and now we love sweet food."

Stella added some advice of her own. "We'll need to get some plastic plates and some good strong cutlery, so that the dishes aren't stolen in the street and so that they themselves don't break anything. If anything does get broken or stolen, they won't dare tell us, they'll just run away." We decided that the kids would take it in turn to come to the residence to pick up the food. The same child would then come back up to us with the dirty dishes for us to wash.

Several weeks later the children already looked healthier and even a little plumper. In some mysterious—and, oh, so African—way, they always knew when I was going out or returning. One morning they weren't there. That evening, too, they were nowhere to be seen. There was no one there to welcome me with a big smile. Where on earth could all ten children have disappeared to?

That evening, one of the Angolan bodyguards of the embassy came to see me.

"You should know that not all the inhabitants of this building are keen on your relationship with these street kids. You do know that this building houses several extremely powerful people; one of whom used his status to call the police, who came and arrested the children," he said.

He hesitated before continuing. As a proud Angolan, he was reluctant to speak against his own people. His service in the Special Police Force, which, until recently had been trained by the Stasi, the East German secret police, had also taught him that it was always better not to talk too much. "These children have to be cared for. So many thousands of orphans are abandoned to wander the streets here and no one cares."

He fell silent again. "I'll see what I can do," he said.

I saw the children the following afternoon, from a distance, their heads newly shaved and shining. They waved, but didn't approach the car as it pulled into the parking lot.

"When children are picked up off the streets they are taken to a police compound, where they have their heads shaved and are forced to wash. They are dirty, you know," the bodyguard told me.

"Afterwards they are ordered to clean out the police offices, showers and lavatories. There are enough children on the streets of Luanda to ensure a constant supply of cleaners for these compounds. The children are usually not beaten or otherwise mistreated and they are allowed to leave after a day or two. Sometimes payment has to be made to secure their release."

"Did you pay anything?" I asked.

"What does it matter?" he replied. "The problem is that there are several VIPs living in this building, who've been complaining that the children are fouling up the staircase, stealing and using drugs. They want the kids to be kept away from here."

"Have there been any burglaries in the building recently? Have they done anything wrong?" I wanted to know.

"On the contrary. Since we've been feeding them, the kids have actually been protecting us. They know exactly who comes to visit the ambassador. They wouldn't touch a car belonging to any of your friends. They even make sure that kids from other groups don't pester your guests. But ..."

"But what?" I demanded.

"There are several senior army officers living in this building. You know those huge new buses that park here every night? Well, they belong to one of them. A few nights ago someone slashed all the wheels. That's not right. The general was furious. He even forced the soldier who was supposed to be guarding his private fleet of buses to face a military tribunal."

For a week, Julia and Stella were obliged to take food down to the street and collect the dirty dishes themselves. The children kept their distance. The building's elevators were, as usual, out of order and we all had to climb up and down nine floors in a dark and filthy staircase. I met the general on a landing between the fifth and sixth floor. We exchanged the usual pleasantries; we were, after all, neighbours in an up-market apartment building. We discussed the 'situation'. I told him (as if he didn't know) about the strange incident in which the police had rounded up 'my' children. I said that with the elevator out of order, I was especially in need of the children's help in carrying my groceries up to my apartment. I ended with one of those bits of hypocrisy that are so often voiced at diplomatic receptions: "Those poor children. What will become of them? This terrible war. When will it end?"

"With your help," said the general, "we plan to win it soon."

"We all hope so. We're all with you. And, until then, I am obliged to feed those children. You know who they are, those orphans who live here, under our apartment block."

"Such an important matter," the general agreed. "Helping those children is tantamount to helping Angola."

We parted. My bodyguards were smiling. The children returned to our building.

It was a small victory, though one that achieved no significant change. The children continue to sleep in the street, to wear rags, to steal from time to time to survive. But our building was now better 'protected'.

As in other cities throughout this enormous country, thousands of juvenile street gangs, like ours, roamed the streets of Luanda. The children joined forces because they knew that they had no chance on their own of winning the cruel war of survival. Each gang included one or two members who were skilled at stealing from under the nose of the white man, while one of their friends drew attention away from them by holding out a begging hand and a third child wailed pitifully and showed off a bleeding wounded leg, the result of fierce gang warfare over territory. Naturally, the stronger the kids, the easier it was for them to establish a permanent pitch at the better places in town.

What was considered a 'good' pitch? Obviously, this was a place where it was easier to steal and where the handouts were more generous, a place where the largest numbers of white people walked past—all white people being wealthy, of course. The fiercest fights were over pitches near the large hotels, which housed the employees of the international oil potentates, the wealthier parts of town, where the diplomats lived, and in the areas surrounding the United Nations offices.

The VIP building that housed the Israeli ambassador's residence was very close to the Presidente Meridien Hotel, just a few steps away along Luanda's prestigious Marginal Boulevard. Our children weren't assertive enough to settle right in front of the hotel. They had been pushed aside by groups who were more determined than they to a place a few yards further down. But their place had higher status than that of thousands of other children who had to make do with survival alongside piles of garbage or inside sewage tunnels, where the smaller kids were able to hide safely from the older, stronger ones who were too big to crawl in through the openings on the road. Every evening large numbers of small children could be seen emerging from the sewage tunnels, to beg for handouts.

Their pitch was a small piece of asphalt on which the children could spread out pieces of battered cardboard on which to sleep, beneath a ceiling provided by the first store of a building, where they could be protected from the tropical rain. If they were fortunate enough to avoid the scrutiny of the building's guards, they could even steal over to a faucet at the back where homeowners' cars were washed. When there was no water in the tap—and water cuts were a frequent occurrence in Luanda—the children would wash in the filthy water of the lagoon, opposite the Marginal.

Wherever anyone parked a car, a raggedy child would immediately materialize, promising to protect it and even to wash it in return for a few kwanzas. This was supposed to be the main source of income for these juvenile street gangs. Inhabitants of the buildings were familiar with "their" children and more or less trusted them and the children were even prepared to fight and die in a war against invaders. A car owner who refused to accept the children's offer of protection would usually find his car burgled or damaged in one way or another when he returned. Thus, the car owners also learned that it was worth their while to contribute to the survival of the children of Luanda. The young members of our gang had set their own inviolable rules, one of which was that they did not do drugs. Anyone who did would be expelled from the group, but we could all see that skinny little Chiquito was unwell. His eyes said it all. He was on drugs.

Vazia, our security officer, explained that the children were too poor to be able to buy real drugs for themselves, even marijuana. They simply sniffed petrol. They would remove the fuel tank caps of cars parked in the streets and inhale the poisonous fumes. On an empty stomach—and they are almost always hungry—the effect of the gas fumes was stunning.

We had warned Chiquito on many occasions, but it was no use. From day to day he became thinner and more confused. In the end his friends decided to expel him from the gang. Sometimes, I would see him waving to me from his new place, next to the UN building. There were a lot of other children there, too, all stronger than he was. It's a well-known fact that, after all, anyone who works for the UN is wealthy. Competition was fierce and little Chiquito didn't stand a chance. It wasn't long before the children told me that Chiquito had died.

Agostinho

The street children were constantly occupied with survival, earning some kwanzas here and there. They stole, they begged, and they worked, washing cars, brushing shoes, carrying heavy loads, whatever came their way. Every foreigner or well-dressed Angolan passing by in the street was greeted with twisted faces and miserable looks. One hand would point to the belly in a circular movement, while the other would be held out, with the plea: "I am hungry." They would do so even just after having a meal. If a person they identified as suitable walked by in the street, they would quickly clean their faces of porridge and run after him, shouting: "I am hungry, I am hungry." When they saw me, they would give me a shy smile which I interpreted as: "What can we do? This is our job."

Behind the tough appearance they adopted, they were only children. Small children craving love and attention like every other child in the world. Their heart went out to any adult man or woman that did not treat them like dirt or as a nuisance.

One day, on the way from my apartment to the ministry, on the Marginal Boulevard, Paulo approached me. He was one of the youngest boys in the group. He showed me his finger and whimpered. It had a small scratch on it. "It hurts a lot," he said with a solemn expression. "Maybe you have a bandage?" I went back home, brought a plaster bandage and dressed his finger. He looked most content, and immediately ran to show his friends. Soon it became a regular habit. Every few days Paulo would come to show me a small scratch, some of which were hardly visible, and I learned not to leave home without plasters and bandages. It became our little ceremony and we both enjoyed it. Agostinho, one of the older boys, and an exceptionally handsome one, became the leader of the group. Agostinho rarely spoke. He had a severe stutter, but it took time to notice. He had his own unique way of conveying a message, communicating, and leading. It was something in his eyes, in his smile, and in his self-confidence.

The street children could not read or write, but they learned from an early age how to get around and how to survive. They recognized all the different vehicle makes, and they knew how the various car protection systems worked. They could dismantle a stolen car radio and install it in another car. They could not read road signs, but they remembered each and every place by name, and all the different ways to reach it, including those routes that only they knew.

Agostinho wanted to learn to read and write, but to register at a school he needed a birth certificate or some other formal identity document. He had none. He was not registered anywhere. He never said where his parents were, or if they were still alive. He did not volunteer any details about his life before he reached the hard and dirty pavement of the Marginal Boulevard of Luanda, not even his age. Eventually, however, his registration with a school was somehow arranged. He proudly carried his notebook wherever he went. From time to time he scribbled something in it. His studies were not consistent, however. Once there was a strike, because the teachers had not received their salaries since the beginning of the year, and at another time the roof of the school collapsed after a heavy rain. Often, Agostinho simply preferred washing cars to earn a few more kwanzas.

Following Agostinho's example, other children of his group also wanted to have lessons. A priest from the Catholic church offered to teach them how to read and write. I met two of the older children in the street and they asked me to buy them notebooks and pencils. I went with them to a nearby stationery shop. At the shop entrance one of the two children retreated and remained outside, while the other went in with me, nervously scanning the place with a terrified look.

Usually, when the street children entered a shop, they would be chased away with shouts and often even beaten. Sometimes, policemen or private guards were called to deal with them, which often left them bruised. More than once they really did enter a shop with the intention of stealing. However, this time the boy felt protected in my presence, the foreigner. He chose two notebooks and two pencils, for him and for his friend, asked me for the required amount, and stood in line to pay.

The shop assistants and their customers treated him with disgust and other customers jumped the queue to the cashier, who ignored the bewildered boy.

I had to interfere. "Excuse me, this gentleman was here before you," I said loudly to a pushing customer. To the cashier I said: "Why don't you serve the gentleman? He was here first." Wide stares were moving between the rag-dressed child and me.

"Are you … ahm, together?" the cashier finally choked out.

"Yes," the boy answered loudly, and then added proudly: "This is my madrinha [godmother]."

He was served immediately and we left the shop. Outside, he waved his bounty, as he and his friend ran back to join the rest of the group.

When I told Agostinho that I was going home to Israel on leave, he asked me to take a photograph of him reading a newspaper and to give it the ambassador to show her that he had already learned to read. He stood in front of the camera with the newspaper in his hand. In the photo he may have been reading, or maybe he was just staring into space.

He can now sign his name, but he still lives in the street.

TR

CHAPTER FIVE

Great women

Women. They carry Angola on their backs.

Almost without intention, as women, Angolan and foreigners alike, found ourselves befriending each other. We found it comfortable to work together, since we understood each other in that special way that only women share. We also liked to meet after working hours, for long chats.

More than once we found that men were envious of this special sisterhood, and we often heard them comment resentfully that the women ran the country. They were wrong, of course. The women only try to survive and repair some of the man-made destruction. The last word always belongs to those who carry the arms.

Benvinda

Benvinda, whose name in translation means 'welcome', was the first woman I met the day after I arrived in Luanda.

Deep in my heart I am absolutely certain that the warm welcome I received in Angola was due to her.

Decades of war had completely destroyed the traditional structure of the African family and a new breed of women has evolved. These women are fiercely independent; they are willing to take their fate in their own hands, and they are self-confident and proud. Benvinda was such a woman. She had a straight back and tall stature, a loose walk, shining doe eyes and an engaging smile, but her tongue was razor sharp. Like a wild creature, she had a habit of arriving and departing in a storm. She was one of those people with whom it was almost impossible to make a firm date, but she was there whenever she was needed. She was a successful lawyer, but as a young woman, she had been an officer in the army of the MPLA. She travelled to Cuba, where she studied military science, excelled at Krav Maga and, back in Angola, she instructed groups of youngsters. She never took part in real battles, but always chose to serve in the frontline bases. They called her the Panther.

Even when she was engaged to work for an international, capitalist construction company, her revolutionary spirit never left her. She would immediately begin lobbying the management on behalf of the company's employees and I was convinced that her Portuguese bosses were reluctant to dismiss her because they were afraid that if they did, all their workers would walk out on strike in protest.

When we were introduced she told me that it was 'really very nice' that her government had decided to enter into diplomatic relations with Israel. "But I want you to know," she said, "all of us here in Angola support the Palestinian nation's struggle for independence."

Benvinda supported every liberation movement in the world and was extremely critical of what she called American imperialism. At every opportunity, even at official receptions, she enjoyed asking the US ambassador embarrassing questions. The US ambassador was not her only target for criticism; she was equally outspoken with the Russians and never forgot the injustices caused by the dictator Joseph Stalin.

But most of her criticism was directed inwardly, at her country's government and at her fellow party members. "How dare they," she asked, "travel in those fancy imported cars with the dark windows? Don't they want to be seen? Or maybe they have those dark windows installed to avoid having to see their fellow countrymen rolling in the mud and filth?

"Have you heard about the palace the general is having built for himself?" she would ask. "It's all being paid for with the nation's money. And he's been going around preaching equality and progress. How can he forget all the comrades who fell in the battle for the homeland?

"Whatever has happened to Comrade José Eduardo? How come he's allowing crooks to get away with corruption? We used to admire him for his humility. After all, he was picked by late lamented Dr Agostinho Neto as his successor over all the other, younger candidates."

Neto was the first and much-loved president of independent Angola. When he died after a brief illness, José Eduardo dos Santos was elected by the party to succeed him. By the time I arrived in Angola, dos Santos had been the country's president for more than twenty years.

Those in government circles heard her criticism, but they said nothing.

She was never arrested and she was never called in for questioning by the police or the secret service. No one ever tried to rein in her free and tempestuous spirit. Benvinda reminded them all what they had themselves once been, but were no longer.

Everywhere she went, she took her beloved nine-year-old son Patrick along with her. I never asked who the father was and she never said, but it was obvious that motherhood was a great source of pride to her.

One evening, mother and son arrived, very agitated, at my home. "We've seen your little boy Antonio, wondering around near the house, his face covered with a rag. He tried to escape, but we caught him and brought him to you. Look how swollen his face is!"

Benvinda interrogated Antonio mercilessly. Apparently, a boy from a rival gang who was jealous of him had hit him in the face and broke several of his teeth. Antonio hadn't wanted to turn up at home with a battered face. An infection had spread throughout his mouth and he wasn't a pleasant sight, but Benvinda kept her cool. She called a dentist friend of hers, informed him of what had happened and told him that he was to receive the child for emergency dental treatment

"The street kid has no money, but he deserves the best possible treatment," she told the dentist. "He is a victim of this lousy war of ours. It's not his fault."

They took Antonio to the dental clinic. It was late and the treatment lasted a long time. She returned with him before midnight and forbade him to go out. "I'm going to buy you some antibiotics. I won't allow you to die."

Benvinda knew that the medicine had to be bought on the black market and she railed against the government, which "doesn't give a damn", but we took care of Antonio for two weeks. Benvinda and Patrick came to visit every day, to make sure the boy wasn't running off back to the streets. "Once you are well," she said to him, "you can do whatever you like. But you'd better know that I won't save you a second time," pinching his ear playfully.

Antonio recovered and returned to his friends on the streets and Benvinda disappeared. I knew, though, that she would turn up again at the right moment, curse the entire world—and save another lost soul.

TG

Fatima and Bela

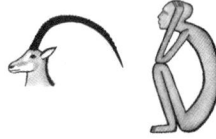

When I started my work in Angola, I felt very protected. I had three strong 'mothers', or rather, matrons: the Israeli ambassador, Tamar Golan, who helped me get there, received me warmly, and spread a safety net upon my arrival; the Minister of Fisheries and Environment, Fatima Jardim, with whom I worked in close cooperation and friendship; and the Norwegian ambassador, Bjorg Leite, who enthusiastically encouraged her government to employ me as a consultant as part of their support of the Angolan government. She offered her help, invaluable advice and companionship, throughout her tenure.

Two years later, over a period of only three months, Tamar left Angola, Bjorg's posting there was terminated, and Fatima was replaced by another minister and was 'out of the game'. I felt as if I had been orphaned.

Women in Angola occupy a major role in the country's day to day life, publicly and behind the scenes. They are the real power.

TR

The women labour in the fields, while the men are busy in their endless wars, killing and being killed. It is said that the number of women killed and maimed by the landmines scattered throughout the country equals that of the soldiers killed and injured in battle. Single-handedly, they raise their children with courage and awe-inspiring capacity. Women are the tenacious merchants who bring the sparse harvests of the fields to the small markets. Without them, malnutrition would be even more acute. How many countries in the world have six or seven women in their governments? Not only in traditional female jobs, such as education and society, but, for example as Minister of Petroleum, in a country where 80% of the income comes from exporting crude oil?

The former Minister of Fisheries and the Environment, my 'sister', Fatima Jardim, is a member of one of the 'fighter families', the family of the MPLA, the liberation movement, that the west coined Marxist-Communist, and fought fiercely against the enemy movement, Unita.

Fatima joined the liberation movement as a girl and, with the declaration of Angola's independence, she began filling political positions in the party, the parliament and the government. With a background like this she might even give the impression of a hardheaded Golda Meir, who had been referred to as the 'only real man in the Israeli government'. But Fatima is a beautiful woman, soft and feminine, a pleasure to spend time with, the kind of person who immediately makes you feel at home, even when she is receiving you in her spacious, elegant, marble lined office. Her velvety voice is low and captivating. The warmth emanating from her personality can melt any heart; but make no mistake, not only does Fatima work extremely hard and is in full control of everything she does, she also knows how to be very tough when the need arises.

Fishing is one of Angola's most important industries. Between the Benguela current in the south and the Guinea current in the north, fishing is very good, with Spain and Russia competing for fishing franchises. To help regulate the industry, Angola's small and under-equipped navy came under the command of Fatima, whose ministry funded most of its budget.

One of my tasks as ambassador consisted of preparing the visit to Angola of Israel's first military attaché. A non-resident attaché, based in the South African capital, Pretoria, he was responsible for about a dozen states in southern Africa. That made it impossible for him to travel to remote Angola for longer than three or four days at a time. Obviously, Israel was interested in exporting military equipment to all branches of the Angolan army. When I set about preparing one such prestigious and important visit, I assumed naively that his agenda would have to include meetings with the Defence Minister, the Chief of Staff and senior military commanders. I thought that he would be happy to exchange information with his colleagues, the military attachés of the US, Russia, Cuba, Britain, France and Brazil, all of which had security and strategic interests in Angola.

"Is Israel interested in exporting warships to Angola?" asked one of my African colleagues, who had been serving in the country for many years.

"Why do you ask?" I replied carefully.

"I just wanted to point out that if you really are interested, the navy commander is not the most effective person to approach. Your attaché should meet the Fisheries Minister. She's the one with the real power. Just a friendly tip."

I got it.

Our military attaché, a tall impressive man in his formal uniform was received by Angola's Minister for Fisheries and Environment. It was a meeting that proved useful to both sides. My friend, the African ambassador, had been quite right.

When I introduced Tamar Ron to Fatima at one of those women's evenings at my residence, I was sure they would find much in common. I hadn't imagined what a wonderful friendship would evolve from that meeting.

19

Only when we worked together did I learn to appreciate the real value of Fatima, the sharp and creative politician and professional, a marine biologist by education. Fatima was dedicated to promoting the issues and people for whom she had responsibility. She worked relentlessly, and frequently left her office at about midnight. Our business meetings were usually held in her office at night, after she had discharged her other commitments, or during long weekends on her farm, some distance from the city, in the company of her family.

Fatima had served for many years as the fisheries minister. She used her time in office to build up a team of professionals whose studies abroad were paid for by the ministry, which then offered them competitive conditions upon their return, to dissuade them from leaving for the private sector. Even today, the ministry still enjoys an exceptionally strong team of professional staff.

For a brief period, Fatima also served as the Environment Minister. During that time she promoted national awareness of environmental issues and nature conservation. Part of her policy was to support the activities of the young local environmental organizations. She also supported the first programme on national television, TPA, that was dedicated entirely to environmental issues. The great popularity of this programme was surprising, considering that at the time the country was submerged in a devastating armed conflict.

One of Fatima's most impressive talents was her ability to mix with everyone, from VIPs to the poorest fishermen and villagers. She was sincere and warm-hearted to all, including those people who other government ministers may not even notice. This attitude was demonstrated at a meeting of the environment ministers of southern Africa, held in Luanda, at her behest. Most of the region's environment ministers attended. Often, ministries send the directors of their ministries or the senior advisers to such events. However, this time they all arrived in person, and with the same declaration: "I had to change many important plans and commitments in order to get here, but I could not miss a meeting organized by Fatima Jardim."

At the end of the meeting Fatima invited all the ministers to lunch at the peninsula of Mussulo, the main recreational beach near Luanda, about twenty minutes away by boat. After the lunch the ministers were presented with T-shirts and caps with the ministry logo and the slogan: 'For a better life, preserve the environment'. The distinguished guests returned to Luanda, wearing their shirts and the caps.

On the short journey from the port to the car park, there were several fishermen in rags, trying to sell their meager catch. One of the fishermen recognized the minister, waved a hand covered in black oil and fish scales, and called: "Ministra, Ministra!"

The illustrious party deliberately ignored the calls, and everybody proceeded toward the cars. Fatima turned around, approached the fisherman and asked him what he wanted. "Ministra," he said, "I want such a cap." Fatima called one of her assistants over and told her to give the fisherman a t-shirt and a cap. The surprised assistant opened the bag with obvious discontent, and announced with a contorted face; "There are none left."

Without hesitation, the minister removed her own cap from her head and handed it to the fisherman. She asked him about his catch, wished him luck, and departed from him with a warm hug and a kiss on his cheek. Only then did she join her waiting guests.

TR

On the other side of the divide stood a relative of Fatima, one of the leaders of the rebel movement Unita. As a girl, Bela Malaquias (her full name was Florbela, which means 'fair flower') had been exquisite. Even through hard times in prison and in the guerrilla camps she managed to maintain a dignified mien. Bela's amazing voice had made her a successful newsreader and presenter on Radio Angola even before the declaration of independence.

Angola's history is steeped in tragic stories in which members of one family find themselves in conflict, not only against colonial rule, but also against each other as members of rival liberation movements. At the height of the war between the two movements, the pro-Soviet and pro-Cuban central government in Luanda conducted Soviet-style purgings in areas under its control, helped by independent Angola's new secret police, which had been trained by the East German Stasi. At the same time, Unita leader Jonas Savimbi cruelly set about murdering anyone suspected of opposing him. The result was that everyone killed everyone else in the name of national unity.

At the time of our first meeting in 1997, Bela was already tired of the trials of her life, but she was still impressive. She told me how it had all begun.

"Even before independence, I was sent to Lisbon, the colonial capital, to continue my academic studies. I began moving in Angolan student circles, out of which the future leaders would evolve on the long road to independence. Many of them were arrested and accused of insurgency by the mighty secret police of the dictator Antonio Salazar, the notorious PIDE."

Even then, during the struggle for independence, rifts and quarrels were rife among the underground movements. Bela fell in love with a brilliant young man, Eugenio Manuvakola, who was active in Unita. Her relative, Fatima, a leader in the rival group, MPLA, did not like this forbidden relationship. But each of the cousins married a man from the opposite camp. As the wife of Eugenio Manuvakola, one of the Unita movement's leaders, Bela did not relinquish her journalistic career and was now working as a senior newsreader on the rebel radio station, Radio Vorgan, which broadcast from deep in the bush. Anyone tuning in to this radio station from areas under government control risked being tried for treason. The most famous voice in the country became that of the enemy.

I met Bela in 2002, at a family gathering organized by Fatima, shortly after the peace accord was signed between MPLA and Unita. The event was held on a beautiful Saturday morning on the beach. The rebellious sparkle in Bela's eyes caught my attention and we started to chat. It was not long before she told me about her life as a member of Unita. "I was a sixteen-year-old girl when I entered the bush," she told me. "I lost my youth there. I came out of the bush a mature and toughened woman, the mother of four children, all born in the midst of a horrible war." She talked about her difficult life at the headquarters of Unita in Jamba. The women and the children suffered the most. "It is difficult to describe that awful place," she said. There were tears in her eyes. "It was a world without God."

She served the movement loyally and only returned to Luanda after the first peace accord in 1992. Then, after sixteen years of complete separation, she renewed contact with her beloved brother. He lived in the USA and like Fatima, was a member of the rival movement. Unita's spies discovered their relationship and suspected her of treason.

One day a messenger from Unita arrived at Bela's home. He informed her that she must accompany him on a short visit to one of the provinces, to help with Unita's public campaign. As a loyal member of her party she immediately agreed without question to undertake the task. Only when she realized that the flight was taking far too long did she suspect that something may be wrong. The plane landed in Unita's headquarters in Jamba. She was taken straight from the landing strip to a field trial, where she was convicted of treason and sentenced to imprisonment.

At first she was held under house arrest in Jamba. Several days later, one of Unita's messengers arrived and ordered her to get in his car. A number of armed Unita rebels were sitting there. She firmly refused to enter. She knew that if she did, she would not return alive. Eventually, she was tied up and dragged to a cell, where she was held in solitary confinement. As soon as her brother heard about her arrest, he informed international media channels and organizations, and started a campaign for her release.

"I owe my life to the international journalist organizations," she said.

"If it were not for their intervention, my life would have ended there in Jamba, as happened to so many others. Jonas Savimbi knew that it would be very bad publicity for him and Unita if the throat of a person well known to the international media was found cut."

She continued to be held with her father and sister for some time under house arrest in Jamba. A unit of armed rebels guarded the house, to ensure that they did not try to escape.

T R

In the meantime, her husband continued to climb the ladder of command in the rebel movement, until he was appointed secretary-general of Unita. Twice, peace agreements were signed between the two rival groups, brokered by international agencies. Twice, the agreements were not honoured and war broke out anew, each time with greater intensity. There was no end to the bloodshed.

The second agreement was signed in 1994 in the Zambian capital: the Lusaka Peace Agreement. This time it was brokered by the United Nations and representatives, while the superpowers witnessed the signing ceremony. Angolan President Eduardo dos Santos flew to Lusaka for the event and everyone waited for the arrival of Unita leader, Jonas Savimbi. But he never came. Instead, the movement's secretary-general, Eugenio Manuvakola, was sent to sign the treaty on behalf of Unita.

As he signed, Manuvakola knew he was signing his own death sentence. No one was more familiar than he with the omnipotent and exquisitely cruel leader of his movement. Nonetheless, he returned to the region under the control of his rebel movement where he was immediately arrested and accused of treason by the very man who had sent him to sign. He and his family were placed under house arrest.

The war was resumed with greater intensity and hundreds of thousands of people were killed. Thousands upon thousands became refugees and the UN was helpless. Only in 1997 did Manuvakola manage to escape mysteriously and make his way to Luanda with fifteen members of his family, including Bela and the children. She returned to broadcasting, this time for the national radio station.

T g

Three lady ambassadors

We were three: the Swedish ambassador Lena Sundh, Bjorg Leite the Norwegian and me, the Israeli. Israel's Foreign Office had been the first to dare dispatch a woman to war-torn Angola. Lena and Bjorg arrived sometime after me. Later on it became easier. Britain, the Ivory Coast and other governments no longer hesitated.

Lena is a big, blonde, beautiful woman, with warm, smiling eyes. She has about her a shyness and modesty which makes everyone feel immediately at ease in her company. From the very beginning of her tenure, she was never reluctant to invite members of the Angolan opposition to receptions at her home, alongside representatives of civil rights organizations, controversial clergymen and journalists who spent much of their time in police interrogation offices. Her receptions usually took place in the garden behind her house, with muted lighting and a relaxed atmosphere that dissolved the initial tension that was inevitable at a meeting between government members and those who opposed them.

At every meeting with the Angolan authorities it was always Lena who started discussions about sensitive issues. On one occasion it was the case of refugees in a remote camp who were not receiving food; another time the debate was over the demolition of buildings in a poor neighbourhood that had been handled too roughly. She would discuss these issues in a gentle and non-aggressive way until even her sharpest critics in the government had to admit that she was doing it because she really cared and not simply to butt the authorities.

Sweden enjoys a special status in Angola because it was the first Western state to take a stand alongside the MPLA against colonial rule. For years the government of Sweden had been sending food parcels to the Angolan freedom fighters in secret camps in neighbouring countries. When Angola won independence in 1975, the Swedes continued to grant their full support to the Marxist MPLA government in Luanda and its struggle against the Unita rebels. Over time, the freedom fighters became government ministers and important leaders, but they never forgot how, during Angola's long struggle for independence, Swedish emissaries had risked their lives to visit those far off hideouts.

Bjorg's blonde hair, in the meantime, had turned silver. She was always elegant. Her figure was youthful, her movements lithe and her blue-grey eyes and direct gaze scrutinized those of her counterparts as if announcing that she was not one to be fooled. Even before she had uttered a single word, her steel grey eyes put every man in his place, however important he may be in his own esteem. She aroused immediate respect, maybe even a touch of awe.

After all, Bjorg represented a country whose enormous oil reserves were greater than those of Angola. Norway is a world-class fishing superpower to be reckoned with. Moreover, Norway has always been one of the bigger contributors to the communist government in Angola, whether directly or via its welfare agencies, whose workers were dispersed throughout the country. Bjorg's country was one of the main financiers of the UN activities in Africa. She had no reservations about reminding the American ambassador that his country had supported the Unita rebels and that it was only in the 1990s that the USA had opened an embassy in Luanda.

We made a habit of meeting in the evenings at the end of a stressful day's work. We felt the need to discuss the terrible things that were happening around us, to exchange information and opinions, and to consider the next steps to be taken, individually, but also for the three of us together. News of a particularly vile massacre of civilians, a horrific mine explosion, or starvation in a remote refugee camp caused us to be restless. We were incapable of being nonchalant at the receptions that are part of a diplomat's life, though we were able to appreciate the value of such events. After all, it was at such occasions that we obtained information, exchanged views with cabinet ministers and settled important issues on behalf of our countries. We all wanted to take action on behalf of the innocent victims and were unable to make do with polite small talk. Often, we would leave the reception early and make for one of our homes to mull over what we had heard and to plan what we could do.

We asked ourselves what it was about women ambassadors that distinguished us from our male colleagues. Why did we become so emotionally involved?

Lena and Bjorg had been born and raised in the feminist tradition of their Scandinavian homelands. They were infused with the certainty that men and women were equal. With all our hearts we believed that one thing that differentiates men and women is our ability to identify with the suffering of others who are weaker than us. One word was common to us all—empathy.

Angola was a blood-soaked country, ruined and hurting. At the height of the civil war, during the 1970s and 1980s, about 50,000 Cuban soldiers and 10,000 Soviet so-called experts fought alongside the government forces. Against them stood the rebel Unita movement, backed by the well-oiled war machine of South Africa's Apartheid regime, together with the direct or indirect involvement of the West—the US, UK, France and Israel. The civil war in Angola was part of the war between the Eastern and Western blocs. Inspiration, funding, weapons supply, strategic command—all these came from external sources.

All this was due to the fact that Angola was blessed—or cursed—with immense natural resources and a vital strategic location on the way to South Africa. Everything in Angola could be counted in millions: landmines, civilian casualties, refugees, paraplegics and murderous weapons. The profit from the crude oil and diamond industries are counted in billions of dollars.

Much has been said and written about the human tragedy that was Angola. Donations arrived from the West for the refugees and IDPs, but it was cold self-interest that dictated which side in the conflict would receive the deadly weapons, the cost of which was many times that of humanitarian aid.

It would be unfair to say, though, that male ambassadors acted purely out of strategic motives, while we, the women, acted only out of humanitarian motives. I have already pointed out that Norway had important interests in Angola. Even Israel had such interests, if relatively modest, in finally recognizing the central government in Luanda in 1992. Obviously, we women took care of our own country's interests in a way that was no less devoted than that of our male colleagues. Moreover, and with all due respect to diplomacy, I have to admit that in an age of electronic communications, the importance of the ambassador is not as great as it once was. The foreign offices of most of the world's states aspire to carry out their policies by remote control rather than allowing their representatives in the field too much freedom of action. The ambassadors of the poorer countries, who are not equipped with state-of-the art communication systems and who often can't even pay their telephone bills, are the only ones who still enjoy free movement in the field.

In Angola, the ambassadors were even more restricted. When fighting broke out, most of the ambassadors received similar instructions from the military: that it was forbidden to leave the capital until the situation became clear. These instructions were even more stringent for the Americans. Whenever there were rumours about attacks or violent uprisings, the American Embassy would be closed for a day or two. This, of course, was intensified after September 11, 2001. There were those within the diplomatic corps who were happy to receive these restricting orders, which spared them the need to fly to dangerous locations in the Angolan military's ramshackle aircraft or those of international humanitarian organizations.

There were an alarming number of fatal air crashes in Angola. Exact information about the causes of such accidents usually arrived only a long while after the event, or not at all. In the meantime, horror stories were heard in Luanda about the number of casualties, the appalling delays in extending medical assistance and the types of missiles which brought down the aircraft. In most cases, the cause of the accident was simple: the aircraft were old and poorly maintained and access to the scene of the crash was very limited. Then there were the Soviet pilots, at times drunk on vodka, who flew these airborne death traps, Ilyushins and Antonovs whose airworthy certificates had long since expired.

The bitter truth is that it was impossible to rely on official information. Even though we were all full of respect for its stubborn stand against the rebels, the government in Angola never excelled at providing accurate reports. The government's methods of distributing information related directly to the days of colonial rule under the dictator Antonio Salazar in Portugal. It was completely compatible with the idea of the freedom of the press under the dictatorships of the Eastern Bloc. The voluntary foreign aid agencies and representatives of the churches were afraid to use the available communications means to report on military events. They did not want to be suspected of assisting the enemy. To them, the most important thing was to save civilians.

The only way to find out what really happened was to go out in person and look. Bjorg said in her usual decisive way that she needed to check for herself. "I can't rely on official reports. Moreover, we have people out there from the Norwegian voluntary associations and I have to go out to them."

When Lena heard that a lot of attacks had occurred in the Malange Province, she said that she had to go out to meet with 'her priests' and get a proper report. "There is no way we can allow such blatant violations of human rights!"

We all wanted to know what the clergymen were saying. Whether they were Angolan or foreign, they had been there, in the field, for many years. They knew what was really going on and they were reliable and enjoyed a certain degree of immunity. Except for a few years during which the revolutionary communist regime outlawed religion, usually referring to it in terms of Karl Marx's phrase, as the opium of the people, religion has always been an inseparable part of the Angolan way of life. It is worth noting that the first Catholic church in Africa was built as long ago as the 15th century in M'Banza Kongo.

Clerics and members of voluntary organizations agreed to conduct their conversations face-to-face only; and only with people they were sure they could trust. Lena and Bjorg were among the few really reliable people.

Another source of information, if unreliable, was the diamond merchants. In Luanda, we had heard some bloodcurdling stories from them about things that had presumably happened to them and what they had seen there. Whether it was to be believed or not was another matter.

When Lena and Bjorg set out on their tours of Angola, they would not make do with meeting local governors and senior officials or with the military command. They made their way straight to the miserable clinics in the poor quarters, to the half-demolished churches in the villages and to the neglected offices of the rural womens' associations. Only thus could they expose the tales of suffering and day-to-day struggle for survival of Angola's poor population—the real victims of the war—and achieve a general awareness of their needs. They were the first to help alleviate the suffering and others followed in their wake.

I envied them. Due to the special restrictions imposed on us as Israelis, I was frequently prevented from joining them. Sometimes I succeeded with the help of various UN agencies, who agreed to overlook the strict rules that forbade the bearing of weapons on humanitarian flights. They made it possible for me and my ever-present bodyguard to reach disaster areas deep in Angola. In-between such visits, I stepped up my activities in Luanda.

One day, a man in a wheelchair appeared at the embassy. He was accompanied by a woman who had lost one of her arms. Their arrival proved problematic. The building in which the embassy was located was not equipped to enable handicapped people easy access and because public transport was hardly available in Luanda, a truck driver had brought them as far as the entrance.

The young man (his name was Yves) apologised for arriving unannounced. "We come to you because we know that you will understand," he said. "We have no car of our own, nor a telephone line. You know, of course, what it's like to be handicapped in Angola.

"I want you to know that we haven't come to ask for money. We want only recognition and respect. We are human beings," he said.

The purpose of his visit, Yves said, was to get help to establish an association for handicapped people that would create awareness for their special situation.

"We don't want only crutches, prostheses and wheelchairs. We are not even asking for reparations. In our country the term 'disability benefits' is unheard of. We have come to ask your help in getting Angolan society to recognize us and to understand that even a man in a wheelchair can be a schoolteacher and that a one-armed woman can work in an office and set up a home."

He listed a few simple steps, such as the kind that are taken for granted in most of the world's developed countries. First on his list was that all future buildings should include wheelchair access; next, he demanded that handicapped people be allocated land for agricultural cultivation, in the same way as are all other army veterans; and that handicapped people be invited to participate in media debates, just like every other citizen of the state.

The young woman with him, Helena, recalled the mine blast in which she had lost her arm while she was out collecting firewood to prepare a meal for her family in a small, central Angolan village. She explained the reason for coming to the capital. "In the village," she said, "they treated me with pity. I felt I had become an insufferable burden on my impoverished family. I want to learn a trade, to be a part of society. I believe I can do it."

There was fire in their eyes and pride in their words. We started working together. The first function took place in the ambassador's residence. I invited colleagues whose minds and hearts were open, including, of course, my two sister ambassadors. We also invited the minister responsible for national rehabilitation, business people whose generosity I had experienced, and representatives of the local media. The guests were welcomed by a line of wheelchairs, crutches, white sticks for the blind and a group of people with sparkling eyes and smiling faces.

The handicapped people broke the ice. None of them asked for pity. They mingled easily with the other guests and exchanged pleasantries. Yves's speech was brief and ended with the request, "Please help us to restore our self-esteem. We are all people just like you, even if some of our limbs are missing."

From that evening, members of the country's handicapped community became local media heroes and results soon followed. The government granted the association a plot of fertile land near the capital and helped in its agricultural development, establishing a successful cooperative at which everyone employed was handicapped. The government passed a number of laws on behalf of the handicapped, but, in the end, most of them remained on paper.

Now and then, when foreign visitors arrived in Angola, especially those who were expected to make some donation to the people Angola, a visit was arranged for them to the Commune for the Disabled. Government officials would strut proudly around the place as though it were theirs. Yves smiled and said nothing. After all, it's the result that counts.

T G

CHAPTER SIX

Four sons

There is no greater honour in Angola, we felt, than to be called Mother. The mother is the anchor, the warmth, the home.

Even the toughest and most stone-hearted men, and there are many in Angola, will always keep a warm place in their hearts for their mothers.

Sometimes this obliging title is endowed upon a woman who is not the biological mother.

We were thus privileged.

João Bernardo

In Angola I derived more satisfaction from my maturity than from all the prestige and distinction afforded by the title of ambassador. Africa, it seems, is the last place in the world where advanced age is still considered an advantage. Here they still believe that the elderly must have experience and wisdom, and are worthy of respect. An Angolan mother enjoys a position of distinction long after her hair has turned white and her back is bent with age.

Even though I have no children of my own, in Angola I had many children, especially three who were like sons to me and a great source of pride. They were talented, intelligent, extraordinarily handsome and successful, each in his own way.

One of them addressed me by the French word for mother, Mère. The second called me the almost universal Mama, and the third chose the Portuguese version, Mai. In any language the word 'mother' has a wonderful ring to it.

My first son was Angola's Foreign Minister, João Bernardo Miranda. The second, Abel Chivukuvuku, was one of the leaders of the Unita rebel movement and the third, João de Matos, is Angola's former Chief of Staff.

The privilege of being called 'mother' did not come about in one day, but once we started referring to each other in terms of mother and son, we knew that the trust between us was complete and that it did not depend on skin colour, nationality or status.

When I arrived in Angola, João Bernardo Miranda, the first one to call me 'mother', was serving as Deputy Foreign Minister. João was relatively young, fluent in French, and had a modest manner and a charming smile. I decided that it would be easier to invite him on an official visit to Israel, than his superior, the minister, a veteran member of the ruling party who had a habit of constantly pointing out that Israel had supported the wrong side in the civil war. I knew that the minister was reaching the end of his career and that the president trusted the younger man.

Zvi Mazel, the Deputy Director for Africa in the Israeli Foreign Office at that time, organized the first visit to Israel of an Angolan cabinet minister— a deputy minister, as it happened—for an official state visit in every sense of the word. The ceremony included a red carpet at the airport and a motorcycle cavalcade racing in front of the official car. The agenda included many important items, but João made it quite clear that he wanted to pay a visit to the old city of Jerusalem and to walk up the Via Dolorosa.

He showed me a battered prayer book and told me that his mother would not believe him when he said that he was going to Israel and that he would be visiting Jerusalem.

"She said Jerusalem is in heaven. She entrusted me with her prayer book and I promised her that I would pray for her wherever she asked me to."

Miranda didn't have a camera, but his devoted bureau chief, who accompanied him on his journey to the Holy Land, was fully equipped. On the last day of his brief visit, he took his mother's copy of the New Testament, went to all the holy places, opened the book, read out of it and said to the video camera: "You see, mother, here is where it all happened. Here, on earth, in the Holy Land, not in heaven."

Miranda returned to Angola and became one of the most devoted friends Israel has ever had. Many believed that it was because of his successful meetings with President Ezer Weizmann, Prime Minister Shimon Peres and Foreign Minister Ehud Barak. I knew that it was because of his mother who had said to him: "My son, God, to whom I pray daily, brought you to heaven and to Jerusalem on earth. You brought me the holy water. Now I can die and, beside me in my casket, you can place the olive wood crucifix that the lady ambassador sent me."

Even when her son was appointed to a senior government position, became a member of the ruling party's central committee and was considered a force to be reckoned with in the country, Miranda's mother refused to move to the big city. She had no time for a government car, servants, or bodyguards. All she wanted was to remain in the small house in which she had always lived, close to her husband's grave.

A few months later, Miranda called me from Harare, the capital of neighbouring Zimbabwe. He was visiting Zimbabwean President Robert Mugabe and his aides dared not interrupt his meeting. When he came out, they told him that there had been a call from Luanda to say that his mother was in a serious condition and that her life was in danger. He decided to set out immediately for home. Fortunately the president placed his private jet at Miranda's disposal. The young minister was on the verge of tears.

I quickly called my colleague, US Ambassador Joe Sullivan, behind whose polished diplomatic façade hid a man who was sensitive and attentive. It was his first mission in Africa and he found it hard, at first, to get used to the unique kind of interpersonal relations common on the continent. But this time, he understood the gravity of the situation immediately. He contacted South Africa and the rescue services of the US Embassy in Luanda. Within minutes, arrangements were made to hospitalize Miranda's mother in Pretoria. We set out together in our car to Miranda's private residence, where they were already familiar with the Israeli embassy's official car and our bodyguards. The gate opened immediately. Miranda's wife ran out toward me, weeping. No explanations were necessary. Miranda's mother would not make it to South Africa. It was too late.

Miranda arrived a few minutes later. He burst into tears and led us to his office. We sat on either side of him and held his hands.

"She was not just a mother," he said. "I owe her my life. I was a 13-year-old boy. My father, who opposed the oppressive Portuguese colonial rule, ran away from home and joined the MPLA rebels. We didn't know where he was or if he was even alive. We lived off the land.

"One morning I heard a strange sound from up above. I ran out of the hut to see what it was. I had never seen a plane before and it was very impressive. But mother ... she just ran to me and threw me down on the ground, under a giant tree trunk. She lay on top of me, covering my body with her own. A few steps away, something exploded with a horrible noise. It was a Portuguese fighter aircraft and the first such explosion I had experienced in my life. When everything was quiet, my mother stood up, covered in dust, and wiped away the blood from a few scratches. My mother had saved my life."

It was the first time I saw tears in João Bernardo Miranda's eyes. Afterwards the house filled up with more and more Angolan mourners. We left. On our way out we were followed by the kind eyes of those present, embracing us to their hearts.

João's mother was buried in the village, next to her husband, who had not lived to see his son follow in his footsteps. In her casket, they placed the olivewood crucifix from Jerusalem.

Ever since, before the whole world, João Bernardo Miranda has called me Mère.

TG

Abel

Abel Chivukuvuku was born with a silver spoon in his mouth. His aristocratic family belongs to the Umbundu tribe which inhabits the fertile highlands of central Angola. Since early childhood, he has stood out for his exceptional beauty and intelligence; a real prince.

The Umbundu people have been known since the 16th century for their noble stand against the Portuguese invaders of Angola. Even after surrendering to the colonial conqueror, this tribe maintained its national pride and, against all odds, rose up whenever harsh new laws were imposed on them. The Umbundu is the largest tribe in Angola and the Portuguese were particularly heavy-handed with them.

Throughout the struggle for independence in Angola, which began in the 1960s, the Portuguese fought against three guerrilla groups, divided not only by ideology, but also on an ethnic basis. Unita is the movement of the Umbundu tribe.

In keeping with a scion of a noble family, it was only natural for the young Abel to join the rebel movement. After completing his basic training, he demanded to be allowed to join the fighters; but his leader, Jonas Savimbi, had other plans for him and appointed him as foreign minister in the shadow government. It would have been hard to choose a better representative than this handsome, impeccably educated prince.

The first multiparty general elections took place in Angola in September, 1992, after the international community and the United Nations imposed a treaty on the warring sides. Savimbi absented himself from the signing ceremony. Unfortunately, many in the international community chose to ignore this provocative act, preferring to move on with the process until the general elections.

Jonas Savimbi sent the young Abel Chivukuvuku to Luanda as part of his movement's negotiating team. Within a short time, he managed to endear himself to many in Luanda. Even his rivals in MPLA were obliged to admit that he was a moderate, tolerant and fair negotiator. The international media were eager to interview the young man who came across so perfectly on screen and had such a good command of English, French and Portuguese.

Savimbi finally arrived in Luanda from his headquarters in the bush in time for the first round of elections. He was surrounded by a large number of armed bodyguards. In truth, Savimbi did not really appreciate the fact that his handsome young spokesman was taking centre stage. He said nothing, but young Abel was too naïve to read the writing on the wall.

The results of the first round of elections came as a surprise to many. Savimbi, the cruel and charismatic warlord, lost to his long-standing rival, José Eduardo dos Santos, the enigmatic, introverted, incumbent president. Savimbi was not about to concede to this stinging defeat and decided to return to war. Accompanied by two or three of his closest associates and a few devoted warriors from his elite fighting unit, he made a clandestine retreat from Luanda.

The civil war flared up again. This time it was not only in the far-off bush, but in the very heart of the capital. Inhabitants of Luanda organized themselves and took up arms. They formed themselves into a bloodthirsty militia and set out in search of Unita rebels.

Within a few days thousands of people had been slaughtered, their bodies left strewn about in the streets. Savimbi had not bothered to inform the senior members of his movement that he was leaving Luanda and that he was returning to battle. When they finally realized that they had been left behind by their leader, they tried to escape from the city to join him. Many of them were captured and killed.

Abel Chivukuvuku and another senior party official earmarked to head the Unita parliamentary (faction) group were among those attempting a getaway. They managed to locate a car and a reliable driver from their clan and started manoevring around the city's side streets. They were stopped and identified at one of the junctions and the militia opened fire.

The parliamentary leader died at once. With an injured leg, Abel got away from the junction under cover of darkness. The shots rang out from all directions. He did not have much choice. He limped up the stairs of a nearby apartment block and knocked on one of the doors, not knowing if a friend or an enemy would open it. The householders identified the injured young man. Although they were from 'the other side', they took him in and administered first aid. Several days later, when he knew that the war was back on in full force, he said to them, "Enough. You've put yourselves in enough danger. It's time to hand me over to the authorities."

Abel Chivukuvuku became the government's most famous prisoner. After he had recovered and was discharged from hospital, he stayed on in Luanda, though his status was obscure. Was he a prisoner? A rebel? Or, perhaps the way of liaison between the rebels and the government?

When I took up my position in Luanda, I knew that I must avoid all contact with Unita. For several years Israel had maintained unofficial ties with the rebel movement. Diamonds, like arms and money, have no smell. Even if there had never been any official recognition of these ties, they were very harmful to Israel's position in Luanda and it is no coincidence that it was only in 1992 that Israel and Angola recognized each other. The embassy in Luanda was inaugurated only in 1995.

When I landed in Angola as Israel's first ambassador, I was aware that the government was scrutinizing my every move and I had no intention of arousing suspicions. I had heard of Abel and of Isaias Samakuva, Unita's senior representative in the renewed peace talks. I had seen them from afar at diplomatic functions, but it was my colleague, the then American ambassador, Donald Steinberg, who introduced us officially at a reception in his residence. Without hesitation they said immediately: "You are evading us. Are you ostracizing us?" I admitted that this was indeed the case.

They called the following day and asked for an audience to be arranged at the embassy. I hesitated, but agreed. After all, Angola was in the middle of a renewed peace process, under the auspices of the international community. Under such circumstances, it is important to talk to all sides in the conflict. I was surprised by the enormous sympathy that Abel and Isaias enjoyed in diplomatic circles and among the various United Nations representatives, especially considering their past experience with Unita.

I feared for them. They were too committed to the peace process, too moderate and too enlightened. I had no faith in Savimbi, their suspicious and vengeful leader. I feared he would be unable to stomach the sight of his representatives talking with world leaders at diplomatic cocktail parties, while he, the supreme leader, was somewhere far off in the bush.

He was located in the middle of the forest, watching and listening—with some difficulty—to his representatives over the satellite communications. While they were holding their whiskey glasses, Savimbi was grasping his faithful Kalashnikov.

We met again one evening at a reception at the American ambassador's. The following day, it was announced that the Unita representatives at the UN negotiating committee would be leaving the capital to the province to supervise the disarming of a guerrilla camp. In accordance with protocol, representatives of the conflicting sides had arrived in a UN plane accompanied by diplomats from the American, Russian and Portuguese troika, who were there to ensure that the agreement was observed to the letter. UN soldiers in blue berets guarded them all.

During that time, after Unita had suffered a series of military defeats, Jonas Savimbi had no choice but to agree to lay down arms.

"Isaias," I said, "I don't think you should go tomorrow. I have a bad feeling. Something could go wrong. You are taking it too fast."

To Abel I said: "You go, Abel. I'm not worried about you. You have luck on your side."

Patiently, Isaias explained that he was the one who had to go. The UN was pressing for swift implementation of all the clauses calling for the collection of weapons. Savimbi had agreed to it, though from afar and not in writing.

Abel said he was offended that I thought that he was in no danger.

At dawn, the white UN plane took off for the Malange province. The blue berets were deployed in the field and the team of international supervisors moved forward slowly. Isaias Samakuva walked before them. He was supposed to talk to the soldiers in their own language on behalf of the organization to which they all belonged. UN television cameras and the local media teams recorded the historical moment.

It all happened very quickly. Someone threw a stone. Others started shouting: "Samakuva the traitor." Shots were fired and UN troops were running around, unable to decide who to defend first, the diplomats, representatives of the troika, or Samakuva. Blood flowed from his brow and the UN soldiers regained their composure. They pushed him into one of the army barracks and stopped the bleeding from his wound, which wasn't serious. Within a few minutes all was quiet.

The UN plane returned to Luanda. That evening, everyone watched it all on television, including Samakuva with his head in a bandage. A couple of days later, Abel and Isaias appeared at my residence. "You were right. How did you know to warn Isaias? You have the mysterious insight of a mother looking out for her offspring."

The telephone rang a few mornings later. A strange voice—I don't know whose—said an attempt had been made on Abel's life at the entrance to his home.

Abel wasn't hurt, but I left my office and had my driver take me straight to Abel's home. We drove in an embassy car flying the Israeli flag, which got us through police roadblocks quickly.

Police and soldiers surrounded the house. Inside, we found the family congregated in a back room. It turned out that Abel himself had not even been in the car that was attacked. His wife had gone out with the two small children on the way to the kindergarten. An anonymous assailant shot at them at the entrance to the house. Two shots hit the car, but no one was hurt.

I took Abel's wife and children and brought them to my own residence where they spent the day, wrapped in our love. Needless to say, the assailants have not been caught to this day.

In retrospect, I know that my behaviour had not been exactly ambassadorial. Nevertheless, from that day on, Abel and his wife called me Mama. The children referred to me as 'Meme', grandmother.

TG

João

I met my third 'son' on one of Angola's battlefields. His name is João Baptista de Matos. He is the highly respected former chief of staff of the FAA, Angola's national army, and was a hero in the war against Unita. On the day we met, the entire diplomatic corps had been flown to the army's main base in Catumbela in the Benguela province. It was seen as an especially gracious gesture by the army, whose commanders had always preferred to keep all information about their activity to themselves. De Matos maintained a stubborn silence and honoured only a few of us with a word or two. There were even those who joked that it was easier to meet the president than to arrange an interview with his Chief of Staff.

Such exaggerated secrecy was part of the Soviet heritage and, indeed, it was the Soviet Union which had trained and equipped the Angolan army since independence. Earlier, the Soviet Union had also supported the underground MPLA movement in the struggle against Portuguese colonial rule. The veil of secrecy turned attempts to obtain reliable information on the military situation into one of the main activities of the diplomatic community in Angola.

The Cubans, Angola's long-time allies, spoke to the Russians only. The Americans were new in the region and they were met with suspicion. The Europeans tended to spread unreliable rumours and were generally kept out of the picture. The African ambassadors knew a little more, but they, too, were told only what the Angolans wanted them to know. The local media released only what the government would allow them, whether it was true or not. Foreign journalists were more often than not refused entry into the country. In any case, no one could reach the battle zone. The roads and the bridges had been destroyed and civilian airports had been almost completely shut down. Although the UN owned a few ancient aircraft, painted in a sparkling white, they too were allowed to take off only with permission from the military and then only from an air force base near the international airport.

We had all heard about mysterious crashes of UN aircraft way off in the centre of the country. The government blamed Unita for firing surface-to-air missiles, while Unita accused the government of trying to get aerial photos of its military bases, and the UN of cooperating with its enemies.

A bloody war raged in this huge country and no one could say for sure which side was winning, the very intelligence sought by our governments. We were, therefore, very happy to receive a rare invitation to visit the most important air force installation of the Angolan army.

The top brass in the military welcomed us warmly at a spotlessly clean camp. Military attachés examined the aircraft parked on the tarmac and the military equipment deposited alongside the runways as though it was a parade. And then the Chief of Staff made an appearance in his impeccable uniform, wearing a small moustache. He moved like a panther and had a penetrating gaze. He summoned us into the command room, where maps had been fixed to a huge board. De Matos delivered his lecture with a thin baton in hand, explaining the whereabouts of the enemy and the way in which the army had succeeded in closing in on them. We all realized that we would not have been privy to such a presentation had the Angolan army not truly been in the lead.

"Next to the runway, we have prepared an exhibition of enemy weapons that fell into our hands during recent battles," said the Chief of Staff and added with a smile, "I am sure that some of those present here will find equipment made in their countries ..."

Some of my colleagues visibly paled. The booty on display included weapons and equipment manufactured in the Western states that were helping Jonas Savimbi. This was typical of the way the chief of staff exposed the violators of sanctions without actually naming names. On the runway, there were also two well-used fighter aircraft, freshly painted in the colours of the Angolan air force. The planes were produced in Eastern Europe and their purchase had been based on Israeli counsel. Before we took off on our way back to Luanda, the Chief of Staff pulled me aside and thanked me. "I appreciate what your people are doing here. I am especially thankful for the fact that absolute discretion is maintained. I think we can now meet officially in my office at GHQ in the capital."

During our first visits, we spoke through an interpreter. My Portuguese was still very basic and, for the sake of accuracy, I preferred French. The interpreter did a terrible job. I noticed that de Matos had an excellent command of French, but that he enjoyed watching the official interpreter perspire and fidget with discomfort.

Not many African military commanders have gained international recognition. Fewer still advance to a position in the UN's Peace Forces, but when such an appointment is made, the blue beret places them beyond suspicion in their own countries where even the appearance of an appetite for power could spell trouble. Service in the United Nations Peace Forces is considered the most respectable and secure way out for an African officer.

Even in Angola, where no coup had been attempted, rumours were rife and, as in the way of rumours, it was hard to discern who or what was behind them and how much truth was in them. One rumour held that the Russians, who had helped build the war machine in Angola, wanted to crown the Chief of Staff as president. Others claimed with great confidence that, in fact, it was the Americans who identified him as a rising force and that it was they who were in a conspiracy against the president, who had already celebrated two jubilees in office. Another rumour said that the army had become disillusioned with the ruling system and that it was owed a debt for its victory in battle and deserved to be handed the regime.

De Matos ignored the rumours, though the rumours did not ignore him. At that time he was deeply involved in a dispute with the president over an important security issue. The two had worked together for many years and, although they had not developed a personal friendship, they respected and trusted each other.

President Eduardo dos Santos is an introverted, rather taciturn man. He is not one of those presidents who draws the masses behind him with fiery, demagogic oratory. His power lies in his inner strength, his talent is for profound thought. He is rather like a chess player planning his next move and anticipating those of his rivals before they have even touched a piece on the board. He never raises his voice, never demonstrates anger, but he remembers everything forever.

The Chief of Staff, too, is one of those players who knows how to plan their moves. Supplication is alien to him and, once he is certain of the need for a move, he does not hesitate. This time he was sure he was right and he waited for the president's reaction.

Several weeks passed during which the Chief of Staff did not appear on state television with the president in the usual ceremonial way before or after important military campaigns. That was significant to those of us who had learnt to read the signs in this secretive country.

Some of those people referred to by the media as 'senior observers' had already noticed the omission, which might have been the origin of the latest wave of rumours coursing through the political and diplomatic establishment in Luanda. At our next meeting I told the Chief of Staff that it could not go on. He knew what I meant without asking.

"I am waiting for his answer," he said.

That led to an intense conversation about justice, power and government. It was not enough to have justice on his side, I told him. He was not living in an empty space. Whether we liked it or not, this world was made up of ups and downs. The most important consideration was what was best for Angola, and with that in mind it was up to him to make the first move.

De Matos asked for an audience with the president and he was received immediately. Later, on the television news we saw them shaking hands and, for a while, the rumours dissipated. In any event, de Matos had never considered toppling the regime, either by force, or through a general election. He wanted to learn and to broaden his horizons. Not long afterwards, the president relieved him of his military duties.

I eased his transition from being the most highly praised general on the African continent to becoming the top student in a prestigious institute of higher learning in London. We took our leave at an intimate dinner party in the company of the ambassadors of the USA, UK and Israel. The Russian envoy was not present.

Shortly after the meeting between the president and the Chief of Staff, de Matos' aide-de-camp arrived at the Israeli embassy with a buff envelope in his hand. The Chief of Staff had invited me to dinner at his private residence. Such an honour, I knew, was extended to very few people.

A pampered Siamese cat met me at the gate. From the interior of the residence came the strains of classical music. What a contrast between the introverted army man I had known and the gracious gentleman who now welcomed me to his home.

This time, de Matos spoke only in Portuguese. "You've been in Angola long enough and our official language is Portuguese. It's about time we spoke in the local language. You are already one of us."

He pointed at a staircase leading upstairs. It was a little awkward, but I went up with him to the bedroom. Next to the bed, there was an old black and white photograph.

"I wanted you to know my mother," he said. "She died when I was fourteen. She is the most important person in my life. She taught me determination and the importance of sticking to my objective. She couldn't read or write but she had plenty of genuine wisdom—the wisdom of life. We were poor and the soil in our village was very infertile. Mother told me that only education could save poor people like us. She told me that I could get an education at the church school or in the army. 'What you have in your head, my dear son, no one can take away,' she said. "And always stand with your back straight".

The blurred photograph—there was only the one—showed a deeply wrinkled face, white hair and piercing eyes, gazing out fearlessly. The eyes her son had inherited. João's father tried to raise his five children on his own after his wife's death. Life was harsh and, in the end, he married a second wife, with whom he was able to share the burden. The boy, João, left home a few days after the arrival of his father's new wife. He had never been fond of the white priests and nuns and he joined the army.

That evening I became acquainted with João Baptista de Matos the man. We both knew that from that day on we were committed to complete loyalty and honesty toward each other. In an African ceremony, we then carved an irreversible covenant. Once again, I had come to know an African mother who had the unwavering love of her sons and daughters. I never believed that the day would come when this tough military commander would call me 'Mai', the Portuguese word for mother.

79

Abias

"Tamar!" Abias sounded excited. "You are the first person I call. Congratulations. You are a grandmother. I have a son." This was how I was honoured not only with the title 'mother', but now even "grandmother".

My friendship with Abias Huongo, a very special young man, began during my first visit to Angola. Any mother would be proud of such a son. He was one of the founders of the local environmental youth organizations. Finding these NGOs in Angola was one of the most exciting surprises for me. They convinced me that it is possible to protect the environment and the biological diversity of Angola, despite all the so-called objective evidence that it was merely a dream.

Many people, Angolans and foreigners alike, reacted cynically. "What?" they would say. "Are all the problems here solved already? Is there no more poverty? No war? No corruption? No street children, unemployment or misery? Is it nature conservation that matters now?"

I have no doubt that the protection of Angola's special natural treasures and rich biological diversity is the key to a better future for its citizens. It was difficult to persuade sceptics who viewed Angola as no more than a cradle of human disasters and who, at best, were occupied only with relieving immediate suffering and, at worst, were out for a quick profit without a care about the destruction that they left behind.

It was very easy to fall into despair. More than once I wanted to leave it all and go home, especially after an encounter with selfish officials who were responsible for protecting the environment, but were only interested in their own promotion, salaries, foreign travel and internal power struggles. There were only a few of them, thankfully, but they created a bleak atmosphere that adversely affected those who were committed to their work.

No less depressing were the countless unsuccessful attempts to mobilize financial support for our work from international bodies. Time and time again

I had knocked on the doors and found myself in front of impenetrable walls. Foreign companies that gain a great fortune from Angola's natural resources, while damaging the environment, do not rush to open their purses to contribute to the country's environmental protection. Even international organizations and countries that genuinely wanted to help Angola were unwilling to direct resources at environmental issues, which they gave a low priority during a time of armed conflict.

Getting to know the young and determined volunteers of the local environmental organizations was a breath of fresh air and a balm to the soul.

After every meeting with them I felt guilty and ashamed of my own defeatist thoughts. They renewed my strength to carry on and to believe that, together, we could succeed. I knew that despite all the ills in Angola, within and without, as long as there was such a dedicated, loyal, wise and determined youth here, there had to be hope for a better future.

The organizations were founded by young volunteers for whom environmental issues and nature conservation were matters close to the heart. They spent days and nights developing special environmental education programmes and went from school to school in Luanda to spread the word. They established excellent working relations with all the media channels and broadcast their message through specialist television and radio programmes and through newspaper features.

They were not spoiled kids, looking for some arbitrary new interest to keep themselves occupied. Many of them had come from the musseques, the poverty stricken quarters of Luanda, and were themselves struggling to survive. And yet, they dedicated every free minute to their passion. They struggled hard to find financial support for their work, and they collected it one kwanza at a time. Here they got a modest contribution from the Swedish embassy for one of their educational activities, and there they received support from a Portuguese organization to set up and run their tiny office.

Abias was elected the president of the leading environmental organization, Juventude Ecologica Angolana, JEA (Ecological Youth of Angola). With uncompromising commitment, a creative mind, exceptional communication skills, a good deal of nerve and a lot of charisma, he and his colleagues had succeeded in turning JEA into a prominent national environmental organization. Through JEA's initiative, articles on endangered species were published in every newspaper and journal programmes about the danger of uncontrolled logging and climate change were broadcast on every radio station. The school children in their multitudes entered the Environmental Olympics, an environmental quiz, which had also received ample media coverage. They held demonstrations and marches to raise public awareness of key environmental issues.

All that during a period when the country was ravaged by civil war.

From time to time, a story about the importance of saving the sea turtles or the tropical forest even found its way into the daily news edition of what was then the only national television channel. The daily newscast was usually dedicated to issues of the highest importance, such as the festive opening of seminars and workshops on a variety of subjects, ceremonies for the laying of cornerstones, or the inaugurations of beautiful clinics, devoid of any medical equipment, or of new classrooms in half-built schools. Sometimes, several classrooms in the same school were honoured each with their own inauguration ceremony, to give adequate media coverage to all of the deserving senior officials. If there was an excess of VIPs who needed honouring, it was always possible to find something else to open or inaugurate. The newscasts during the war were full of ribbon-cutting and ceremonial speeches, in front of tired-looking audiences. Obtaining news coverage for environmental issues was a real achievement. More than once it was a direct result of Abias's personal efforts and the contacts that he had meticulously nurtured in the corridors of the national television station.

To encourage the youth of Luanda to join up as volunteers, JEA recruited the 'Misses', Angola's beauty queens, dating from the late 1990s. Abias had excelled at this. Almost every year he convinced the winner to join up. Whenever I met him he was accompanied by yet another amazingly gorgeous girl, who gazed at him in admiration. He would present them with a flourish. "This is Miss Luanda (or Benguela, or Bengo, or some or other province). She has just joined our team of ambassadors." The popular pageants had been transformed into a platform for impassioned speeches by beautiful young women about the dangers of desertification, climate change and the illegal hunting and trade of wildlife. Abias's appearance is rather conspicuous, with his characteristic flamboyant and bizzare taste in clothes. He tends to choose a combination of bright colours that dazzle the eyes, with preference to those that also cause a slight nausea, but his special charm is captivating and he uses it for the service of nature and the environment.

I knew that he lived in poverty, in a part of a small room which he rented at the top of a rickety staircase in a semi-derelict building. There was no doubt that if he had devoted his great energies to his own purposes, he would have improved his financial situation considerably. But he chose otherwise. As the years passed and Abias's youth started to slip away, I knew that he regretted not being financially stable enough to get married and support a family. Still, nature conservation was more important to him.

My great love story with Abias and his friends started when I first taught a series of courses on biodiversity conservation at the Ministry of Fisheries and Environment. The courses were intended for the ministry's staff, but very few officials attended the first day and even fewer the second day. On the third day only two had arrived and they, too, disappeared soon enough. But at the party to celebrate the end of the course, a great many had arrived, some of whom I had never seen during the course. Yet, the lecture hall was packed out every morning, during the two months of the course. The youth members of the organizations were always there to absorb every word about the subject that was so close to their hearts.

Since then, a special relationship developed between us. We shared the same goals: promoting nature conservation in Angola and raising awareness of its importance, and we collaborated in achieving those goals.

Whenever I wanted to give up and leave, Abias would call me for a pep talk. "We continue to struggle," he would say, "despite all the difficulties, and with so much personal sacrifice. And you, you want to leave? After all, you are not subjected to the same pressures that we, as Angolan citizens, have to face on a daily basis. If you do not want to continue, where does that leave us?"

He was right, of course, and so I stayed, for a year, then another year, and another. Once Juventude Ecologica Angolana had established a strong foundation in Luanda and had several hundred members, they started to extend their activities to the provinces. Abias and his colleagues used every possible opportunity to join the UN flights and those of the aid organizations to get to the remote provinces. There they met the local youth, brought them printed material and education kits and helped them to establish local branches.

One day I was invited to an interview at the local radio station in Bengo, the province encircling Luanda. I asked Abias to join me and, as always, he agreed. During the interview I noticed out the corner of my eye that Abias was deep in conversation with one of the programme producers, an impressively good-looking girl, like all his misses. About an hour later, after the interview, I discovered that Abias had persuaded her to establish a new provincial environmental organization in Bengo, and that she should add a permanent daily programme on environmental issues during the station's morning schedule.

When I was asked to recommend an Angolan candidate for the UN Environmental Programme's special award for world-leading environmental activists, UNEP Global 500, I could not think of a more worthy candidate than JEA, headed by Abias. It was the first time that anyone from Angola had received such a prestigious international environmental award. The local media covered the story enthusiastically, and the organization's representatives were invited to a special meeting with the president, who praised them, and thanked them for the honour that they had brought to their country.

Abias went to China with one of his colleagues to receive the award. The video of the ceremony was broadcast in Angola later. As appropriate at such an important formal event, we saw Abias wearing a suit, but underneath, you could just glimpse a glossy shirt in psychedelic colours. It is perhaps better not to dwell on the interesting tie that he chose to go with it. I was glad to see that he remained our same colourful Abias.

When Abias and his friend returned with the UNEP certificate, it was clear to all that JEA now had a leading role in promoting environmental issues in Angola. Abias himself had become a well-known public figure. He was invited to formal events throughout the country and to international conferences. But the publicity and success did not change him. On the contrary, he used them for one goal only, to promote the protection of the environment and nature conservation. He now felt more confident in expressing his views publicly, and even to openly criticize the government's actions (or lack of them), in environmental affairs, something which required special courage.

JEA's success contributed to the popularity of all of the environmental organizations in Angola. Abias made a point of representing them at every event and during media coverage. He knew that the greater the public recognition, the closer they would all be to achieving their common objectives. From a marginal group of teenagers involved in education, whom nobody took too seriously, they turned into a real force for environmental good and for bringing these issues onto the national agenda. It was no longer possible to ignore them.

One of the highlights was Abias's memorable presentation at the World Parks Congress in South Africa. Many notable professionals in their fields attend this prestigious congress, which is convened once every ten years by the World Conservation Union (IUCN). The moderator of one of the discussion groups had invited Abias to lecture about the budget shortfalls and requirements for the rehabilitation and management of the national parks and nature reserves in Angola. Abias studied the subject thoroughly and collected valuable information and documents from various government departments and other sources, even some from as far back as the colonial era. Slowly but surely he prepared and assembled his first presentation for an international event of this sort. He was the first Angolan to give a presentation at the World Parks Congress. He was given the option of delivering his speech in Portuguese, with the services of an interpreter. However, although his self-taught English was somewhat rough, he chose to speak in English to maintain contact with his audience, even if it meant there would be some inaccuracies in his delivery.

When it was time for his presentation he seemed terrified and he looked ready to run away. The hall was full with standing room only. I followed him in, worrying about the grey tinge to his face. I was afraid that he was going to faint. His knees were shaking and his lips were trembling. But as soon as he started the presentation, he was magically transformed. He stood there confident, controlled the presentation skillfully, and detailed in great clarity, in his special English and within the allocated time, the problems facing the protected areas in Angola and the investment required for their rehabilitation. He was applauded and I felt so proud of him.

"Before I conclude", he said', I want to thank the expert that invited me, the people that helped me collect information, and … I also have a mother here, in the hall."

ooo

Despite discontent among some of her ministry's senior officials, who viewed the environmental organizations as a nuisance, the Minister of Fisheries and Environment, Fatima Jardim, saw them as real and valued partners. She understood the importance of their public and educational actions and appreciated their commitment and willingness to volunteer. She made a point of allocating resources to support their activities. Without this assistance, most of the organizations would probably have collapsed financially.

After they had received the UNEP award, the minister summoned Abias and some of his colleagues to a meeting at her office. She told them many new organizations were emerging, almost daily, following the award. "The ministry cannot support them all, but we cannot discriminate between them either. There is only one solution. You must accept the initiative to establish one network association for all of the environmental organizations in Angola. The ministry will maintain contact only with this umbrella association, and you must resolve all the internal issues among you within this framework."

This is how Rede Maiombe—Maiombe Network—an umbrella association of the environmental organizations came to be, an idea that was first raised in the late 1990s. Abias was elected democratically, and almost unanimously, as the president of Maiombe Network. The ministry's support was increased, and the minister requested that the UNDP project of support for environmental promotion and biodiversity conservation in Angola include a modest budget to help with the operation of Rede Maiombe. This budget was used to acquire basic equipment for the establishment of an office, and to finance several of the educational activities, mainly in the remote provinces.

Shortly after the UNDP project was launched, the Ministry of Fisheries and Environment was closed down, and replaced by the new Ministry of Urban Affairs and Environment, with a significantly reduced budget. Maiombe Network and its member organizations were the first to suffer from the budget cuts. But by then they were able to continue with their work through the assistance they now received from UNDP and other sources.

Abias asked me to meet him. He looked distressed.

"So many years I dedicate myself to nature conservation," he said, "and I do not take care of my own livelihood. I am not so young any more. I will never be able to have a family, if I do not start to work for my living. I cannot continue to work so hard without any income. I must find a real job. I do not want to neglect my activities for the environment, but I think that I have to start working in a bank."

It was the first time that I had noted signs of defeat in Abias's voice. It was also the first time that he had asked for my assistance, not for nature and the environment, but for himself. I knew that I had to find a way to help.

About a month after our conversation, two senior representatives of an international environmental organization, Natural Heritage Institute, arrived in Angola. They had won a tender to establish an extensive environmental and social project in several neighbouring countries, and were looking for a local project coordinator. It was the opportunity that I was waiting for. I arranged a meeting for them with Abias, and they were obviously very impressed. There and then they decided to employ him as the local representative and Abias received an international contract and a salary in a foreign currency.

Meanwhile, the situation at the new Ministry of Urban Affairs and Environment had deteriorated. Several officials at the ministry, whose main aim seemed to be to obstruct others who were committed to their work felt that they had found a new opportunity to achieve their ends. To promote their own interests, they were conducting a slander campaign, using anonymous letters. Dedicated ministry personnel, who fulfilled their duties to the best of their ability, were now living in constant fear of losing their jobs. No one knew what was being said about them behind closed doors or what was written about them in obscure letters. They could not tell who would believe the lies or whether they would be given the opportunity to defend themselves. With an aching heart, I watched the distress mount among my dear friends at the ministry. Some were moved from their positions onto marginal jobs. Yet, those responsible for this witch-hunt were flourishing.

The anonymous letters and slander campaigns did not pass me by, either. Those responsible for the ministry's deterioration were the same officials who resented the special cooperation and friendship that had developed between me and the former minister. They also opposed our efforts to help the local environmental organizations. They took advantage of a new minister who knew none of us. After all, who is an easier target than a foreigner who had been close to the previous minister?

I wanted to leave Angola. Abias met me again for one of his pep talks. This time he understood me very well. He, too, was very concerned about what was happening at the ministry. "Don't worry," he said. "Just do your work, and I will take care of the rest. You can trust me, you know that."

Several days later the new minister called me to his office. He asked for my professional view on several issues, and then, to my surprise, thanked me for my good work in Angola, and asked me to carry on. I did not understand what caused this dramatic change in his attitude. Only much later one of my friends at the ministry told me what had happened. Abias had convened an emergency meeting of the members of the environmental organizations. They decided to submit a joint letter to the new minister, telling him how I supported them and asking that he saw to it that I continued my work in Angola. They also mentioned in the letter that they knew that there was someone who wanted to get rid of me, and who had been spreading malicious rumours, which were lies that the minister should not believe.

On the next anniversary of the founding of Juventude Ecologica Angolana, Fatima Jardim and I were invited to join the organization as honorary members. The ceremony received extensive media coverage. "They needed a lot of courage to honour you, the foreigner, and the former minister, and not the current minister and senior officials," I was told. "Instead of trying to win the hearts of the new administration to get further support, they chose to show their gratitude to those who had assisted them so far."

Several months had passed. Abias's work for the international organization continued to be praised and he also worked relentlessly in conservation and education in Angola. He was still wearing bright clothes, but at last he had succeeded in improving his standard of living. He had moved to a larger rented room in a reasonably pleasant apartment block.

One day he called and asked to see me urgently. "I want to get engaged," he said. "But I cannot do so until I have presented my bride-to-be to you."

Neusa was, of course, a beauty queen from one of the provinces. I was pleased to see that she was not only beautiful but also intelligent, and a leading JEA activist in her province. About a year later Abias called to inform me excitedly and proudly that I had become a grandmother.

T R

CHAPTER SEVEN

On the ocean and in the river

Angola's wonderful natural treasures reach beyond the terrestrial territory of the country, into the rivers and lakes, through the coastal zone, and out into the ocean. The fisheries resources in the Atlantic Ocean, along Angola's long coastline between the Guinea and Benguela currents, are abundant and varied, thanks to the large marine eco-systems. Rare and unique species live here, and attract global interest in terms of conservation. These include, among others, the manatees in the coastal rivers and lakes, the sea turtles that nest along the coasts, and the dolphins and whales out in the ocean. The information about them is scarce, but there is great reason for concern.

Sea turtles

They run blindly and eagerly straight toward the sea; their little feet stumbling over the sand, their heads tilted forward on their slender and wrinkled necks. With great effort they carry their tiny bodies, covered with a still-soft shell, up and down the sand mounds. Onwards, always onwards, to the sea. Without hesitation, they propel themselves into the foaming surf and are swallowed by the ocean, carried far out into the dark night.

There is something heart-wrenching about the sight of the little hatchlings as they head out with great intent straight into the dangers awaiting them. They have just hatched, having shed the eggshells from their bodies and emerged, bewildered, from the depth of their nest in the soft sand, and here they are, already running. They do not know that most of them are doomed. Only one or two of these dozens of hatchlings will ever reach maturity. Most of them will meet their death tonight, others over the next few days.

Nature is overwhelmingly beautiful, but there is a great deal of cruelty, as well. Man's actions are the cruellest. He will destroy all of the turtles, even before they hatch. He will rob them even of the smallest chance of reaching maturity. He will even prevent the turtle mother returning to sea. He will take her life too.

The female turtle leaves the sea and starts crawling up the beach with an immense effort, there to dig a nest and lay her eggs. Every step is difficult for her. She drags her heavy body on her flat awkward flippers. They are intended for swimming, not for crawling on the sand. One heavy step slowly follows another. She groans and carries on, one laborious step at a time, until she finds a suitable place for the nest, high above the tideline. She has arrived here after swimming for many days, sometimes from one end of the Atlantic to the other. She navigates that immense distance just to return to lay her eggs on the same beach where she hatched.

After laying her eggs she abandons them and returns to the sea, leaving behind her a wide line of tracks like those of a little quad-bike. Sometimes she returns to the beach over several consecutive nights and lays more eggs in several nests. From here she will go on her long journey back to where she came from, deserting her offspring, leaving them behind in the nest to their inevitable destiny.

As soon as the little turtles hatch, many predators covet their small, soft, unprotected bodies. Many dangers lurk on the beach and at sea. Large monitor lizards devour them with their long tongues and jackals gorge on them. Seagulls dive to catch them and fly off with their bounty in their beaks. Crabs wave their gross, red claws greedily, while large fish open their mouths wide and disappear with them into deep water. It seems as if all of the sea and the beach creatures take part in this feast. All, except for the turtle hatchlings. They are the feast.

When the hatchlings that have survived the journey from the nest across the beach arrive at the sea, they jump into the waves and start swimming quickly, propelling their tiny bodies, only a few centimetres long, far out into the ocean. And so they swim for days and weeks, without stopping. Despite all the dangers, a few of them will make it into the deep ocean, where even fewer will survive to maturity. Then they will spread throughout the ocean and look for a niche in which to feed and live, sometimes at great distances from where they hatched.

About fifteen or twenty years later, as large adult sea turtles, they will return to the same beach where they hatched to lay their own eggs. About two months after, a new generation of hatchlings will emerge from the sand, running again toward their destiny. Some species may return to nest annually, others once every few years. It is a cycle that has gone on for many millennia.

How do the adult turtles know to return, after so many years, to the same beach where they themselves hatched? This is one of the great mysteries of nature, and there are several theories. It is possible that they use a magnetic sense that enables them to navigate. Maybe they remember the special combination of the scent and the taste of the sand where they hatched, and maybe there is some other mystery yet to be revealed.

No less interesting is why they do it. There is something that makes us feel great respect for an animal that swims many miles and crosses oceans, at great risk, to return to the same place where it hatched to have its own offspring. More so, when it is an animal that has overcome many dangers and attained maturity against all odds.

The sea turtles that return to the coasts of Angola find no respect, sympathy, or compassion, only a hard struggle for existence, a fight for survival, with many losers and very few winners. Wildlife, including the turtle, is invariably on the losing side. Throughout the nesting season the fishermen are waiting for them on the beach. Most fishermen are war refugees, internally displaced people from other provinces, unemployed and living in extreme poverty. Every morning, before dawn, they throw their tattered nets into the sea, often ending their hard day's work after midnight. Sometimes they gather a meagre harvest of fish, although it is rarely ever enough. They try to sustain themselves and their families, but it is no easy task.

Capturing a sea turtle is a great prize for a hungry fisherman. It is a large amount of meat, it is considered tasty and it is relatively easily obtained. One turtle can feed a whole family and there may even be something left over to sell. The fishermen spend every night patrolling the beaches during the turtle nesting season. When the adult female emerges from the sea, they wait until she has laid her eggs. Then, when she is slowly dragging her exhausted body back towards the sea, they catch her with their bare hands, cut open her belly, cut out her flesh, and prepare it for cooking. In Luanda and in other markets, the shell will also be sold. Craftsmen carve it into artifacts to be sold to foreigners and the country's elite. After killing the mother, the fishermen will also dig out all of the eggs from the nest. Some they will keep for their family's consumption, and the rest they will sell. This way the life of the female turtle will end, one of so few to survive and return to lay her eggs on the Angolan coast. Of all her offspring, not even one will survive.

Shortly after I started working in Angola, we visited several nesting beaches during the turtles' nesting season with ministry staff and members of the environmental organizations. It was during the war, and we had access to only a few zones about sixty kilometres north and south of Luanda. We could see the conspicuous remnants of turtle shells from a distance as we approached these beaches. This was all that remained from their encounter with man after so many years of a persistent battle for survival.

We met the fishermen. Many of them were internally displaced people from other provinces in Angola. The sea turtles and their eggs had become an important part of their livelihood and a source of scarce protein. Those who struggle for their own daily subsistence and for the sustenance of their families find it difficult to consider the distress of another species.

There are only seven species (some say eight) of sea turtles in the world, and they are all threatened with extinction, at some level or other. Six of the species occur in the Atlantic and reach the coasts of West Africa. All of these have, in the past, been recorded in Angola. Only four species have been observed in Angola in recent years, and their numbers are smaller than previously reported. The most common species in Angola is the olive ridley (*Lepidochelys olivacea*). On some of the beaches there are also nesting green turtles (*Chelonia mydas*), loggerheads (*Caretta caretta*), and leatherback turtles (*Dermochelys coriacea*), the latter being the largest turtle species in the world. It is critically endangered.

We launched an extensive awareness campaign about the importance of sea turtles and their conservation. Most of the Angolan media channels helped to transmit the message. By the end of 2002, several months after the peace agreements had been signed in Angola, and when it became possible to travel safely on the roads, we embarked upon a preliminary beach survey and started an awareness campaign among the fishermen, from Luanda all the way south to the border with Namibia, in Namibe Province. The Cunene River, which forms the southern border of Angola with Namibia, is also the southern distribution limit of sea turtles in the Atlantic Ocean coast of West Africa.

Over a two-week period we travelled along the war-fractured coastal roads. The skillful and careful driving of Adelino Nunes, the UNDP driver, saved us more than once from undesired adventures. Occasionally other saviours came to our rescue. There was not much difference between driving on dirt roads and on the main roads, except that the dirt roads were smoother. At least, it was reassuring to know that the roads along the coast had not been mined.

We travelled through breathtaking and varied landscapes, between golden and reddish beaches, sandy and rocky coastal stretches, and the high cliffs east of the coast. We stopped frequently to meet fishermen and to randomly survey short stretches of the coast for turtle spoor. Some of the fishermen were descendents of the old communities that had lived there for many generations, and others were war refugees. They all had one thing in common: extreme poverty and an arduous daily struggle for survival. One scene repeated itself everywhere: the macabre graveyards of the turtle shells planted in the sand.

We persisted with the awareness campaign, but it was clear that the only effective way forward would be to provide the fishermen with real support, by helping them to develop alternative livelihoods.

During the next turtle nesting season, several private beach owners decided to protect the turtles and their nests. In that way, about twenty kilometres of Angola's 1,650 kilometres of coastline were protected.

In Cabinda province we developed a special programme in cooperation with the provincial government and the local organization, Gremio ABC. We went from village to village along Cabinda's coast and asked the fishermen for their help and participation. After all, the turtles' successful return to reproduce on these same beaches where they hatched would mean that there would be a turtle presence in the future for these fishermen and for their children. If the extermination of all of the females and their nests continued, eventually not even one turtle would remain to return to these beaches.

The fishermen had more urgent considerations.

"When I walk on the beach at night," one fisherman opened the debate, "after pulling the nets all day, with a meagre yield of a few small fish, and there on the beach I find a large turtle, it is like winning the lottery.

"Leave it there?" he said. "Give up all this meat and the opportunity to sell something and make some profit? And leave the eggs, too?" He sighed deeply. "This is difficult, very difficult!"

"Only if you could help us develop alternative livelihood sources could we give up the turtle harvest," said another.

"And what about the nets?" asked a third fisherman. "During the nesting season many turtles get entangled in our nets and destroy them as they try to free themselves. It is impossible to repair a net that has been torn by a turtle, because the damage is too great. If I take the turtle to market and sell it, I can buy a new net to replace the damaged one, but if I return the turtle to sea, who will give me a new net? How will I then be able to fish and provide for my family?"

Together with the provincial government, the UNDP and the oil companies' association in Cabinda, we raised a modest sum to help the fishermen purchase new fishing nets. Every fisherman who could prove that he had turtle-damaged nets and had returned the turtle to the sea after it had been caught up in them, received a new net as a replacement. The provincial officials checked every call where a fisherman reported a captured turtle.

The national television station and other media channels in the province enthusiastically supported the awareness campaign. Time and again the provincial news programmes, television and radio stations and journals showed huge female turtles dragging themselves by their flippers back into the sea, after being released. Sometimes the images were presented on the national channels as well. The camera would then move from the freed turtle to the fisherman, as he presented his torn net to the camera, next to it the new net that he had just received, while talking excitedly about his part in saving the turtles.

"Look," one fisherman turned proudly to the camera, "this turtle has made a very long journey to get here, of all places, to my beach, where she was born, and to lay her eggs here. She did not go to any other place. She is a real patriot. I want my children who were also born here, my grandchildren, and their children, to meet her offspring here too. I do not want them to see turtles only in photos."

Despite all the efforts, there is still a very long way to go before the turtles that reach the Angolan coast are adequately protected, as they are in other parts of the world. Fishermen in other countries enjoy the fruits of eco-tourism, enabling them to provide for their families by protecting the turtles, rather than harvesting them.

Studies show that the economic status of villagers that are involved in eco-tourism specializing in turtle watching is several times higher than that of subsistence fishermen who hunt and harvest the turtles and their eggs.

For more than a hundred million years the sea turtles have arrived on the beaches, laid their eggs, and returned to sea. During the past few decades they have been driven rapidly towards extinction. One species—man—is responsible for their demise. In the coming years the destiny of the sea turtles in Angola will be determined: irreversible extinction and loss, or recovery.

TR

The manatee

I searched for the manatee (*Trichechus senegalensis*), the 'sea cow', or as it is locally called manatim, dikunji or peixe-mulher (fish-woman), since it first brought me to Angola. When I told people that I was trying to find this animal, some smiled pityingly and chuckled: "But you surely know that the fish-woman does not really exist. It is a myth."

Throughout history, the manatee has been the subject of myth and legend. Perhaps this is a result of its obscure lifestyle and behaviour. The animal tends to disappear beneath the murky waters of rivers and lakes, where it feeds on aquatic weeds, and reappears above the surface only briefly to breathe air or to feed on bank vegetation. Maybe the tales about it are a remnant of an old maritime belief in mermaids, though it may be that the stories about mermaids, fish-women, and even the legendary and magical Kianda were only accidentally associated with this large, round and slow-moving mammal.

One such myth is related, of all places, to a main street in Luanda. The Marginal, the esplanade of Luanda, stretches along the coast and has many ministries, embassies, prestigious offices and business premises along it. But along this road there is also a multitude of open potholes, leaking pipelines, and many other hazards. On the pavement, directly in front of one of the ministries, there is a permanent pothole that is always flooded. During the rainy season it is filled with rain water, and during the dry season, with water that leaks into it from the underground systems. Despite many efforts over the years to fix the problem, the pothole always re-floods within a couple of days. I have heard a variety of reasons for the state of the pothole and forgotten most of them, except for one: in the port of Luanda, across the road from the pothole, lives a mermaid, a fish-woman. When the port was built, many years ago, during the Portuguese colonial era, her home was destroyed. In her rage, she went out one night, and created potholes along the road. Since then she has continued to take

205

her revenge for the destruction of her home by keeping this pothole always open and flooded, thus reminding people of the wrong they did her.

We started searching for the manatee during my first visit to Angola, as a consultant to the then Vice-Minister of the Environment, Professor João Serodio de Almeida. We had requested the help of the fishermen in the villages around the lakes and the rivers, within a radius of up to 100 kilometres from Luanda. A delegation consisting of the vice-minister, several officials and myself reached the first village on the bank of Ibendwa Lake. The village was in the heart of a picturesque landscape of large, tranquil, deep blue lakes, nestled in green wooded valleys surrounded by a yellowish-green savannah, dotted about with small cassava fields and banana plantations. Only a few of the original inhabitants had remained in the village. Most of the residents were internally displaced war refugees from other provinces. They lived in hastily built straw and wood shacks with corrugated iron roofs. In the middle of the village there was one brick construction, the church which was both the spiritual and community centre. "You see," one of the ministry's officials whispered. "In this village only God has a real house."

The vice-minister asked the village head, the Soba, to convene a meeting of all the villagers. The fishermen assembled under the large jungo, the debating shed, near the Soba's home. Here they continued to work on their fishing nets as they watched the vice-minister with an air of indifference.

"Do you know who I am?" Serodio opened the discussion. The fishermen shook their heads. A small and noisy transistor radio was the only means of communication in the village. Serodio was not one of the senior ministers that most people recognized. These refugees, who spent their days from dawn to dusk fishing for their subsistence, could not have known him. The vice-minister presented himself and the fishermen nodded and continued with their nets.

Serodio talked with great enthusiasm about the manatee and the importance of its conservation. He explained at great length about the eco-tourism that could evolve around it, and its potential benefits for the economic development of the communities. To illustrate his words, he showed brochures and publications of tourist sites with luxury lodges near other lakes in Africa. These sites offered the very best facilities for the pleasure of rich tourists, who were supposed to bring with them financial opportunities and jobs for the villagers. Here, among the rickety shacks, in this village of poor fishermen refugees, at a time when the civil war was still taking its daily toll in the country, these descriptions and photos must have seemed as a legend. The fishermen watched the vice minister with obvious disbelief, thanked him politely for his visit, and carried on meshing their fishing nets.

Serodio then passed around photos and drawings of the manatee and asked the fishermen if they had seen this animal in the lake. The fishermen discussed this and eventually the Soba confirmed that such an animal did exist in Ibendwa Lake, but was very rarely seen. Only a few experts knew how to find the dikunji and to hunt it. This expertise was passed from father to son, and remained the legacy of a few families. If a fisherman who was not a member of one of these families hunted for a manatee, he would not only fail, but risk bringing disaster upon himself. The Soba told us that in this village there was only one manatee expert and only this man could show us the dikunji. His name was Mr Rodrigues, one of the original villagers. He was not there on the day of our visit, but we were told that if we returned in exactly one week, we could meet him early in the morning, before he went to fish in the lake.

We returned a week later, early in the morning, and Mr Rodrigues was waiting for us. He was glad to meet the vice-minister and confirmed that he was indeed the only expert in this area who could hunt manatees. He even showed us bones and other remnants of manatees that he had killed recently.

"To see a living manatee," he said, "you must join me in my canoe, on my daily work in the lake."

Three of us returned the next day without the vice-minister, who had business elsewhere. That day we spent several hours exploring the lake in the hunter's little canoe. We returned the next day and the next, and for many more days after that. We did not see any manatees. Here and there we found proof of their existence, such as the browsing marks on a water hyacinth and half-eaten plants.

After one of our visits to the lake, Mr Rodrigues asked us to take his young son to Luanda, where he was starting school. The boy had just returned from fishing, dressed in rags, and covered in mud. He went into the little hut and ten minutes later came out clean and wearing a neatly pressed school uniform. His shiny new appearance, in a white shirt and even a little tie, was a mystery to me. After all, there was no running water in the whole village, definitely no electricity, or an iron, or even a dry and clean place to store clothes. On the way to Luanda the child told us that his father was saving all of his meagre income from selling fish and manatee meat to finance his schooling and that of his brothers and sisters. He did not explain his metamorphosis which occurred under our marvelling eyes.

We searched for the manatee in Ibendwa Lake and further afield, asking the advice of fishermen in other villages near lakes and rivers around Luanda. We heard the same story everywhere: yes, there were manatees there, but only a few experts, who passed on their expertise discreetly, from father to son, could find them. We spent many days in the experts' rickety canoes, seeing signs of manatee activity, but we never actually saw one.

One of these specialized hunters, in a village near the bank of Lake Quilunda, told us that the manatees there were nocturnal and that they were active only shortly after dusk and again just before dawn. "You will not see them during the daylight hours," he said. "You should come with me to the lake in the evening, then spend the night in the village, and before dawn we will go out to look for them again. You will be able to see the manatees with the upper part of the body raised above the water to browse in the vegetation on the bank."

The next afternoon, two of us arrived in Quilunda, another refugee village. In accordance with the custom, we brought some small presents for the village and for the Soba, and we asked for his permission to spend the night in the village. The villagers gathered around to watch us as we erected our tents, and discussed our presence among themselves. In the evening we went with the manatee hunter for a trip around the lake. We used powerful flashlights to light the bank and the lake surface and disturbed several birds from their sleep, but saw no sign of the manatee.

We returned to the village in the cold night air. While I was preparing my sleeping bag in the tent one of the village women appeared with a blanket in her hands. "You will be cold tonight," she said. "You will need the blanket." I showed her that the sleeping bag was thick and warm, and only then was she convinced and returned to her hut.

I was warm that night, but my body was shaking. The people of this neglected refugee village had lost all that they had, experienced terrible hardships and lived in extreme poverty, struggling from day to day for their very existence without help from anyone. Yet, here, of all places, a woman who had never met me before, offered me what little she had. If I had accepted the blanket, someone would have spent the night shivering with cold.

Several hours later we tripped around the smooth, dark lake again, until grey shades of orange tinted the water in the mist of the dawn. In the vegetation on the bank we could see fresh foraging signs of manatees, but we never saw them.

The manatee expert was embarrassed. "There is a secret that I did not tell you," he said. "I hoped that things would work out differently, this time. The secret is that it is possible to see the manatee only when you do not look for it, when you do not intend to see it."

How can I search for the manatee, without wanting to see it? Everything here contains contradiction, and the contradiction is the thing itself.

The information we collected during our visits to the lakes and rivers and in our conversations with the fishermen and manatee hunters helped me later in the preparation of an extensive programme for the study and conservation of these rare mammals in Angola. The status of the manatee, similar to that of many wildlife species in Angola, has deteriorated significantly during the decades of armed conflict in the country. The old traditions that had protected them were no longer respected. Many manatees were shot from the air and their population had declined. It was now essential to implement an emergency programme for their conservation and to stop the poaching to protect the few that remained. The reproduction rate of manatees is very low. A female calves only once every two to three years. The conservation programme that we developed was based mainly on the cooperation of the traditional expert hunters in the study and protection of the manatees. Later, when I returned to Angola for a longer period, as a general consultant to the government on biodiversity conservation, there were so many other pressing issues that the manatee was pushed from the top of the list. However, I still jumped at every opportunity to search for it in the rivers and the lakes along the coast. The surveys for the manatee were continued by Miguel Morais, a young biologist and one of the manatee's leading supporters from the Agostinho Neto University, the national university, in Luanda.

The years passed, and shortly before my UNDP mission in Angola ended, a friend invited me to join him for a weekend on a small boat in the great Kwanza River. He was going to fish, and I joined him to enjoy the boating and to view the forest along the river bank and the impressive mangroves at the river mouth. It was a great opportunity for bird watching and with a bit of luck we could see the odd antelope coming to drink. On our way upriver, we visited several small and picturesque fishing villages. These villages, which had been inhabited for generations, were easy to distinguish from the refugee villages. Their huts were well built from mud, wood and straw.

The day passed lazily and pleasantly. Suddenly a small round wave rose in front of our boat in the middle of the river. The ripples spread wider and wider and a large rounded head appeared in their centre. There was a noisy blast of air, like a great sigh, and then the head disappeared at once. Some bubbles rose to the surface and the ripples died away. That was it. This whole scene took merely seconds.

It was a manatee that raised its head for a quick breath of air, and immediately disappeared in the murky river water, without a sign.

Thus it happened ... or did it?

TR

In the ocean

High cliffs descend steeply onto red sandy beaches that slope smoothly to the sea, caressed by the slow, monotonous movement of the waves. We are on a research cruise heading south, along the coastline of Angola. Great waves pound steel-grey beaches and small rocky islets break the coastline, encircled by shades of turquoise and deep blue. A tern accompanies our vessel.

These beaches have probably appeared the same since the first Portuguese seamen arrived here more than 500 years ago. What must have passed through their minds as their caravels drew near these remote coasts of what was then called the Black Continent? Such a different world from the one they came from. I try to picture them in my mind—seamen, merchants, adventurers, people drawn here by curiosity, an irresistible passion to explore distant lands, or by simple greed. Maybe it was despair of their own world that drove them to such distant shores.

Exhausted from the long journey across the Atlantic, they were surely not prepared for the shock of their first encounter with Africa.

The distance from their familiar life in Europe, the length of time that had passed since they had last seen their families, the hardships of sailing the open sea, maybe even aggression fuelled by crowded masculine company, the unfamiliar, strange and dangerous place they had reached—all these must have hardened their hearts. They came to Africa to take whatever they could.

And what did the Africans feel, those who were taken to be sold as slaves? What went through their minds when they saw the coast of their homeland disappearing over the horizon? Chained, beaten, shocked, the only life they ever knew was taken away from them, along with their freedom. Greedy, strange hands coveted their world and sowed destruction and loss. Africa and her sons and daughters were led against their will on a journey from which there was no return.

Our ship turned away from the coast toward the open ocean. We entered a quiet desert of grey-blue water, as the land receded into the distance. I surveyed the sea with my binoculars. Above the surface there was no sign of life. However, below, it was teeming with life.

This is one of the most productive seas in the world. This ecological system is known for its richness and abundance of fish, crustaceans and other species, because of the special combination of environmental conditions created by the confluence of the cold Benguela current from the south and the warm Guinea current from the north.

We stood on the mast deck of the Nansen, a research vessel named after Dr Fridtjof Nansen, the founder of the Norwegian fisheries study project in the Atlantic Ocean along the west coast of Africa. The research cruises in the territorial waters of Angola are conducted in partnership between the governmental Marine Research Institute of Angola and the Norwegian Marine Research Institute of Bergen. This part of the cruise is repeated twice a year, from north to south. The objective is to monitor the dynamics of fish populations and the effect of commercial fishing. I used the opportunity to initiate a preliminary survey of marine mammals—dolphins, whales and seals. I joined the cruise on two occasions. The first year we sailed in the northern part, from the Congo River to Luanda, and the next year, the southern part, from Luanda to the Cunene River.

It was a cold morning. Heavy clouds had hidden the sun and a thin, annoying rain swept the decks. The Norwegian crew lowered the sampling nets into a grey and gloomy sea. Everyone on deck was enveloped in rain gear and silence. About 20 minutes later the net was drawn back onto the deck. The catch was poor. The Angolan research team went on board to sort the fish and record the data. Their disappointment over the catch was obvious from their sombre expressions. The very small but mature horse mackerel in the net were an indication that the fish population was in decline. The nagging drizzle added to the heavy atmosphere on board.

Since this research was first conducted in the 1980s, a general decline had been recorded in Angolan offshore fisheries. It is the result of uncontrolled over-exploitation over many decades. Fishing vessels, both Angolan and foreign—Russian, Spanish, Chinese, Korean, and others—have pillaged the treasures of Angola's waters with alarming efficiency. We encountered several such vessels on our voyage. At times we saw them very close to the shore, in areas where commercial fishing is prohibited. The large trawling nets, which are lowered all the way down to the bottom of the ocean and sweep everything in their way, are especially destructive.

Marine biologist and head of the Angolan research team, Nkosi Luyeye, said he believed that Angola would lose an important source of food and income within a few years if strict measures were not taken to enforce fishing regulations. "The rich and productive zone, which is influenced by the Benguela current, may irreversibly turn into an undersea wasteland."

A large foreign trawler was fishing a short distance from the Nansen, spreading its trawling net and lowering it close to the coast, in an illegal commercial fishing area. The slave ships that sailed here several hundred years ago came back to my mind. Greed has many faces, but the goal is the same: take. Easy profit, here and now. The destruction left behind is a matter for the soft-hearted only.

The Nansen was slowly emerging from the heavy rain clouds. The grey shade of the sea was replaced by vivid blue, and on the horizon the sky was brightening under a light cloud cover. A flying fish jumped out of the water, hovered above the surface for a few seconds and landed with a splash. The sun's rays penetrated between the spreading clouds and were refracted, splitting into myriad little shards of light, shining and flickering on the small waves.

"There is hope," said Nkosi and his expression softened with a smile. "The government of Angola has decided to prohibit trawling in large parts of the sea off shore of Angola. If we keep the ban for several years, long enough to allow reproduction, there will be a chance for the fisheries of Angola to recover. Similar measures will also enable the recovery of the crustaceans and other species that have also been subjected to over-exploitation over many years. It is also very important to have a good law enforcement system in place, to ensure the implementation of the new regulations and other legal fishing instruments. It may still be possible to save the once-rich and productive waters off Angola."

Two Namibian girls, young cadets who had been training as ship's crew for four months, climbed up onto the deck. They had paint tins and brushes and were painting the rusty patches, dancing their way from deck to deck, and humming cheerfully. They had been on the cruise for the whole research route, from Morocco to Cape Town.

We sailed on, heading south. Between the sky and the sea there was no life to be seen. The sea was quiet. Suddenly a vertical rounded spout appeared in the distance. It was what I had been searching for with my binoculars for hours: a whale. Immediately another one appeared next to it. I called Ole, the captain, on the radio and he steered the ship towards them. As we approached we saw they were two humpback whales. It was easy to identify the conspicuous and somewhat humped dorsal fin on the rounded back emerging briefly above the waves and diving back. The whales disappeared into the water. We thought they might have been swimming away.

And then we saw it—the white ventral side of a long flipper came clear out the water in a round movement and then landed back, beating strongly, at a distance of a few dozen metres from the ship. A strong exhalation was then heard on the other side of the bow. A second whale was also very close. It dived again leaving behind a large oily patch, with a strong smell of fish oil. The flipper of the first whale beat the water forcefully again, and then a head emerged. The whale's arched back leaped into the air, in a magnificent breach, landing back and ending with a powerful beat of the tail.

There are several theories around the reasons for breaching. It may be to get rid of annoying parasites, or to improve breathing or catching prey. Maybe it is a signal to other members of the species, or perhaps it is just for fun. Whatever the reason, to witness such a spectacular sight, even for one brief moment, is well worth a cruise of many days in a seemingly desolate sea. It is difficult to comprehend the great flexibility and agility of such a giant creature.

The pair of whales dived back and we carried on. I was busy recording the details of the sighting in my notebook when we heard another air blow very close, and then another. Suddenly the ship was surrounded by more than 20 whales. Some were very near. Their characteristic ventral pleats and the tubercles around their mouths could be clearly distinguished. We could see the white and black patterns that are unique to each individual, from the white ventral side of the body, the flippers and the fluke, to the black dorsal side.

They dived, surfaced, blew air, swam, breached, and landed, hitting the water with explosive force. The great whale show was all around us. Such power and grace. And then, at once, they all disappeared, diving, surfacing after several minutes some distance away. They continued on their migration route, and we went back on our survey route, all heading south.

The sampling net continued to come up with worrying catches. Every morning I went up to the highest observation point on the mast deck, where I spent the day surveying the sea for cetacean movement. I had a small table and chair, a camera, binoculars, a GPS receiver, maps of the route, field guides of sea mammals and birds, observation recording sheets, a water bottle and a radio to inform the captain whenever I spotted anyting. Every evening I packed it all up and went down to the laboratory. There I transferred data from the ship's computer to my laptop, such as the daily route and the weather and sea conditions, and added it to the coordinates of each sighting and to my detailed observation records.

It was gradually getting cold and stormy as we sailed south toward Namibia. The winds were stronger and the waves higher. Constant seasickness had begun to affect me. The heavy Norwegian food, unpalatable to my Mediterranean palate (and as it seems, to the Angolans as well), did not improve the situation. A greenish hue began to spread on the faces of the Angolan researchers, and on mine too. I dreamed of terra firma.

Between the silent Norwegians and the homesick Angolans who were longing for solid ground under their feet, only the two Namibian cadets were flourishing. They moved cheerfully between the decks and the rooms, painting, learning to navigate, helping to roll the nets, and adding much needed colour and lively spirit to the gloomy atmosphere. Ole, the captain, also maintained his good mood and tried, without much success, to cheer up the others. "I myself," he said, "suffer from seasickness only on land."

Bjorn's baby face was getting paler every day. The head of the Norwegian research team's previously constant kindly smile became more and more rare. "The fishery status findings are alarming," he said. "There has been severe deterioration over the past few years. If Angola does not take urgent measures to protect the little that is left, the country may lose the opportunity to recover the abundant fish stocks of the past."

He and Nkosi were preparing their joint report and recommendations to the government, but they were not optimistic about its reception. Politicians in most governments tend to have short-term, short-sighted objectives and are seldom willing to sacrifice today for the better good of future generations.

Several days passed with no close sightings of cetaceans. All we saw were some whale spouts in the distance. The long hours on the upper deck passed slowly. I comforted myself with the memory of the previous exciting observations. I surveyed the sea again with my binoculars. All I could see were small greyish waves all the way to the horizon. Suddenly, I saw several dozen tiny black triangles riding up and down the waves. "Dolphins!" I shouted excitedly into the radio. The captain directed the ship toward them.

As the Nansen drew closer to the pod, we saw to our surprise that there were pilot whales swimming among them. These toothed whales, closer relatives of the dolphin than of the large baleen whale, are easy to identify by their large rounded heads and their characteristic wide dorsal fin. There were around twenty-five pilot whales swimming with a small group of bottlenose dolphins, the most common and well-known dolphin species globally.

The pilot whales swam in an organized structure, all very close to each other. In the centre of the pod were four mothers with calves. The dolphins were more scattered, jumping with the waves. The two species are known to coexist in mixed pods in the ocean.

Every day, we saw the small rickety boats of the fishermen from the coastal villages making their way into sea, overloaded and at the mercy of the storms. The danger was obvious, but the fishermen had no choice. Extensive commercial fishing has caused the decline of the catch near the coast, so to get something in their nets, they had to go further out to sea and even then they often returned empty-handed. The sight was heartbreaking. Fishermen wearing rags sailed into the open sea with small boats they constructed from odd collections of planks. They tried to find their way among the gigantic commercial fishing vessels, and threw their patched nets into the sea, hoping to catch something to sustain them and their families for one more day.

As our ship sailed southward, more and more sea birds joined our passage. The Cape gannets became an integral part of the view. The adults are conspicuous with their white bodies, ornamented with black wing and tail tips and a yellowish-orange shade to the head and the neck. Their beaks are strong and pointed, and their clear and beautiful eyes are emphasized with a fine dark outline. They patiently flew around the Nansen. Whenever the sampling net was lowered into the sea, they folded their wings and dived into the water as swiftly and powerfully as arrows, beak first, immediately resurfacing with their fish bounty still kicking. Albatrosses glided along in wide circles, with their long wings spread and their bodies close to the surface of the water.

The small common terns arrived in a large flock and settled down at convenient observation posts on the deck railings and on the horizontal spars attached to the mast. The first to arrive perched comfortably, at a generous distance from each other, but they were soon joined by others and slowly the spaces inbetween filled up until the spars and railings were crowded with lines of roosting terns, all facing the direction of the ship. More terns arrived. Now no more space was left in the rigging, yet another approached. It landed on the tail of another and beat its wings forcefully, kicked with its feet, and pulled the tail feathers of the roosting tern with its beak, until the harassed bird took off and the new arrival took its place. More and more terns arrived, each trying to occupy a place, continuously driving each other out in a winged game of musical chairs. Each expelled tern looked for a victim of its own to chase out and take its place. Eventually some of them gave up and flew away. It was an instructive lesson in hierarchy—for us and for the terns.

One tern dived into the water and returned with a large fish stuck in its beak. The fish was nearly as big as the tern and half of its body was still hanging out of the beak, with the tail flapping violently. The tern nearly choked, but would not let go. It found a place on a spar, tilted its head back and tried to swallow.

It was immediately chased away by another tern and flew off, but it still had its flapping booty.

In the south we also saw many Cape fur seals, migrating north from Namibia in search of food. From time to time, a seal or two passed by, drift-sleeping on the waves, head resting on one fore-flipper, while the other was raised in the air. Some were float-resting on their backs, with both fore-flippers folded on their bellies. As soon as the screech of our ship's net mechanism sounded, they would wake up and approach the ship rapidly from all directions. Dozens of them would arrive and dive with agility under the net, pulling out fish and feasting with great appetite. When the net was pulled back onto the deck they would quickly disperse.

The survey terminated when we arrived at the Cunene River, the southern border of Angola with Namibia. The Nansen came about and headed back rapidly. We all abandoned our observation posts in the cold wind on deck and went below to gather in the dining room. There we found reviving hot chocolate awaiting us with home-made Norwegian waffles. The atmosphere was pleasant. The chat was flowing in English, Portuguese and Norwegian. Someone from the Angolan team asked to listen to Hebrew music. I chose a Riki Gal disc.

"At the end of the sky and the edge of the desert, there is a place far away ..." she sweetly and softly sang the Jonathan Geffen song.

"A place far away, a place of worry ... God is sitting there watching, thinking on all that he created ... It is not allowed to pick the flowers of the garden ... And He is worried, very worried ..."

T R

CHAPTER EIGHT

Some facts on Angola

We have written but little about the Angola we know. This chapter provides a short background to the stories, some dry facts about the history of Angola, the present, and a wish for the future.

Milestones

At the end of the first millennium, tribes belonging to the Bantu ethnic group inhabited the region now called Angloa. The Bantu lived in a lush tropical forest that covered the huge area of the Congo River basin. From what is now Cameroon and Gabon in the west, on to the east to Zambia and Zimbabwe, an agricultural and trading society flourished. They were familiar with fire and iron, out of which they fashioned tools for working the land and weapons for defending both their commercial routes and their kingdoms.

The largest of the Bantu kingdoms was the Kongo, which ruled over large areas and had a highly developed social structure, comparable with the kingdoms of medieval Europe. The Kongo Kingdom had ties with the N'gola and Mbundu kingdoms, with a relationship based on commercial competition.

The first white men to arrive in the region by sea towards the end of the 15th century were daring Portuguese sailors, merchants and adventurers from a small and impoverished country in southern Europe. The Portuguese sought a sea route to India and most of the earliest 'discoveries' are accredited to them. Of course, the term 'discovery', which is in common use to this day, is inappropriate and misleading. Africa and its people have been here since the beginning of humanity.

In 1482, the Portuguese sailor Diogo Ciao arrived at the estuary of the Congo River, the world's fastest flowing river. Near the estuary, he planted a stone pole and made friends with the local people, who told him all about the great King Mwani Kongo, whose kingdom was spread around the capital, M'Banza Kongo. News of this unique and very wealthy kingdom reached Lisbon, the capital of Portugal.

According to a Portuguese evaluation of the time, the population of M'Banza Kongo was about 50,000 people.

In 1490, the Portuguese government decided to dispatch an official ambassador to the African kingdom. The first Catholic missionaries to reach the region accompanied him in his ship. They were very successful in their mission and the king and many of his subjects were baptized into Christianity.

In 1534, the first Catholic cathedral on African soil was built at M'Banza Kongo. The Portuguese explorers continued south along Atlantic shore.

The year 1576 saw the first buildings in Luanda, which was destined to become the capital of the colonial Portuguese government and, eventually, the capital of independent Angola. The white invaders tended to avoid penetrating deep into the country and most of their interests focused on the slave trade. The Congo River basin was known in those days as the Basin of Slaves. The Portuguese made full use of gunpowder, their great advantage in squashing resistance to their endeavours.

Between 1641 and 1648, the Dutch drove Portuguese settlers out of the Luanda area. Under the leadership of the fiery Queen Ngola Nzinga, the local Africans helped the Dutch against the Portuguese. The Portuguese subsequently returned to capture the town and the fort built by the Dutch. The Queen and her followers withdrew to the highlands in the centre of the country. From there, they continued their struggle against colonial rule until the queen's death in 1671.

From the middle of the 15th century and up to 1830, Angola was the most important source of slaves, who were rounded up and exported to Portugal and North and South America. The first destination was Brazil, although large numbers of slaves were also sent to the United States. The slave trade continued even after 1830, when, under international pressure, Portugal was forced to officially announce that it would no longer be trafficking in slaves. Most of the slaves from Africa were employed on huge farms and plantations where their masters grew cotton, sugar cane and other crops. Later, they were also sent down mines. Throughout the centuries of colonial rule, the Portuguese controlled only the coastal region and the areas along the banks of the rivers.

Germany's Chancellor Otto von Bismarck—the 'Iron Chancellor' who united Germany—created the concept of Realpolitik and sought to establish Germany a as colonial power. He convened the first international congress on the issue of Africa. The 1884-1885 Berlin Conference established regulations for the acquisition of African colonies, and for ending hostilities and military conflicts between the European countries in Africa. Needless to say, the Africans themselves had no representation whatsoever at the negotiating table.

The delegates at the conference all strove to obtain control as much as possible of the continent, especially where natural resources such as copper, gold, iron and diamonds were abundant.

Extensive areas of the African hinterland had not been exposed to the presence of white people at that time and the maps over which the experts pored were inaccurate. But that was of no concern to the Europeans in their efforts to divide the continent. The way in which the rulers drew the borders between one country and another was arbitrary. To this day, the straight lines that traverse nations and kingdoms serve as the internationally recognized boundaries of the independent states in Africa.

Portugal, whose explorers were the first to land on the shores of Africa, did not succeed in appropriating the lands it had hoped for and became a weak second-league player in the struggle among the European nations. Bismarck, on the other hand, managed to grant his friend, King Leopold II of Belgium, access to the ocean. The estuary of the Congo River was given to the Belgians and the enclave of Cabinda, on the west (Atlantic) coast of Africa was formed. More about that later.

Angola became a Portuguese colony, joined by the Cabinda enclave on the other side of the Congo River, surrounded by the Belgian Congo and the French Congo.

In 1890 Portugal began penetrating deep into the hinterland of Angola, in accordance with the conditions set by the Berlin Conference, which stated that to continue colonizing African lands, European countries were obliged to demonstrate active occupation of the land.

Thus, a forced labour system replaced slavery. Portugal established giant farms, owned by white people, this time in Angola itself and not across the sea. It wasn't before 1961, by which time most of the African countries had already won their full independence, that the Portuguese colonial regime ended the laws of forced labour.

In 1930, the oppressive right-wing dictator, General Antonio Salazar, seized power in Portugal. He was soon to declare that the Portuguese colonies in Africa were no more than overseas provinces of Portugal. Portuguese colonial rule was the harshest in Africa. The dire poverty in Portugal drove many Portuguese to migrate to the colonies. By 1900, about 10,000 Portuguese were living in Angola. After World War II, their number had risen to 80,000.

With the end of World War II in 1945 and the consequent reduction in the power of the main colonial powers, Britain and France, a nationalist awakening occurred in Africa. In all the colonies, with the exception of those belonging to Portugal, Africans were beginning to establish welfare associations, trade unions and political parties. These bodies were to lead to a first wave of independence in Africa. Ghana, which gained independence in 1957, was first, and between 1960 and 1963, most African countries had won their independence with almost no bloodshed.

In contrast, Portugal intensified its colonial rule in Angola. General Salazar announced the principle of Lusotropicalism, under which all the colonies and their people had to be integrated into Portugal. In fact, only a few—mainly people of mixed race—became Portuguese citizens. The rest of the so-called natives were obliged to continue living under an oppressive colonial rule until they could prove that they were worthy of citizenship. In other words, they had to fulfill conditions, such as fluency in the language, embracing the Catholic religion and so forth. Those years saw violent clashes between Africans seeking freedom and equality and Portuguese security forces. The notorious secret police established by the fascist regime in Lisbon, the PIDE, intensified its activity in Angola and among Angolan students studying in Portugal. Many thousands of Angolans were arrested and some of them were the victims of cruel torture.

In 1961, encouraged by the wave of independence washing over Africa, the freedom fighters in Angola decided to risk establishing a liberation movement of their own. The Angolan War of Independence would become the longest and bloodiest war in the history of the continent and would last until the end of 1975.

FNLA, the National Front for the Liberation of Angola, was the first movement of its kind to be established in March 1961 under a different name, which was changed following a rift. Its founding members came mainly from the country's north, where most people belonged to the Bakongo tribe, descendants of the ancient kingdom of Kongo. Holden Roberto was its leader. For many years the movement's hinterland bases were in Congo-Kinshasa (Zaire). With the Cold War in the background and under the influence of the then ruler of the country, Mobutu Sese Seko, the movement obtained aid and assistance from the West.

There is a continuing debate about liberation movement seniority from a historical perspective. Today, with the MPLA being the ruling party in Angola, it has claimed seniority, but my view is to favour the FNLA. In any case, it is worth bearing in mind these dates are somewhat contrived. A liberation struggle does not begin with a formal declaration, but with secret meetings of a small group of determined people.

MPLA, the Popular Front for the Liberation of Angola, began its activities several months later. Its power base consisted of the intelligentsia of the capital, Luanda, and members of the Kimbundu tribe who lived in the district. Many of the MPLA's founders were of mixed race, which granted them access to higher education. Students with left-wing sympathies who lived in Lisbon joined them. After internal struggles, the movement finally settled down under the leadership of Agostinho

Neto, a physician and a poet, who was married to a white Portuguese woman. From its early days, the MPLA followed a Marxist-Socialist ideology and, in time, it turned to the Soviet Union for assistance, not only as a liberation movement, but also as a faithful proselytizer of Soviet doctrine.

Unita, the Movement for the National Unity for Full Independence of Angola, was established in 1964, following a rift in the FNLA. At the head of the secessionists stood Jonas Savimbi, a member of the daring Ovimbundu tribe from the fertile highlands at the centre of the country. In the movement's early days, Savimbi turned to communist China for support, under the rationale that it was the only country to have mustered a peasants' revolution. Since most Angolans work the land, Savimbi considered China to be the most appropriate model to follow. A few years later, when the struggle for independence intensified, Savimbi chose political expediency in making a pact with the Apartheid regime in South Africa.

1961 to 1975 were the long years of struggle for independence in Angola. It was a struggle that was influenced by the Cold War as well as the desire of the superpowers to win for themselves a portion of the country's wealth of natural resources.

Many thousands of people were killed during those years, many thousands more fled to neighbouring countries to escape the terrors of colonial rule and the war. Thousands were left to rot in jail. Although the freedom fighters received massive aid from both sides of the Iron Curtain, in time, they turned into their sponsors' prisoners. The struggle between the three liberation movements complicated the war against the colonial ruler. Also, this turned the first day of independence, November 11, 1975, into the beginning of a civil war. This war would continue until 2002, when Unita leader Jonas Savimbi was killed by MPLA-led government forces.

In April 1974, shortly after the death of General Salazar and the appointment of one of his close aides Marcelo Caetano in the Estado Novo regime, a group of young Portuguese army officers decided that they had had their fill of the bloodshed in the colonies and of the fascist regime in their own country. The Carnation Revolution (named after the flower worn by some of the army officers or put in their gun barrels) took place with virtually no blood being spilled. The young officers granted independence to Angola and Mozambique and led their country to its first democratic elections, won by socialist leader, Mario Soares, who returned to Portugal from exile in France.

Under the auspices of the young Portuguese army officers, leaders of the three rival Angolan liberation movements met for the first time in Lisbon in early 1975. After conducting lengthy and difficult negotiations, they signed an agreement of cooperation and division of power. On the face of it, it seemed possible to achieve a smooth transition from Portuguese colonial rule to civil government by citizens of an independent Angola, but, in fact, none of the three movements was prepared to relinquish its vision of exclusive rule, reflecting the relationships of the external forces which supported each of the movements. The seed of iniquity had remained, though everyone chose to ignore it and hoped for the best.

Portuguese citizens in Angola, who had until the last moment not believed that 500 years of colonial rule had come to an end, now clamoured to get out of the country. There was no proper handover of government files, ownership records, water and electricity systems, health services, air traffic control or any manifestations of organized government. The Portuguese, who had never allowed Africans to hold managerial or supervisory positions, left behind them a country in chaos.

November 11, 1975: Independence Day in Angola and the day on which civil war erupted among the three liberation movements.

At midnight, by torchlight, Dr Agostinho Neto, leader of the MPLA, raised the flag of independent Angola. The national flag of Angola, in black and red with a gold sickle, a sword and a star printed in its centre is, in fact, a combination of the flags of the former USSR and Communist China. It differs very little from the flag of the MPLA party that ruled the capital.

All the countries of the Eastern Bloc and Scandinavia immediately recognized the new state and the MPLA regime. Angola was granted a seat at the United Nations, but a group of Western states, led by the United States, refused to recognize the Marxist regime in Luanda.

The Cold War between the East and the West was now being fought on Angolan soil. The newly born African state turned into the largest inter-bloc battlefield since Vietnam. The cruel war would continue until 2002 and the number of victims would reach the one million mark and greatly exceed the number of victims in the drawn out war of liberation.

Another front, in the south, opened on the very day that independence was declared when South African troops invaded Angola from what was South West Africa, now Namibia.

Before finally achieving independence in 1992, Namibia was known as South West Africa. Formerly a German colony, it had been handed over under mandate to South Africa, a British dominion at that stage, after the German defeat in World War I (1914–1918). South Africa retained the mandate, even after it left the Commonwealth in 1961.

Regular army troops and members of racist South Africa's special units crossed the border into Angola to support Jonas Savimbi's Unita movement in its attempts to gain control of Angola.

Initially, South Africa supported FNLA as well.

The northern front was opened shortly afterwards. FNLA fighters started moving out of camps in the region and in Zaire and from the northern provinces toward the capital, Luanda. Their objective was identical: to seize control of the government. Holden Roberto, whose traditional supporters, led by the United States, were not prepared to provide direct military aid, did not enjoy sufficient backup. Nonetheless, the first FNLA units managed to make it to a northern suburb of Luanda, where they were defeated. The Americans and their allies withdrew their support for the FNLA and transferred it to Unita, and Holden Roberto went into exile in Europe. The movement was disarmed a short while later and its leader returned to Luanda; the FNLA then turned into a parliamentary opposition party.

227

The Soviet Union did not remain far behind the developments and, from the first night of Angolan independence, it began operating a colossal air lift, transferring heavy military equipment from Eastern Europe to the airport at Luanda. Soviet advisors, experts from East Germany and technicians from all over the Eastern Bloc operated weaponry along the battlefront, although none of these countries sent soldiers to fight alongside the Angolans.

The actual fighting on the side of the MPLA troops was carried out by thousands of soldiers from Cuba. At the height of the battles, some 50,000 Cuban soldiers were fighting on Angolan soil. It was the first time that Fidel Castro had demonstrated such intense international involvement. The Cubans were not seen as invaders and soon earned the admiration of their Angolan counterparts. They spoke Spanish, which is similar to Portuguese; they were easygoing, were neither condescending nor racist and mingled effortlessly with the local population. To this day, thousands of Cuban-Angolan children bear testimony to the presence of those soldiers.

Between 1975 and 1987, the war continued to rage throughout the country. But the biggest showdown, the most symbolic of them all, was the Battle of Cuito Cuanavale, which was the biggest in the history of sub-Saharan Africa. For many months, the little town was divided among the fighting forces, who entrenched themselves there and battled over every house, every yard, every tree.

Cuito Cuanavale was razed to its very foundations, and thousands of soldiers and civilians lost their lives in the town in the Kuando Kubango province of southeast Angola, on the way to Jamba, the provisional capital of Jonas Savimbi. Unita, together with its South African allies, planned to forge northward to Luanda. The intention of the MPLA and its Soviet and Cuban supporters was to halt the invasion at all costs.

The exact numbers are not known, but the South Africans claim to have fought against an overwhelming force consisting of 20,000 Soviets, East Germans, Cubans and Angolans. These were equipped with heavy T-55 tanks, various kinds of SAM missiles, Mig-21 and Mig-23 fighter jets and MI-24 helicopters, Howitzer cannons and radar receivers operated by Soviet experts.

The South Africans admitted to having at least 4,000 regular army soldiers at their disposal, 8,000 Unita troops, French-made Mirage F-1 fighter jets, helicopters provided by several Western states and Stinger missiles, supplied by the USA. Both sides laid landmines over huge areas and took advantage of the Angolan war to try out their state-of-the-art weaponry.

The advance of Savimbi and the South Africans was blocked in Cuito Cuanavale, but the war continued to rage in other regions. Many thousands were killed, thousands more starved to death and millions were displaced from their lands.

In 1989, the collapse of the Soviet Union was followed by profound changes on the African continent. Following American pressure and under the auspices of the United Nations, an agreement was reached for the mutual withdrawal of South African and Cuban forces from Angolan soil and for renewed negotiations between the warring sides.

The Bicesse Accords were signed in Portugal after exhausting negotiations. According to the agreement, thousands of troops from the United Nations peacekeeping forces would be dispatched to Angola, with the mission of upholding the cease-fire and organizing and securing the first democratic general elections in the country.

September 20, 1992 was the day of the first round of multi-party elections in Angola. If no outright majority was achieved in this round, a second one was planned to take place two weeks later. Savimbi had gained control of almost half of the country; but the MPLA and its leader, President Eduardo dos Santos, held the capital, Luanda. Savimbi demanded the right to be allowed to come to the capital with a group of bodyguards from among his guerrilla forces. The demand was met. It appears that Savimbi's aggressive behaviour, constantly accompanied by formidable bodyguards, caused him more harm than good. The first round of elections, which were held under UN supervision, determined that dos Santos had won 49% of the vote; Savimbi had received only 40%. A second round was inevitable, but Savimbi refused to accept the results. He left Luanda secretly, in a great hurry and returned to Huambo, the capital of the Ovimbundu tribe, and the war resumed. In the streets of Luanda, a witch-hunt was staged for those of Savimbi's supporters who were left behind when he fled and left them to their fate.

Thus, the tragedy began anew—refugees, mines and stubborn guerrilla warfare. A growing number of Western states withdrew their open support for the guerrilla leader who refused to accept the results of an election that was recognized as legal by United Nations invigilators. The place previously held by the Western states was now taken over by traders in blood diamonds, who continued to purchase the stones from the area under Unita's control, with the help of secretive dealers and from the West and international villains.

In 1994 the government forces succeeded—after much bloodshed—to change the balance of power in their favour. Again, an agreement was signed with Unita. This time the signing ceremony took place in Lusaka, the capital of Zambia. And again, it happened under the auspices of the United Nations. The troika, which consisted of the United States, Russia and Portugal, also signed the agreement. Savimbi himself did not honour the ceremony with his presence and it should have been obvious to objective observers that he had no intention of doing so. And the fighting continued, with thousands of United Nations Peace Forces stationed on Angolan soil. It was neither war nor peace.

The election of Nelson Mandela, South Africa's first black president, increased Savimbi's isolation. During the Clinton presidency, the United States decided to cease all US support for Savimbi and to cooperate instead with Russia to bring an end to the war. Angola's army, FAPLA, became one of the strongest and most experienced fighting forces in Africa.

On February 22, 2002, soldiers in the Moxico province surrounded a small group of Savimbi's fighters, who were searching for shelter in the tangled bush. They were making a desperate attempt to escape across the border into Zambia. Savimbi didn't even have time to draw his gun before being shot to death. The remains of his forces—hungry, wounded and exhausted—surrendered. The end of the war was declared two months later at a ceremony in Parliament House in Luanda. Jonas Savimbi's generals swore an oath of allegiance to the Angolan army, the FAA. Those Unita members who had been elected to parliament in 1992 took their seats on the opposition benches.

○○○

The enclave of Cabinda is a classic example of the adverse effect colonialism still has on Africa. As we know, it was Portuguese sailors who were first to set foot on the shores of Africa in general and, especially, in that part of the continent's central-western region. At that time, Cabinda was part of the kingdom of Angola, which had been under Portguguese control from the 16th century until the 1885 Berlin Conference. At this famous conference, the African continent was parcelled out at random among the various colonial powers and its history was thus subjected to ineradicable change. The original population of the continent did not, of course, have any representation and its voice was not heard. The instigator of the conference was Otto von Bismarck, the Iron Chancellor of Germany, who felt himself strengthened after having completed the unification of Germany under his baton.

In those days, Britain and France were Europe's two superpowers and ruled over waterways and many countries in Africa, Asia and the Americas. They, of course, received the lion's share of the continent. Bismarck personally appropriated several juicy chunks, even though Germany had never had a large sea fleet and it did not take control of large areas.

Belgium's King Leopold II was a personal friend of Bismarck and although the country he ruled was small and relatively poor, his aspirations greatly exceeded the modest dimensions of his own monarchy. It was he who sent Henry Morton Stanley to seek out the sources of the Congo River. On the way, Leopold imposed on Stanley the task of forging covenants with local chiefs and, through them, to grant franchises to the international mining companies. The problem was that those regions which Stanley colonized on behalf of Leopold had no access to the sea. It was here, therefore, that Bismarck came to the help of his royal friend. The Berlin Conference decided to create a corridor and to grant Leopold ownership over the estuary of the Congo River. The protests of the relatively weak Portugal were to no avail. Thus, the Cabinda enclave which was part of the Portuguese colony of Angola, but severed from it by the two Congo colonies, the Belgian and the French, came in to being.

This random apportioning remained in effect throughout the colonial era and continued to be a part of African reality after independence. Having no choice, the African states decided to honour the colonial divisions and to recognize them as their national borders. The French Congo, whose capital was Brazzaville and the Belgian Congo, whose capital Leopoldville (later Kinshasa) on the other side of the river, won their independence in 1960. The people of Angola continued to struggle against Portuguese rule for many more years and achieved their independence only in 1975. During those years of enormous political upheavals and civil wars in the Congo basin, the international oil giants went from strength to strength. They provided the new African regimes with a large part of their income, which subsequently allowed them to finance their cruel wars. In the chase for money there is no place for ideology.

Today most of the world's larger oil conglomerates still operate in Angola. But the country's wealth of natural resources has not yet brought salvation to its impoverished population. The profits go mainly to making the international oil companies richer still and to a thin layer of the country's elite.

ooo

Angola: fourteen years of struggle for independence and twenty-seven years of civil war. The cost: a million dead, four million displaced, one and a half million people starving in refugee camps; many thousands of orphans, thousands more amputees, nine million landmines, dozens of bridges blown up, whole towns razed to the ground; scorched earth and fields that will not provide a harvest for years to come.

Angola: a mélange of courageous, hard-working women, children returning gradually to their homes in the villages, a bright smile lighting a sad-eyed face and an amazing ability to be genuine human beings, in spite of it all.

Tg

Oil and diamonds

One of the wisest things my 'father', the late Ivorian President, Felix Houphouet-Boigny, used to say, was that it was our great good fortune that the country was not blessed with natural resources. "We have no oil and we have no diamonds; we have only coffee, cocoa and pineapples. For this reason, we are left to our own devices. How good it is to be poor."

So far, Angola's almost unbearable natural wealth has always been more a curse than a blessing. It has drawn to it greedy foreigners, provided a reason for bloody wars and served to corrupt many an Angolan political leader. It is not possible to understand Angola's modern history without a study of the effects its diamonds and oil resources have had on the country. We can only hope that one day, in the not too distant future, the inhabitants of this sad country will, themselves, have the good fortune to enjoy their own treasures.

Portugal, a small, rather weak country, was never able to exploit Angola's vast treasures on its own. Out of the Industrial Revolution in the late 18th century, coupled with the rise of capitalism, there evolved huge international oil potentates, who became the real overlords of Angola's natural resources. It was thus during the period of Portuguese colonialism and it continued to be so after November 11, 1975, the day on which the country officially received its independence. The people of Angola do not possess any real control over their country's many resources, while the power of the multinational companies continues to grow.

After Nigeria, Angola is the second largest oil producer in Africa. But the two countries differ in two essential ways. First, while Nigeria has a population that exceeds 150 million, Angola's population is only about twelve and fourteen million. Also, Nigeria's oil deposits are concentrated inland, around the delta of the Niger River, whereas those of Angola are mined in the ocean in deep waters. It is for this reason that, in Nigeria, violent clashes often erupt between the local population and the international oil companies—mainly Shell-BP—that result in upheavals and production halts. Oil production in the ocean depths off the coast of Angola, on the other hand, has never stopped and continued at full force even when the civil war was at its height. Although some problems arose with the local population in Cabinda, these were not serious enough to disturb the international oil companies.

Crude oil provides the main source of income for the Angolan economy, with a production of close to a million barrels a day bringing in more than seven billion dollars a year. The revenue from oil exports constitutes more than 80% of the country's gross national product.

The USA is Angola's major customer with more than eight percent of the oil imported into the United States originating in Angola. Imports are conducted via several enormous conglomerates, headed by Chevron-Texaco. Angola is also the main supplier to the French-Belgian oil giant, Total-Fina-Elf.

In most oil-rich Third World countries, revenues rarely make their way down to the general population. In this respect, Angola is no exception and the oil industry is handled there very much in the same way as we have witnessed in Saudi Arabia and Kuwait; although recent years have seen some positive changes in a few of the oil-producing countries in South America, where efforts are being made toward a fairer distribution. Africa is yet to witness the arrival of these changes.

The activity and conduct of the international oil companies is the subject of sharp criticism. These organizations find it comfortable to deal directly with the heads of centralized regimes. Representatives of these companies say they are merely carrying out business transactions with the official regime and that they have no intention of involving themselves in the country's internal affairs.

The fact that oil production is capital intensive and employs relatively few people means that most of the revenue finds its way straight into the state's coffers—or into the pockets of its leaders. For years, the International Monetary Fund has been complaining that billions of dollars in oil revenue have not been accounted for in the Angolan state budget and have simply disappeared into thin air. The IMF has begun pushing Angola on transparency and more disclosure of their oil revenues and has made this a condition for Angola to be allowed back into the organization. During the civil war, the government in Luanda had proclaimed that, for security reasons, all information on its oil revenues was classified. But even after the war was over, Luanda was in no hurry to fulfill the IMF's directives and negotiations have been haphazard. Meantime, oil has made a few people in and out of Angola extremely wealthy, while millions of the country's citizens are still living in squalor.

Yet, despite all that has been said about the injustices caused by the oil industry, they are less than nothing when compared with the death and destruction inflicted on the Angolan people by the diamond industry.

'Diamonds are a girl's best friend', goes the famous slogan coined by the marketing department of De Beers, the South African diamond conglomerate—the largest in the world. Hollywood has made these stones famous and millions of men the world over have learned that the best way to express their love for a woman is by giving her diamonds; millions of women continue to remind the object of their affections of this wisdom. Needless to say, few of them have taken the trouble to ask the opinion of the widows and orphans throughout Africa, the victims in the chase for sparkling stones.

Since the middle of the 19th century, when the first diamond deposits were discovered in South Africa, the hunt for these precious stones had become increasingly cruel. There are people who consider this passionate pursuit of diamonds to be a kind of disease, one that can cause a man to lose his mind. Apart from the diamonds extracted from the giant mines deep below the ground—under close scrutiny of the big diamond miners—many of the diamonds are found by people mining in the alluvial strata close to the earth's surface.

In Angola, this form of artisan diamond mining is known as 'garimpo' and those involved in it are called 'garimpeiros', meaning 'climbing to search'. They mine for diamonds in the foothills of mountain ranges or in riverbeds, using their bare hands or simple rakes to scrape the earth and sand into huge piles. Sometimes these improvised mines collapse and bury the garimpeiros under them. They work in scorching heat and in pouring rain, always hoping to find that one special stone that will bring them overwhelming wealth.

The garimpeiros sold their finds to buyers, invariably foreigners, from countries such as Senegal, Mali, Mauritania and even Congo. The merchants included people from Lebanon, Belgium, South Africa and Israel. Most of the West African buyers snuck into Angola illegally, using various routes, especially via the Democratic Republic of Congo. Others came by other, more sophisticated routes, on direct (if illegal) flights from South Africa. Some of them operated in government-controlled regions, but there were more even who carried out their shady deals in areas controlled by Jonas Savimbi's rebels. Very few of these merchants honoured the country's boundaries and laws, though they shared a single ambition: to get rich, at any price and as soon as possible.

The value of a single cut diamond can fetch many thousands of dollars. It is a temptation that is hard to resist; it is an affliction of thousands of destitute Africans and they are prepared to kill and be killed in order to earn a few kwanzas in payment for a stone. The return on the rough diamond they dig out of the ground is very low and its price begins to rise only when it is purchased by a foreign buyer, has been passed around among the brokers and makes its way to the cutting plant and, finally, to the jewellery shop. Only then is it worth millions. The difference between what the garimpeiros get paid and the price for which the diamond is eventually sold to the wealthy client can be measured in many thousands of percentage points.

Diamond trading has always been considered among the most untamed and cruel of all the many kinds of commercial activities in the world. Diamond traders have never been concerned with international borders, laws, or the sanctity of human life. This trade has funded rebel movements, unscrupulous rulers and mercenary adventurers. In the wealthy and distinguished markets of Johannesburg and Antwerp, Tel Aviv and New York, no one asks to be told the real price of those diamonds offered for sale. These were the blood diamonds against which the United Nations declared war, but this war was declared only after millions of innocent people in Angola, Sierra Leone, and the Congo were slaughtered, injured and dispossessed of their homes. Recently, the Kimberley Process (an international supervisory system) has—at long last—been put into operation to stem the flow of conflict diamonds. The Kimberley Process Certification Scheme imposes extensive requirements on its members to account for the source of each and every stone. It is not a perfect system, because it is easy enough to violate, but it is a start.

Blood diamonds or a girl's best friend? One thing is certain: the day is still a long way off when the diamond becomes the best friend of the girl in a remote African village.

TG

About nature

Angola's real natural assets are not the country's famous minerals. Angola was known in the past for its rich and varied biological diversity. Nowadays, though, it is defined by some as a black hole on the global conservation maps.

Angola is one of the largest countries in Africa, covering an area of 1,246,700 square kilometres. From the Namib Desert in the southwestern part of the country, to the Okavango and the Zambezi River basins in the south and east, up to the tropical rainforests of the Congo River basin in the northwest, Angola has it all. The tropical Maiombe forest, the Miombo and Mopane woodlands which cover more than half of the country, savannahs and grasslands, desert, numerous marine and terrestrial wetlands of various coasts, rivers and lakes, and even such gems as mangrove forests and vast flooded plains, constitute a rich variety of diverse ecosystems. The source of some of Africa's most important rivers are in Angola or on the borders, including the Congo, the Okavango, the Cunene, and northern tributaries of the Zambezi. The narrow escarpment which lies between the coastal belt and the vast inland plateau form a unique ecosystem and a centre of endemism.

The variety of habitats host rich and diverse flora and fauna, including species and sub-species that are endemic only to Angola.

The marine fauna, along the 1,650 kilometres of the Atlantic coast, was exceptionally abundant and diverse. Between the large marine ecosystems of the Benguela current to the south and the Guinea current to the north, special conditions occur which enable the development of remarkably productive marine biodiversity. During the 1950s Angola produced the second largest annual marine catch on the continent, after South Africa. Nowadays, after decades of over-exploitation, the fisheries resources have dwindled significantly.

It was not only the people of Angola and its infrastructure which fell victim to the extended armed conflict; its biodiversity too was devastated. Most of the country's large mammal populations have been exterminated by merciless commercial poaching and systematic shooting by both warring sides. Extreme poverty and famine have driven the people to hunt for their survival; internally displaced people had to sustain themselves in any way possible; and uncontrolled over-exploitation and the looting of the natural treasures on land and at sea resulted in the wholesale destruction of ecosystems.

During the war and even after it came to an end with peace agreements in place, environmental issues in Angola were always neglected. The consequences were severe: water and air pollution, mountains of garbage piling up in Luanda and other cities, a lack of adequate infrastructure, oil spills at sea, further destruction of natural habitats by diamond mining, oil exploration and other mining activities, uncontrolled and irresponsible logging for timber, charcoal, development and agriculture, poaching and commercial trade in wildlife, bush meat, skins, turtle shells and ivory, all with no control or law enforcement. All of this has resulted in the loss of Angola's once rich biological diversity, with its attendant depletion and collapse of ecological systems and damage to human health and livelihoods. The internal displacement during the war caused over-population of the coastal zone, followed by serious degradation of its sensitive ecological systems, soil erosion, and a rapid process of desertification.

International support for the protection of the environment and nature conservation in Angola was very limited. The donor community mostly concentrated on relieving the emergency situations caused by the war and tended to ignore the requirements for long-term sustainable development. The Norwegian government and the United Nations Development Programme (UNDP) were the only entities willing to invest significantly in biodiversity conservation in Angola during the war. This was obviously not enough. We can only hope that it is not too late for Angola's unique and diverse ecosystems to recover.

The knowledge base of the country's fauna and flora is poor. While British and French researchers and naturalists have systematically recorded the biodiversity in their colonies, the Portuguese often neglected it. Such information as existed was collected by a number of pioneering and committed researchers. Most of these records, however, are available only in Portuguese and are kept in archives which are difficult to access.

Between the 1930s and the 1970s, six national parks and seven nature reserves were proclaimed in Angola. They cover little more than six percent of the country's area, which is about half of the international standard. With the outbreak of war, even these formally protected areas did not enjoy any real protection. They were little more than reserves on paper and loggers, poachers, farmers and developers exploited them at will.

In the early 1970s, toward the end of the Portuguese colonial regime, efforts were being made to study the country's biodiversity and to protect it. These efforts were led by, among others, João Serodio de Almeida, João Crawford-Cabral, and other young Angolan and Portuguese ecologists and conservationists, as well as Brian Huntley, a young South African ecologist, who would later become a world renowned authority in his field.

In 1992, Huntley returned to Angola for a short visit, and together with the outstanding botanist Liz Matos and other partners, conducted a brief study to evaluate the status of the ecosystems and wildlife populations in the country. They concluded that most of the large mammal populations had drastically declined and some were already extinct in Angola. However, core populations of many species still survived in areas that had not been accessible to people during the war. Small species with no economic value usually remained intact and even thrived in habitats where farming and human settlement had collapsed.

In 1992, when Angola still enjoyed a short period of peace, the Convention on Biological Diversity (CBD) was launched at the famous Rio de Janeiro Summit. The rising global awareness of the importance of biodiversity conservation and sustainable development penetrated the governing bodies of Angola. A governmental secretariat was established to handle environmental matters and some years later was upgraded to a full ministry.

In 1998, Professor João Serodio de Almeida, then Vice-Minister of the Environment, an enthusiastic ecologist and a vet by education who began his career during the colonial era as a warden in national parks, succeeded in promoting the Basic Law of the Environment in the National Assembly. He went personally to meet each and every one of the members of parliament, and the law was adopted almost unanimously. The Basic Law of the Environment defined the general legal framework for the protection of the environment in Angola. It also passed most of the responsibilities for environmental and conservation matters from the Ministry of Agriculture to the Ministry of Environment. But regulations were still needed for the law to have practical implications.

However, before such regulations were adopted, the Vice-Minister of the Environment was replaced by a Minister of Fisheries and Environment, who was later replaced by a Minister of Urban Affairs and Environment, a nomination that was soon replaced by yet another minister. The regulations were drafted and redrafted again and again and transferred from one legal adviser to another over several years. Meanwhile, even agreement on the division of authority and responsibilities among the different ministries and departments could not be reached. Several officials responsible for environmental protection were often more preoccupied with internal power struggles. Others, who were genuinely making the effort to do the work, encountered near insurmountable obstacles, such as severe budgetary constraints and a lack of means and skilled personnel.

Core populations of many wildlife species found refuge during the war in areas where human movement was restricted or too dangerous. Shortly after the armed conflict ended, many of these areas became more accessible, but they were still not adequately protected. Thus, Angola's wildlife fell victim not only to war, but also to peace. Whenever a so-called state of emergency is declared, in war or peace, environmental protection and nature conservation become the losers while attention is diverted to what is perceived to be more urgent issues.

The young committed volunteers of the national and local environmental organizations continued to make every possible effort to protect nature and the environment, and especially to raise awareness of the importance of these issues. Several researchers from the Agostinho Neto University and other Angolan universities joined them in their efforts. They received modest support from the government and from international aid agencies and organizations.

Now that the war is over, measures must be taken to allow the recovery of humanity and of nature, before they reach a point of no return. Angola's rich biodiversity can still be rehabilitated, returned to its former splendour and used as a source of income through ecotourism and other sustainable uses. Hope for such a future is still possible, provided the leaders and the people of Angola maintain what is left and reject the avaricious schemes of those who only seek personal gain.

The development of transfrontier conservation areas with neighbouring countries, if done well and in true cooperation with local communities and other stakeholders, may also play an important role in promoting biodiversity conservation.

Angola is now at an important crossroads for the survival of the great natural treasures with which the country was blessed. If their systematic destruction is permitted to continue, any hope for a sustainable recovery will be lost, but with concentrated efforts to protect the natural assets in cooperation with the government, citizens, neighbouring countries and international entities, Angola could yet become the heaven on earth it was meant to be.

T R

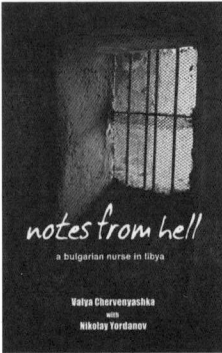

Notes from Hell—a Bulgarian Nurse in Libya

Valya Chervenyashka with Nikolay Yordanov

Born in poverty-stricken Vratsa, Bulgaria, Valya Chervenyashka is married and has two daughters. Her whole life has been dedicated to nursing, most of it caring for children in Bulgarian hospitals. In the 1980s she was posted to Tarhuna, Libya where she received awards for her work with children. In 1998, she was arrested in Benghazi, Libya, transferred to a Tripoli jail, charged with conspiring to deliberately infect over 400 children with HIV and sentenced to death. *Notes from Hell* is her story, covering a decade of torture, cruelty and absolute despair.

978-1920143-47-3; R145.00; Paperback; 166 pages; 198 x 130mm; 50 b/w photos; P&P: R35 local, R135 o/seas

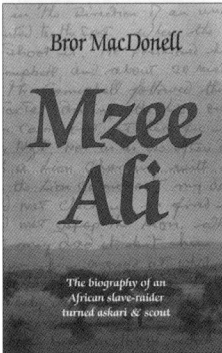

Mzee Ali

Bror MacDonell

Mzee Ali Kalikilima was born near the present-day town of Tabora in western Tanzania, probably in the 1870s to black Muslim parents of noble birth. Aged 14, Mzee Ali led his first slaving safari to the shores of Lake Tanganyikand then some 1,200 kilometres east to Dar es Salaam on the Indian Ocean.
With the arrival of the German colonizers, Mzee Ali joined the German East African forces as an askari. With the outbreak of World War I, he found himself attached to the forces of the legendary German commander, General von Lettow-Vorbeck. He saw action at the Battle of Salaita Hill near Mombasa and was with the General to the end.

0-9584890-5-X; R135.00; Paperback; 224pp; 210 x 148mm; illustrated; P&P R35 local, R135 o/seas

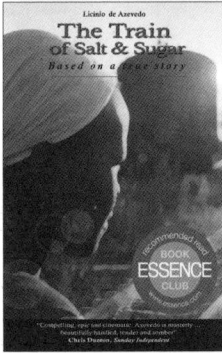

The Train of Salt & Sugar

Licínio de Azevedo

Out of every conflict situation comes myriad of stories; stories about people, set against the backdrop of war. During the bitter and protracted Mozambican civil war there were many such stories, but none so courageous nor so passionate and beautiful as that told in *The Train of Salt and Sugar*. After 30 years of devastating war, on a misty morning in the town of Nampula, in northern Mozambique, a convoy of three trains, loaded with supplies, three garrisons of soldiers and over 600 passengers left relative safety, destined for Cuamba, a town 341 kilometres to the west, bordering Malawi. The harrowing journey is as colourful as its passengers—civilians and soldiers alike.

978-1920143-12-1; R115.00; Paperback; 160 pages; 198 x 130mm; P&P: R25 local, R80 o/seas

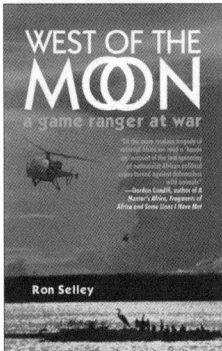

West of the Moon

Ron Selley

West of the Moon—A Game Ranger at War is a sweeping canvas that evokes a bygone era of 1940s colonial Natal through to the cruel intensity of the Bush War that ravaged Rhodesia in the 1970s. The book is in two distinct parts. Part 1 chronicles the author's earlier years—an idyllic childhood spent in the rolling hills of northern Zululand; Part 2 recounts the author's move north across the Limpopo where his love of adventure, hunting and the bushveld lead him to Rhodesia. He becomes a game ranger, dealing with 'problem animals' in the farming areas and the escalating terrorist war in the Gona re Zhou National Park.

978-1920143-32-9; R250.00; Paperback; 284 pages; 234 x 153mm; 200 b/w photos, 4 maps; P&P: R40 local, R165 o/seas

www.30degreessouth.co.za